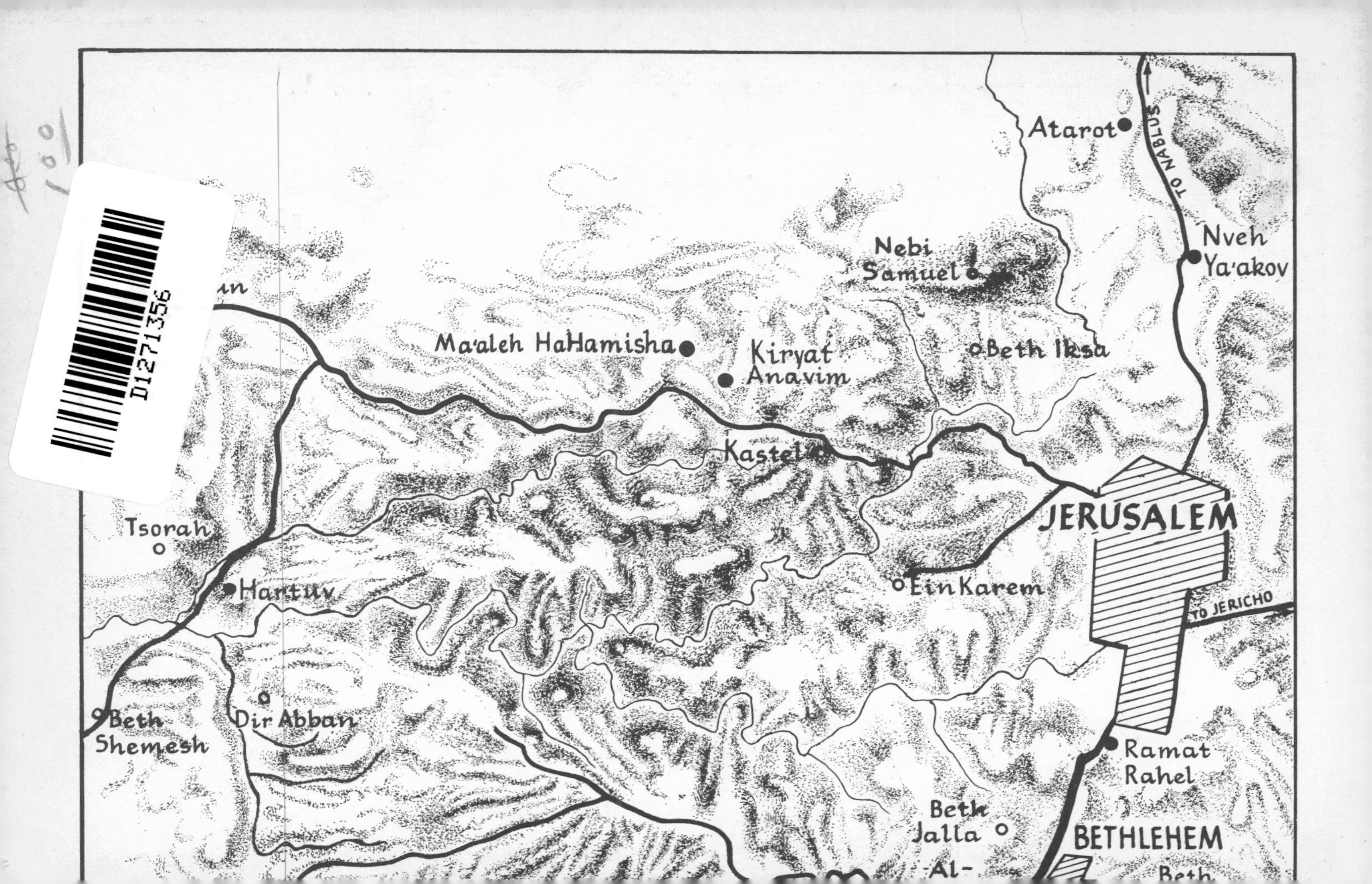
Atarot
TO NABLUS
Nveh
Ya'akov
Nebi
Samuel
Ma'aleh HaHamisha
Kiryat
Anavim
Beth Iksa
Kastel
JERUSALEM
Tsorah
Hartuv
Ein Karem
TO JERICHO
Beth
Shemesh
Dir Abban
Ramat
Rahel
Beth
Jalla
Al-
BETHLEHEM

SIEGE IN THE HILLS OF HEBRON

SIEGE IN THE HILLS OF HEBRON

The Battle of the Etzion Bloc

compiled and edited by

DOV KNOHL

introduction by

ABBA EBAN

evaluations by

Yigael Yadin and Yig'al Allon

New York · THOMAS YOSELOFF · *London*

Library of Congress Catalogue Card Number: 58-8032

THOMAS YOSELOFF, Publisher
11 East 36th Street
New York 16, N. Y.

THOMAS YOSELOFF LTD.
123 New Bond Street
London W. 1, England

Siege in the Hills of Hebron was originally published in Israel as *Gush Etzion BeMilhamto.* This edition in English, abridged and edited by ARYEI FISHMAN, was translated from the Hebrew by ISAAC HALEVY-LEVIN, and prepared for publication by the Religious Section of the Youth and HeHalutz Department of the Jewish Agency.

Printed in the United States of America

"And he said, Take now thy son, thine only son Isaac, whom thou lovest, and go thee unto the land of Moriah; and offer him there for a burnt offering upon one of the mountains which I will tell thee of" (Genesis 22:2).

Abraham asked him: On which mountain?

The Lord answered: Wherever you see my glory dwells and awaits you.

(From the Aggada: *Pirkei d'R. Eliezer,* 31)

Preface

This work was first published in Hebrew in 1954, and a second impression was printed in 1957. Its compiler and editor was a founding member of Kfar Etzion and one of the few survivors of the final battle of that settlement. Though the English edition has been abridged by about a half, it has remained completely faithful to the original. The only significant additions to it are the short introductions to individual chapters, which provide a background for the understanding of events in the Etzion Bloc.

I wish to thank Mrs. Shulamith Schwartz Nardi and Mr. Dennis Silk for reading the English manuscript and for their comments on it. Mr. Knohl checked the manuscript and offered many suggestions regarding its content. I am also grateful to Mr. Sam Bloch of New York, for his valuable aid in the publication of this work.

A. F.

Jerusalem, Israel

Editor's Preface

The course of the Israel War of Liberation was marked by many miracles. Many Jewish settlements and outposts were saved at the last moment under unusual circumstances, which religious persons could only regard as the result of Divine intervention. In the Etzion Bloc, however, events led inexorably up to their logical denouément. Why this should have been so, we cannot tell. The ways of the Lord are inscrutable.

Kfar Etzion, the oldest and the largest of the four settlements of the Bloc, was the base for many of the soldiers who took part in the siege, and housed most of the important institutions of the Bloc. It was the hub of the operations planned and executed in the area in the course of the War, and the final battle centered mainly about it. For these reasons this book is largely the story of Kfar Etzion.

DOV KNOHL

Introduction

This is a story of valor and sacrifice in the hills of Judea ten years ago. It portrays men and women of simple faith in an hour touched by tragedy and exaltation. The memory of these events is vivid in the mind of a grateful nation; and it will certainly be held in reverence whenever the saga of Israel's rebirth is told.

The Etzion Bloc settlements were built amongst the hills and rocks flanking the road from Hebron to Bethlehem. They were inhabited by pioneers, steeped in the tradition of Jewish faith and dedicated to the vision of reviving the land and restoring its fertility. It was here that Abraham had pitched his tent when he entered the Land of Promise by Divine command. Here David had tended his flocks, and the Macabbees had waged their sublime and desperate revolt against the oppressors of their faith. The modern settlers of the Etzion villages were attended by these familiar memories as they set out to clothe the hills with orchards and vineyards, and to merge their toil in the enterprise of Israel's rebirth. In a few years they had brought some life to the barren soil, gathered the first crops, and raised their first families. But their work was only at its beginning when the drama of their people's history overtook them in its course.

On November 29, 1947, the United Nations proclaimed its judgment in favor of Israel's statehood. The Etzion villages were in the area allocated to an independent Arab State which was to arise in cooperation and economic union with Israel. But on the morrow of this international judgment a torrent of Arab violence poured over the land, and the Etzion settlers found themselves isolated amidst the surge of Arab ferocity.

This book depicts the siege laid upon them, notably its last phase. Their mission was to defend their own lives and homes and in that defense to relieve Jerusalem from assault, gaining time to rally protection to the capital. The men and women of these villages, whose temperament lay uniquely in peaceful pursuits, with scanty equipment fought against a savage assault by units of the Arab Legion, a regular army equipped with cannon and armor. After an epic resistance they were finally crushed, becoming the first victims of an attack which the United Nations was to describe in solemn terms as an act of defiance against the law of nations and the judgment of the world.

The record is set out in the simple language of the men and women who saw the fighting through all its tumult. It consists largely of diaries, letters, and messages written in the heat and tension of the fray. The narrative is free of conscious art, but its very simplicity endows it with poetic force. Nobody who reads it can fail to catch something of the spirit which moved these people in their hour of immaculate sacrifice. This book is somber testimony to the kind of valor which brought Israel through the darkness into the new dawn of its freedom. There are many such episodes of siege in the long history of a people to whom the gift of life has never been freely accorded. No monument of words is an adequate memorial to such as these. They belong to the ancient and unbroken lineage of them who were "swifter than eagles and stronger than lions: pleasant were they in their lives, and in their death they were not divided."

ABBA EBAN

Contents

II. JERUSALEM'S SOUTHERN OUTPOST

III. THE SACRIFICE

Illustrations

The illustrations appear as a group following page 160

The Battle of the Etzion Bloc—Calendar of Events

November 29, 1947	The General Assembly of the United Nations votes in favor of the establishment of two States in Palestine, one Jewish and one Arab.
December 6	A Palmah platoon commanded by Danny Mass arrives to reinforce the Bloc.
December 11	The attack on the convoy from Jerusalem; ten passengers are killed.
December 12	The bodies are returned from Jerusalem and supplies are brought in a convoy escorted by British forces.
December 25	A platoon of the Student Company ("C" Company), Mikhmash Battalion of the Jerusalem Field Force, arrives to reinforce the Bloc.
January 3, 1948	A Hagana-escorted convoy brings food, fuel, and cement.
January 5	The mothers and children are evacuated.
January 7	A second platoon of the Student Company arrives.

January 12	A Hagana-escorted convoy brings food.
January 13	Two passengers are killed in the attack on the return convoy to Jerusalem.
January 14	The first mass attack on the Etzion Bloc, by the forces of Abdul Kader el-Husseini, is repulsed.
January 16	The thirty-five members of the "Mountain Platoon" sent to reinforce the Bloc are killed.
January 19	The funeral of the thirty-five.
January 20	The regular parachuting of supplies is begun.
January 24	A five-truck convoy, escorted by British troops, brings food supplies and fuel.
February 2	A truck of supplies, escorted by British troops, arrives.
February 7	An Auster lands for the first time on the air strip.
February 10	A three-truck convoy, escorted by British forces, arrives.
February 19	Another three-truck convoy, escorted by British forces, arrives.
February 21	A seven-truck convoy, escorted by Hagana forces, arrives. Yigael Yadin, of the General Staff, visits the Bloc.

February 24-26	The General Meeting of Kfar Etzion discusses partial evacuation.
March 14	The occupation of the Russian Monastery.
March 21	Mosh Silberschmidt arrives to assume command of the Bloc. Reinforcements from the "Orthodox Company" of the Tel Aviv Field Force begin to arrive by air.
March 27	The giant convoy arrives. "B" Company, Mikhmash Battalion, replaces the Student Company. The convoy is held up at Nebi Daniel on its return journey to Jerusalem.
March 28	Yig'al Allon visits the Bloc. The Nebi Daniel convoy surrenders. Part of its escort escapes back to the Bloc.
April 12	Arab traffic on the Hebron-Jerusalem road is harassed.
April 30	Arab convoys carrying reinforcements for the Battle of Katamon, in Jerusalem, are effectively attacked.
May 2-3	Barriers are constructed on the Jerusalem-Hebron road.
May 4	The Russian Monastery and the Mukhtar's Saddle are captured by the Arab Legion and later abandoned by it.

May 12	The Legion launches an all-out attack. The Mukhtar's Saddle, Russian Monastery, Russian Hill, Hirbet Sawir, Lone Tree Hill, and Yellow Hill are captured.
May 13	Kfar Etzion falls.
May 14	The declaration of the Jewish State in Tel Aviv. The surviving defenders of the Bloc go into captivity.

SIEGE IN THE HILLS OF HEBRON

Prologue

THE HEBRON HILL REGION

The highway running southward from Jerusalem and transversing the ancient inheritance of the tribe of Judah, winds sluggishly over a range of hills, which, as far as Bethlehem, are called the Jerusalem Hills and further south, the Hebron Hills. This region is one of the highest in Palestine, the altitude ranging from 2,280 feet above sea-level in Jerusalem to 3,336 feet in the vicinity of Hebron.

The entire district is cut by sharp valleys and canyons. The crest of these highlands is the watershed, the ravines running to the west draining off the rainfall to the Shorek and Rubin brooks, flowing into the Mediterranean, and those on the east drawing water off to the Jordan and the Dead Sea. East of the main highway, beyond the gaunt mountain peaks, lies the desolate Judean Desert with its meager annual rainfall. Westward, however, where the precipitation is heavy, the flora is lush and green and the soil fertile.

Climatic conditions resemble those of hilly regions elsewhere in Palestine. In the winter, fierce, cold storm winds sweep over the high slopes, which are frequently covered by a dense pall of mist. Sometimes the higher reaches of the hills are covered with snow. In the summer the weather is cool and temperate, while the air is translucently clear. The heavy dew freshens the earth, and the moisture in the heavy, loamy soil is protected from the rays of the sun by a loosely strewn layer of boulders and stones. The annual precipitation varies from between twenty-eight to thirty-four inches.

Here between Hebron, City of the Patriarchs, and Jerusalem, capital of the House of David, the Hebrew nation was cradled.

In the Scriptures a special significance was already attributed to this southern area of Palestine. In this area Abraham, Isaac, and Jacob roamed with their flocks and herds; here they acquired lands; here they purchased their burial place in the Cave of Makhpelah.

After the conquest of the land by Joshua the entire area beyond Beersheba was included in the portion of Judah, the leading tribe of Israel: "Now therefore give me this mountain whereof the Lord spake. And Joshua blessed him and gave unto Caleb, the son of Jephunneh, Hebron for an inheritance" (Joshua 14:12-13). In the days of the Judges and the early monarchy, when the coastal plain was still occupied by the Philistines, large numbers of the Israelites settled in the hill regions, built their villages, and diligently tilled their fields.

In Bethlehem, David, later anointed King by Samuel, was born and tended his sheep on the surrounding slopes. In his flight from Saul he hid among these mountains, and in the bleak desert with which he was so familiar. And later, as Samuel II relates: "David dwelt in Hebron, and the elders of Israel came unto him in Hebron and there they anointed him King over all Israel."

From Hebron the newly anointed King of Israel went forth to conquer Jerusalem, which was to become his capital city. Here his son, Solomon, built the Temple, the spiritual center of the Israelites.

In the Books of the Maccabees it is related that the Hasmoneans fought several major battles against the Hellenistic Syrian armies in this area, and that after peace was restored many Jewish villages were re-established here. The numerous ruins, the stone terraces on the hillsides, traces of which can still clearly be discerned, bear mute testimony to the density of the population and intensive cultivation of the mountains and valleys by the Jewish farmers.

Even after the destruction of the Sanctuary in Jerusalem by Titus' legions, Hebrew villages continued to thrive here. But Bar Kokhba's war, which was waged largely to the south and west of Jerusalem, was followed by the ravaging and destruction of many Judean towns and villages. Hadrian's official historian lists a large number of Jewish villages and towns in these environs which were razed in the course of the war. Those of the Jews who were taken prisoner by the Roman legions were sold into slavery at an enormous fair held near Hebron, and thence, via Gaza, were transported to Egypt.

In the Talmudic era there were still Jewish villages in this region. The inhabitants tilled the soil and engaged in various crafts or in trade, while a considerable number were students of the Law. The Church Fathers, Eusebius and Jerome (in the third and fifth centuries respectively) mention these villages south of Hebron. Significantly enough, there is no reference to Jewish settlements along the Jerusalem-Hebron highway. Because of the sanctity ascribed by Christians to Jerusalem, Bethlehem, and Hebron, a large number of monks settled there and forbade any Jews to take up residence in their midst or in the surrounding district. But there is historical evidence of Jewish community life in Hebron in the seventh and, again, in the eleventh century.

Jewish settlement in the City of the Patriarchs, however, was interrupted following its conquest by the Crusaders in the year 1100 and was resumed only after the victories of Saladin. In the early thirteenth century a group of rabbis from France settled in the Holy Land, and from then on Jewish communal life continued uninterrupted in this city for over seven hundred years.

In the sixteenth century, Hebron was developed as a Cabalistic center by the disciples of Rabbi Isaac Luria, the "Ari." In the first quarter of the nineteenth century Hassidim of the Habad sect settled in the city, and established a Yeshiva called Magen Avot. The Jewish community there soon counted some two thousand souls and expanded beyond the confines of its ghetto, founding new quarters in which institutions of charity and of learning were established.

As a result of the economic depression which followed the outbreak of the First World War, Hebron entered upon a period of decline and the Jewish community was depleted to about seven hundred inhabitants. Even the great influx into Palestine which came in the wake of the Balfour Declaration and the institution of the British Mandate did little to change the face of the ancient city, for few of the Jewish immigrants settled there. In this respect, however, the renowned Knesset Yisrael Yeshiva of Slobodka (Lithuania) showed remarkable initiative by transferring in 1925, a large portion of its institutions to Hebron.

The revival, however, was shortlived. In the riots which broke out in the late summer of 1929 the community was utterly destroyed. Sixty-six Jews were massacred by the

Arab rabble, among them a large number of the Yeshiva students. Many others were wounded and the survivors abandoned the city immediately. Whatever Jewish property remained behind was plundered.

When security was re-established, attempts were made to restore the ancient Jewish community, but the renewed outbreak of countrywide violence and Arab terror in 1936 frustrated them, and Hebron has remained a city without Jews ever since.

When the British Mandate over Palestine came to its close, an estimated eighty-five thousand Arab inhabitants lived in the Hebron Hills. Almost all were Moslems, but the inhabitants of the villages in the Bethlehem area were for the most part Christians. The greater part of the populace lived in villages located on hilltops or near springs, and in hamlets built on the site of an ancient ruin or a holy place, containing no more than several hovels, inhabited by members of a single family. Most of the villagers engaged, as their families had done for generations, in vinegrowing, horticulture and the cultivation of grain and vegetables. Their houses were constructed of stone quarried from the slopes and they conserved water for the dry summer season in cisterns hewn out of the mountain rock. About the villages every patch of soil was cultivated. Stone fences protected the small fields that had been cleared, plowed, and planted, from the ravages of erosion. Many hills, however, the top soil of which had been washed down into the valleys by the heavy winter rains, remained bleak and desolate. In some areas, indeed, the general aspect was of gaunt desolation.

In the summer Beduin tribes from the Judean Desert,

wandering in search of pasture for their flocks, would set up their encampments in this neighborhood.

The main artery of this region was the eighteen-mile tortuous highway running from Jerusalem southward towards Hebron. This road was of considerable economic importance, for besides serving the local villagers, it connected Jerusalem with southern Palestine. The religious and historic sites along it, as well as its scenic beauty, would attract many tourists.

Two miles south of the Holy City stood Rachel's Tomb —a small stone domed building which drew Jewish pilgrims from all over the world. Another mile further south, straddling the road, were the adjoining towns of Bethlehem with a population of about eight thousand, to the left, and Beth Jalla, with three thousand, to the right. The inhabitants of these towns benefited greatly from the large number of Christian pilgrims and tourists drawn to Bethlehem and from the income of the various church institutions.

Eastward of Bethlehem, toward the Judean Desert, lay the village of Beth Sahur, the majority of whose two thousand inhabitants were Christians.

Solomon's Pools were located two miles south of Bethlehem. It is believed that the digging of these pools was begun in the days of King Solomon; hence the name. Large stones of an aqueduct of Roman times for conveying water to Jerusalem had been found there. These pools were still in use and served as a water-reservoir for the area. The tracts of land near the pools were irrigated and cultivated. Vineyards covered the hillsides near the road and in their midst there stood small isolated houses. One of these houses was known as Nebi Daniel.

On the slope of a hill, rather more than a mile east of Solomon's Pools, the ancient village of Artas, counting some five hundred Moslem inhabitants, was situated.

Hirbet Sawir, consisting of several dilapidated buildings, stood some five miles further south, to the right, on a hill dominating the highway. Many tribesmen of the Ta'amra Beduin made it their practice to camp out here and in the neighborhood toward the close of summer. On a small hill to the east there was a lone house, the summer residence of the Mukhtar of Bethlehem.

A side road separated Hirbet Sawir from the Russian Monastery, to its south. The Monastery had been established in 1902 by the Russian Orthodox Church to serve as a hostel for Russian pilgrims traveling between Jerusalem and Hebron. It stood on a hill overlooking the main road and consisted of two buildings erected by the monks, as well as oak and pine woods and orchards of olive and fruit trees.

Opposite the road leading to the Monastery a path turned off to the village of Beth Fajjar, which occupied a bald crest overlooking the Judean Desert.

The highway continued on its serpentine course and came to a Government Experiment Station near which, to the right, was the historic Valley of Brakha. Chronicles II 20:26 relates that after Jehoshaphat's war on the Ammonites and Moabites, "they assembled in the Valley of Brakha, for there they blessed the Lord; therefore the same place was called the Valley of Brakha unto this day." From there the main road climbed to its highest summit near the large village of Halhul, with its twenty-six hundred Moslem inhabitants. There was a British Army encampment nearby. From Halhul the highway wound down to Hebron.

Hebron had twenty thousand inhabitants, the source of whose livelihood was viticulture, arable farming, sheep breeding, the manufacture of cheese, crafts, and trade. This city served as a center for an extensive area and as a communication hub linking Jerusalem, Jericho, and Trans-Jordan on the one hand, with Beersheba and the Negev region on the other.

The Hebron Hills region had for long been considered an Arab stronghold. The villages here were large and prosperous, while the towns of the district, all well-known centers of Arab nationalism, served as a hinterland for the Arabs of Jerusalem. The Arab highlanders were renowned both for their religious fanaticism and their courage, and were regarded as formidable fighters.

Just west of the Russian Monastery, midway between Jerusalem and Hebron, there was a hill known as Dahar-el-Kadis—the Holy Mount. From the beginning of the century the hill itself had been the property of an Arab of the nearby village of Beth Umar, who had built a house there, but as a result of financial difficulties, was forced to sell it. In 1928, the small estate was occupied by German Benedictine monks. The Benedictines built a large roomy house—which later came to be known as the German Monastery—as well as various farm buildings, hewed out water cisterns, and planted fruit trees.

At about the same time the Zikhron David Company, established by a group of orthodox Jews of Jerusalem, acquired land in the vicinity, and proceeded to lay the foundations of a new settlement, to which they gave the Biblical name of Migdal Eder. The new village was to subsist on fruit-growing and dairying. The settlers constructed several wooden bungalows, a synagogue, and a *mikveh* (ritual bath), and settled ten families on the land.

The time, however, was not propitious. In the late summer of 1929, when riots broke out in various parts of the country, and the neighboring Hebron Jewish community was massacred, Migdal Eder was abandoned and later looted by Arab villagers.

The area, however, did not remain desolate for long. Shmuel Holtzman, a citrus-grower of Rehovot, resolved to establish there a settlement based upon fruit-growing, which would also be developed as a vacation resort for the Jews of Jerusalem and elsewhere. Holtzman purchased the Migdal Eder land as well as scattered plots from the neighboring Arab villages, and established a colonization company. He obtained the consent of the leading members of the Russian Church in Jerusalem for the lease of the neighboring Monastery and, in 1935, a group of about forty Jewish workers was brought to the lands and quartered in the Monastery. The workers engaged in various land improvement works and laid out a large nursery of deciduous fruit trees.

In honor of the founder, the new settlement was named Kfar Etzion. (Both *holtz* in Yiddish and *etz* in Hebrew mean wood.)

In 1936, however, the Arabs of Palestine launched a new campaign of murder, arson, and robbery against the Jews. Isolated Kfar Etzion was among the first to suffer. Seedlings and fruit trees were uprooted, and the laborers were subjected to intermittent sniping. At the beginning of 1937 the decision was taken to evacuate the nascent village. The company was, consequently, soon involved in financial difficulties and was compelled to put up the land for sale.

The Kfar Etzion land was acquired by the Jewish National Fund, the Zionist land-purchase organization, which sought to create in this region an area suitable for extensive Jewish settlement. In 1942—in the midst of the Second World War—the Jewish National Fund successfully negotiated for the purchase of the neighboring German Monastery on Dahar-el-Kadis, whose monks had been interned by the British Administration as enemy aliens. There was one drawback, however. The region in which this land was located was designated by the Mandatory Government, under the Land Regulations of the 1939 White Paper, as one in which land transfer to Jews was prohibited. This difficulty was overcome by a simple stratagem. It was resolved to establish a limited company in which both the representatives of the Jewish National Fund and the monks would hold shares. At a later stage only the former were appointed to the Board of Directors of the company, thereby facilitating the transfer of the land to Jewish ownership.

In 1943, Kvutzat Avraham, a collective group affiliated with HaPoel HaMizrahi, and until then occupying a labor camp near the village of Kfar Pines in Samaria, accepted the proposal made by the Jewish settlement institutions that they occupy the land of Kfar Etzion for permanent settlement.

THE KVUTZAT AVRAHAM PIONEERING GROUP

Kvutzat Avraham was organized in 1934 in Lwow, Poland at a gathering of *halutzim* belonging to the Bnei Akiva Organization. This youth movement of HaPoel HaMizrahi had dedicated itself to the building of the Jewish homeland according to the precepts of Torah and labor, and had resolved to embark on a course of self-realization to be achieved in a communal-pioneering framework. Kvutzat

Avraham, named in honor of the then Chief Rabbi of Palestine, Rabbi Avraham Y. H. Kook, was the embryonic body of the *kvutza* to be.

In early 1934, an advance group of nine members of Kvutzat Avraham arrived in Palestine and joined the Shahal pioneering group at Rehovot for a period of training. Six months later they were reinforced by a second group from Poland.

In May, 1935, a group of nine young men and women left Shahal and pitched their tents on a small hill near Kfar Pines in Samaria. The group was to be on its own and to train intensively for the anticipated day of colonization. In this preparatory period its members were to advance their farming knowledge and technical skills, absorb new members to reach the complement necessary for establishing a settlement, and to consolidate the fellowship of the collective, socially and culturally.

Privation and hardship were in store for the settlers in the early period, much of it a result of their inexperience in farming and the absence of suitable guidance. They cleared a small plot of land and out of their meager savings built a bungalow, laid down water-pipes, developed a vegetable garden, and acquired a variety of tools and agricultural implements. Gradually they found employment in the neighboring orange groves and in construction work in the vicinity. A loan extended to the *kvutza* by the Jewish Agency made possible the erection of more bungalows for housing and the development of the small farm.

Additional men and women joined the young collective. Kvutzat Avraham was accepted into the newly-founded Religious Kibbutz Federation of HaPoel HaMizrahi. As the group gradually established itself a number of its members were seconded for work in the Bnei Akiva youth movement and were even sent on various missions abroad.

In the spring of 1938, the *kvutza* was reinforced by a comparatively large contingent of newcomers from a training farm in Galicia. Other groups, from training farms in Poland, from the Bnei Akiva of Czechoslovakia and the Bachad in Germany also joined them. A shortage of housing and chronic unemployment in the Kfar Pines area compelled the *kvutza* to seek work further afield, and a group of members was dispatched to Givat Ada, a small colony in the foothills of Mount Ephraim, to work as hired laborers on the local farms.

In the following year the *kvutza* was again reinforced by religious *halutzim* from Central Europe, who arrived in Palestine on board various "illegal" immigrant vessels. The number of members of the group was now eighty.

In the meantime preparations for the future continued. Members were sent to settlements in the Jezreel Valley to undergo training in the major branches of farming; a carpentry, a cobbler-shop, and a bakery supplied the needs of the settlers; new buildings were erected; the small-holding was enlarged and new agricultural branches were initiated. The members also took part in clandestine Hagana training courses and became adept at handling military weapons.

The outbreak of the Second World War led to a period of crisis and depression. Work in the orange groves, the main source of the *kvutza's* livelihood, abruptly came to a standstill. Once again the position deteriorated and again many of the settlers had to wander far from Kfar Pines to take advantage of whatever employment they were offered.

The continued arrival of new members from Poland and Czechoslovakia, however, who had fled from the advancing

Germans, did much to encourage the settlers. And despite difficult material conditions, socially and organizationally, the group was acquiring cohesion. Cultural work and religious study were expanded to include all members of the *kvutza*. A settlement "Journal" appeared regularly, new books were bought for the library, and a reading room was furnished and equipped. The mutual ties between the members were strengthened, the newcomers were satisfactorily absorbed into the communal structure, and the group experienced a new period of consolidation. In this period the first children were born.

Meanwhile, events in North Africa and in the Middle East threatened the future of the Jewish community in Palestine, and a number of members enlisted in the British Army. Others volunteered for service in the Palmah and the Jewish Settlement Police Force. In all, twenty members of the *kvutza* were on military service in this period.

Towards the end of 1942, the Zionist settlement authorities approached Kvutzat Avraham and proposed that it settle on the abandoned lands of Kfar Etzion. This meant that after seven years of training the group was thought fit to establish itself at last.

This proposal was received with mixed feelings. Many of the members contended that they had trained themselves in the *kibbutzim* of the Jezreel Valley and on the farms of Givat Ada for settlement in the lowlands, and had looked forward to broad irrigated fields, cultivated by modern farm machinery. The hilly terrain of Kfar Etzion was different. The work of improving the land, of creating the elementary pre-conditions for successful farming on the bleak, boulder-strewn hillsides of the dreary Hebron highlands, would require many years and intensive effort. There were no subterranean water sources in the region, and only water collected from the rains or transported from afar could supply the agricultural and domestic needs. The dangers to which solitary settlement was exposed in this unruly Arab district was another factor that had to be taken into account, for the nearest Jewish community would be in Jerusalem, eleven miles away.

Those in favor of the proposal did not ignore the magnitude of the difficulties. They expressed the hope that the national institutions would appreciate their difficulties also and would help them to establish a self-supporting settlement. They stressed, in the course of the stormy debates, that it was a privilege to re-establish a Jewish settlement between Jerusalem, City of David, and Hebron, City of the Patriarchs. Some of the members, remembering the position of European Jewry, spoke of opening up a new area for the settlement of the survivors of the holocaust.

After a good deal of discussion, it was decided to accept the proposal and to occupy the "Holy Mount."

An advance group of thirteen settlers, ten men and three women, took possession of the lands of Kfar Etzion in April, 1943, and set up their home in the German Monastery. They were reinforced by a squad of twelve youngsters serving in the Orthodox detachment of the Palmah, of whom two were also members of Kvutzat Avraham. In addition there were two veteran *shomrim* (watchmen). The occupation was carried out secretly, to minimize and, if possible, to avoid hostile reactions among the British authorities and the Arab community.

There is a significant entry in the Journal of the *kvutza* for that day. It reads as follows:

> For us this day marks the end of one period and the beginning of another—a period of conquest and settlement. We know that the task we have assumed is a difficult one. Every new colonization project demands supreme effort and no little sacrifice from the settlers. The project upon which we are engaged will call for even greater effort, stamina, and consciousness of our duty as *halutzim.*
>
> In Kfar Etzion we shall be opening up a new and exceedingly difficult area for Jewish settlement. We shall have to dedicate all our spiritual and material resources to strike sturdy roots in this area. . . .
>
> It is a terrible period we are living through. Our relatives and our fellow-Jews are experiencing a horrible fate in Europe. Great Jewish communities are being totally annihilated.
>
> We can only seek consolation in our efforts to rebuild our country, to develop a secure homeland, which can serve as a haven for those who survive.

The three buildings of the German Monastery compound, comprising twenty-four rooms, were cleaned and renovated. The walls of some of the rooms of the Monastery were still adorned with crucifixes, religious pictures, and the like but, shortly afterwards, monks of the Benedictine Order came from Jerusalem to remove their property. An Arab, who had been raising pigs on the Monastery grounds, left several weeks later.

The first concern of the settlers was to secure the settlement. A barbed wire perimeter fence and defense posts were constructed and fourteen members of the *kvutza* left for Jerusalem to participate in a special government course for supernumerary policemen. In July, a Settlement Police post was established by the Mandatory Government at Kfar Etzion equipped with twenty rifles. A motor truck was purchased to maintain regular communications with Jerusalem.

The settlers established neighborly relations with the Arab village of Beth Umar and its extension, Saffa, as well as with the few inhabitants of the hamlet of Hirbet Zakaria, barely a mile to the north. They also maintained friendly relations with the occupants of the Russian Monastery—two monks and a Christian Arab family from Bethlehem who had leased the land—one mile to the east. On the other hand, there were hardly any contacts at all with the other Arab villages in the vicinity.

Most of the land was unfit for cultivation and had to be cleared. Boulders had to removed, underbrush uprooted, and terraces laid out. Two wagons and four mules were acquired for field work and land improvement. Later, the Jewish National Fund sent a bulldozer manned by a trained operator to help the settlers in this work. Dozens of work days were devoted to the preparation of each acre.

There were no water sources in this area and it was necessary therefore to rely on the winter rains. It was possible to store twelve hundred cubic meters of rain water in the cisterns of the German Monastery, but the minimum needs of the farm were three thousand cubic meters a year. It was necessary, therefore, to supplement the rain waters with tanker-carried water from Jerusalem.

In the winter of the first year the foundations of the dairy branch were laid. An attempt to sow fodder and cereals failed and it was soon clear that the area was unsuitable for arable farming. The experimental growing of vegetables was hardly more successful. On the other hand, the planting of fruit trees and vines—plums, apples, and grapes

—for which these hills were eminently suited, was carried out successfully, but only after a number of years would the orchards begin bearing fruit.

Gradually the size of the group grew as more and more members were transferred from the labor camp in Kfar Pines to Kfar Etzion. But while the grant which the colonization authorities had placed at the disposal of the settlers was considerable, it still did not permit them to build as fast as they wished. As a result, some of the men, most of the women, and all of the children were compelled to remain for over a year in Kfar Pines. This prolonged separation of families caused a good deal of hardship and unnecessary expenditure.

Ten months after the settlement was founded, the Jewish National Fund resolved to honor Rabbi Me'ir Berlin, the venerable leader of the Religious Zionist movement, by planting at Kfar Etzion a forest of twenty thousand trees in his name. The planting of the first trees was the occasion of a celebration held in January 1944, attended by many distinguished members and leaders of the Jewish community.

The Plantation Scroll, read by one of the members of the *kvutza,* reflected the feeling in the new settlement at the time:

> On this twenty-sixth day of Shvat, 5704, in the fifth year of the Second World War, at the close of the first year of our occupation of this site, we, settlers of Kvutzat Avraham of HaPoel HaMizrahi, are planting fruit and forest trees in Kfar Etzion, observing the injunction of the Torah, "When ye come to the land ye shall plant," for "He did not create it for chaos; He created it for habitation."
>
> . . . The trees we are planting today are a symbol—a symbol

of the path we tread as pioneers of our people, a symbol of our covenant with the soil of our homeland, "for man is like unto the tree of the field." The roots these trees will strike deep in the soil will always remind us to engage in the practical work of construction, of planting, and all manner of labor. The lofty tree tops will inspire us with high thoughts, to know our Creator, to strive constantly to achieve moral integrity, and to sanctify life. This is the way our forefathers trod; it is our way as pioneers of Torah and labor.

Two thousand years ago these slopes reverberated with the sounds of a multitude of trees and life that teemed all about. Today they stand bleak and desolate.

We have taken this oath upon settling in Kfar Etzion: We shall not rest nor know peace until we cast off the shame of barrenness from these highlands, until we shall cover them with fruit and forest trees which together shall give forth a song of rebirth, which the Prophet Ezekiel foresaw: "But ye, O mountains of Israel, ye shall shoot forth your branches and yield your fruit to my people of Israel; for they are at hand to come. For behold I am for you, and will turn unto you, and ye shall be tilled and sown. And I will multiply men upon you; all the house of Israel, even all of it; and the cities shall be inhabited and wastes shall be builded."

Blessed be He who has kept us alive, and sustained us and enabled us to see this time.

The establishment of a new settlement in the Hebron Hills was recognized as an historic event by all sections of the Jewish community in Palestine. The rejoicing of the inhabitants of nearby Jerusalem was naturally greater, and they were frequent visitors. Scholars and rabbis came often to address the settlers. The Fifteenth Day of the Hebrew month of Shvat, the Jewish Arbor Day, was celebrated by school children in this neighborhood.

The Regional Command of the Hagana took advantage

of the isolated position of Kfar Etzion to establish a secret training base there.

Immediately after Passover of that year (1944), Kfar Etzion was the scene of another celebration; this time the occasion was the arrival of the womenfolk and children from Kfar Pines. The village began to seem more than a pioneering outpost. Its population now totalled one hundred and twenty.

The final building plans of the settlement were now approved and the work of construction began. A large new water cistern was hewn out to supplement the reservoir constructed by the monks. Other farm buildings followed: two dairy barns in which some twenty cows were to be housed, and six chicken coops for several thousand hens. Soon a mechanical shop was in operation. A marble quarry was also established on a neighboring hill. A generator to supply the electricity needs of the settlement was installed. A medical clinic was also set up, headed by a doctor from Jerusalem.

In the winter of 1944-45, fifteen acres of new orchards and vineyards and fifty thousand forest trees were planted.

In the spring of 1945, the *kvutza* established a rest resort, for which special buildings had been erected and the necessary personnel trained. The opening of the resort coincided with the inauguration of a regular service by the Egged bus line to Jerusalem.

In the summer of that year a group of Youth Aliya graduates who had undergone agricultural training joined the *kvutza*. A group from South Africa was also absorbed, as were a number of *halutzim* from Egypt. The *kvutza* was also reinforced by a group of young men and women, survivors of the European holocaust, who had undergone training in Belgium and Switzerland.

Another important event in 1945 was the dedication of Nveh Ovadia, a rest resort exclusively for writers and scholars. This was a spacious building, the largest in the village, and it was to serve as the religious and cultural center of Kfar Etzion.

In September, 1946, six children of the *kvutza* inaugurated the settlement's school, housed in a small building specially erected for the purpose.

The isolation of Kfar Etzion was relieved in October, 1945, with the establishment of Massuot Yitzhak, on an adjacent tract of land, a mile to the northwest. Massuot was also a collective settlement affiliated with the HaPoel HaMizrahi Organization. It consisted of young pioneers from Czechoslovakia and Hungary who, after having escaped to Palestine during the Second World War, had been educated in various religious agricultural institutions and settlements. Their village was named in honor of the Chief Rabbi, Yitzhak Isaac Herzog. Several months after its settlement on the land, a rough road was laid down to connect it with Kfar Etzion and the danger of isolation during the heavy winter rains was averted.

Two other collective settlements, Ein Tsurim and Revadim, were also founded nearby. The first was established in the fall of 1946, and was sited two miles to the northeast of Massuot Yitzhak. Its members were native-born *Sabras* who had received their education in the Bnei Akiva Organization. Ein Tsurim (Spring of Rocks) was named after the small spring on the lands of the new village.

The fourth settlement, half-a-mile west of Ein Tsurim,

was established by members of the MiSella training group of the HaShomer HaTsa'ir Organization in February, 1947. This group had undergone both agricultural and military training as a Palmah unit. The name *Revadim* (Hebrew for strata), alluded to the visible strata of bare rock characteristic of the surrounding hills.

In the autumn of 1947, just before the outbreak of the first phase of the Israel-Arab War, the Etzion Bloc occupied an area of nine square miles. The total population of the four villages was four hundred and fifty persons. Kfar Etzion had two hundred and twenty inhabitants (including sixty-five women and fifty-seven children); Massuot Yitzhak one hundred and twenty-three (thirty-three women and twelve children); Ein Tsurim fifty-five (seventeen girls); and Revadim eighty (twenty-seven girls).

I

UNRULY ROADS

"In the days of Shamgar the son of Anath, in the days of Jael, the highways ceased, and the travelers walked through byways."
Judges 5:6

1 "In Thine Own Blood Live"

The resolution passed by the United Nations Assembly on November 29, favoring the establishment of a Jewish State in part of Palestine, brought nearer the realization of a dream shared by all inhabitants of the Etzion Bloc. The rejoicing of the settlers, however, was tempered by their anxiety for the fate of their villages which, according to the adopted Partition Plan, would remain in the proposed Arab State. In view of the hostility of the Arab leaders to the plan and their threats against the Jewish population, the settlers were only too conscious of their shortage of manpower and of the limited arms and equipment they possessed with which to maintain a prolonged defense —if necessary. Meanwhile they persisted in their efforts to foster friendly relations with their fellahin *neighbors.*

From the Journal of Kfar Etzion—November 29, 1947
(Saturday night)

Throughout the Sabbath we were all in a state of suspense, waiting for the decision of the United Nations to be made at Lake Success. During the morning service special prayers and Psalms were recited in keeping with the Chief Rabbinate's instructions. Throughout the day a mood prevailed of expectation of Divine intercession.

In the evening the *haverim* sat bunched round the radio, listening to the bulletins as they came through. About midnight we heard the first news of how the voting had gone. A wave of joy swept through the village. We sang songs of rejoicing on the surrounding hillsides, while an ever-growing circle of *haverim* danced in the farmyard. We lit a bonfire to proclaim the news throughout the countryside.

November 30

The spirit of rejoicing was still apparent this morning. A flag is flying from the roof of Nveh Ovadia. The dining hall was decorated with flowers and fitting Biblical passages. The tables were laid with white cloths as if today were a holiday. We sang *zemirot* at lunch, and just before Grace we sang Psalm 126, "when God returned the captivity of Zion," with great joy. . . .

That Arab from the neighboring village, who professes to be our friend, came to ask why we had hoisted a flag. We told him and congratulated him on the decision to establish an Arab State. He congratulated us in turn. . . .

According to the radio there have been attacks on the road and a number of Jews have been killed. Dougan, the friendly English police officer from Hebron, who came to congratulate us, warned us of a possible attack. . . .

This evening, we all gathered in Nveh Ovadia to celebrate. First we recited the *Hallel* thanksgiving prayer, after which one of our members delivered an address. He took as his theme the sufferings that must be endured before redemption is complete. Then we sang songs of the Ghettoes of Nazi-occupied Europe, of the "illegal" immigration, and of the Hagana.

December 3

News has come through of an Arab attack on the Jerusalem Commercial Center. It is likely that our Bloc will also be attacked. The guards have been reinforced. Last night an armored car approached in the dark. After a careful inspection we allowed it to enter. There were seven British policemen in the car, who had been sent by Dougan from Hebron in case of an attack upon us. They remained until quite late. . . .

The radio and the newspapers report attacks on Jewish traffic on the roads, of the "neutrality" of the British, and also of resistance and of the first martyrs in the cause of Jewish independence. So far we have not allowed the situation to inconvenience us. People go to Jerusalem as usual about their normal business. The Egged bus keeps to its regular schedule, though it has already been stoned. The only change is that our vehicles now travel in convoys, escorted by Settlement Police of the Mobile Patrol. On the surface, at least, everything is quiet in our area, but if the convoy is late in coming the anxiety is felt everywhere.

The tanker goes every day to Jerusalem to bring water for the Bloc's cisterns in case of an emergency, and our buyers are also trying to lay in stocks of food. Our security men are making the rounds of the various institutions of the Hagana, insisting that special arrangements be made for the defense of the Bloc.

Shalom K. has written an editorial for *Alonim,* the organ of HaKibbutz HaDati, on the significance of the events we are experiencing these days. It says in part:

> There is the sound of rejoicing and salvation among the hosts of Israel. The dream of many generations is being realized before our eyes. The State of Israel will soon become a reality, transforming the very foundations of our life in this country and our standing among the nations of the world. . . .

The riots which broke out throughout the country following the proclamation of the establishment of a Jewish State, have not taken us by surprise. We always feared that the birth of the State would call for considerable sacrifice in both blood and property. . . . We are a people experienced in making sacrifices, but today we are inspired by the knowledge that our blood is not being shed in vain. It is the blood of a covenant, marking the beginning of the liberation of our homeland. In the words of the prophet:

"And I passed by thee and saw thee polluted in thine own blood, and I said unto thee: In thine own blood live! Yea, in thine own blood live! . . ."

December 4

We have received reports that Arabs are trespassing in the territory of the Bloc and passing from Surif in the direction of Nahalin and other villages in our neighborhood. The settlements have been ordered to put out patrols to prevent the Arabs from infiltrating. Every evening a squad of men, armed with rifles and sub-machine guns, takes up positions on Rock Hill, overlooking the wood, and Wadi Abu Rish to the west. At midnight they are relieved by another squad which remains on guard until morning.

The settlers of Massuot Yitzhak are stationed on a height in the direction of Jabba. The men of Revadim and Ein Tsurim take up positions in the direction of Nahalin and the feeder road leading to the main highway.

December 5

Today is Friday and reports have come in of thousands of Arabs gathering in Hebron with the intention of marching on Jerusalem. Their route will take them past our settlement and we must be on the alert.

We are a little apprehensive. Can we prepare sufficiently in the few days at our disposal?

December 7

Yesterday at noon we noticed an Egged bus driving along the feeder road. As it was Sabbath we were all very much surprised, and one of the *haverim* went out to determine the reason for this desecration of the Holy Day. Inside the bus was a platoon of the Palmah. Its commander brushed aside our queries with "What questions you ask! I could not sleep all night. I was afraid we should come too late." Apparently we have not realized the gravity of the situation. The platoon has come to reinforce us. . . .

In the evening, while we were putting the children to sleep, we suddenly heard shots fired. The alert was sounded and we ran out with our arms to the defense posts. We lay on the cold earth, waiting for further shots. Shortly afterward the all-clear was sounded. It had been a maneuver.

The *haverim* gathered in the dining hall to discuss the exercise.

This was how Ya'akov A., the District Commander, summarized the results of the maneuver:

> There are not sufficient arms for all the defense posts.
> The men are not sufficiently alert.
> The efficiency of all *haverim* must be increased.

Beside him a short, lean lad with dark, intelligent eyes stood listening. He looked like a senior boy from high school. "Who is he?" someone asked.

"That is Danny Mass, the new Commander of the Bloc," someone else replied. . . .

One of our informers has reported that the neighboring Arabs are getting ready for an attack, but that he does not know any further details. A state of alert has been declared. The guards have been strengthened.

Just before evening a car left the Bloc for Jerusalem. Where the feeder road meets the highway the passengers were attacked by a group of Arabs and robbed of their money. Apparently the band had planned to waylay the Egged bus which returns to Jerusalem at about that time. But the regular bus-service has been discontinued.

December 8

It is Hanukka, Feast of the Lights. A large electric candelabrum has been placed on the roof of Nveh Ovadia. Its lights can be seen from the distance. . . .

In the evening the children of the kindergarten and the school had a pleasant Hanukka party. Parents and other *haverim* who did not have to go out on guard duty enjoyed themselves very much. . . .

In view of the gravity of the situation, the defense posts have been reinforced and a projector has been installed. During the day the womenfolk keep watch at the observation posts and guard various other defense posts in the area. All women who have so far not been trained in the use of arms participate in the training program.

Work on the farm is being reduced to allow for the construction of various fortifications.

December 9

The villagers of Saffa and Hirbet Zakaria are trying to finish their plowing and seeding. They are working with a large number of mules in order to finish the work as soon as possible. They insist that they will do us no harm.

We can hear the sound of firing from the direction of Beth Fajjar. . . .

Our convoy was held up at the Bethlehem Police Station and searched for arms. Nothing was discovered.

December 10

Ha'im M., accompanied by a friend, went yesterday to invite an Arab friend from Beth Umar to his wedding. His Arab friend warned him to return without delay to Kfar Etzion, before the *shabab* (youth) made trouble. On their way back they were stoned by the urchins and it was only with difficulty that they escaped. . . .

Last night there were two weddings. The relatives and the rabbi could not get here from Jerusalem. Tsvi solemnized the marriages. The tables were laid and beautifully decorated and the *haverim* did all they could to be gay in the presence of the brides and bridegrooms. Singing and dancing continued for a long time.

We have been informed of a meeting of representatives of the villages in the region with the commander of the "Arab Rebellion." The villagers were called upon to attack the Bloc. Four of the ten representatives present agreed to the plans outlined. Four others refused to do so, while the remaining two gave no clear reply.

From a report of the meeting of representatives of the Jewish settlements situated in the territory of the proposed Arab State—December 10

The decision taken by the United Nations on November 29, 1947, regarding the partition of the country affects thirty Jewish settlements, which have been left outside the borders of the proposed Jewish State. These settlements are located in Galilee, the Negev, and the Jerusalem district. The resolution has caused some apprehension among the settlers as the villages, for the most part, are remote from the main centers of Jewish settlement, and are unable to support or defend themselves.

For this reason a meeting was called today of representatives of these villages, at the offices of the General Federation of Labor to discuss the situation. Despite the attacks on Jewish traffic all representatives of the villages attended. Among the points on the agenda were fortifications, emergency stores, reinforcements, and added supplies of arms and ammunition.

The major point of concern, as expressed by A. Hartzfeld, was whether these thirty settlements should continue to be maintained on their present sites in the proposed Arab State, or should be evacuated to the territory of the Jewish State. He clearly stated that no one at the moment was considering evacuation.

The Etzion Bloc was represented by four delegates, one from each of our four villages. They were accompanied by Shalom, who is working in Tel Aviv and was especially invited to attend. Shalom spoke on behalf of the Bloc. In his characteristically ardent manner of address he stressed how ridiculous it was for the institutions to continue their peacetime practice of selling Sten-guns for cash to individual settlements. "The villages must be fortified and equipped with arms. We shall settle our account when the time comes," he said. He also raised the question of the proposed national frontiers and insisted on our being included within the International Zone of Jerusalem.

It was resolved that each settlement prepare plans for

development and for the doubling of its population within a period of six months.—NATAN SH.

From the Journal of Kfar Etzion—December 11

A normal day of work. We were engaged in the more urgent jobs, including the perimeter fence and fortifications. Most of us are back at our usual tasks.

At noon an armored car with a crew of British soldiers visited the area.

In the evening we waited in vain for the convoy from Jerusalem. In the distance we saw flames and heard the faint sound of firing. We were very anxious about the fate of the convoy.

From the report of the Commander of the Mobile Patrol and the accounts of passengers of the convoy—December 11

The convoy was made up of four trucks carrying food and water for the settlements. There were twenty-six people in it, including the escort of eight Settlement Police. The truck belonging to Kfar Etzion, on which there were nine people, led the convoy and Revadim's light truck made up the rear. In the latter vehicle there were eight people, including Danny Mass and Yatza, commander of the Palmah detachment.

Beyond the Bethlehem Police Station the convoy was overtaken by a motor-cyclist, dressed in black and traveling fast. He vanished down the road.

Suddenly, near Solomon's Pools, a machine gun opened fire on the vehicles. It was concealed behind one of the terraces to the right of the road, about ten yards from the convoy. The time was 3:30 P.M. Shlomo K., who was driving the leading truck, was hit in the face by the first volley. Others in this truck were also wounded. The radiator was perforated by bullets. The truck came to a stop and blocked the road for the other vehicles. The passengers grabbed the rifles and sprang from the truck, taking cover underneath or in the ditch. Those who were not wounded returned the fire.

Shlomo remained alive for a few minutes, muttering, "Father, Mother!" with his dying breath.

Eliahu, the corporal in command of the Settlement Police, ordered his men to open fire and sprang forward to see what was happening at the head of the convoy. . . .

The driver of Revadim's truck was ordered to hurry back to the Bethlehem Police Station for help. This truck was also damaged but was still in working order. The driver could not turn round on the narrow road and so had to reverse for a mile-and-a-half, with his head out of the window all the time to see where he was going. A number of the passengers in this truck had already been wounded.

The enemy fire grew stronger and the number of our men in the convoy who could still return their fire decreased. Nevertheless, by firing from the ditch where they had taken cover, they were able to keep the Arabs off.

About a quarter of an hour after the beginning of the attack two British traffic policemen, riding on motor-cycles, appeared on the scene. They called to both sides to stop firing but the Arabs refused to obey. One of the policemen thereupon made his way through the line of fire to Bethlehem, while the other took up a position in a ditch about forty yards away.

Suddenly a British military jeep came up and the Arabs stopped shooting. The soldiers agreed to return with Eliahu to Bethlehem to bring help. They arrived at the Police Station before the truck or the policeman. The police officer, however, deliberately delayed for about twenty minutes before leaving with a squad of about ten policemen. One of the *haverim* telephoned from Bethlehem to the Settlement Police office in Jerusalem, reporting the ambush and requesting the despatch of ambulances to pick up the wounded.

Meantime, at the scene of the ambush the firing continued. Shmuel K., who was wounded in the head and lay under his truck, pleaded with those about him to take his revolver out from under the driver's seat, but before long he was hit by several more bullets and ceased breathing. Shalom K. stood by the truck, very pale, but firing away. Raphael H. crawled along a terrace to the leading truck and shouted, "They are surrounding us! We are lost!" Then he was hit by a bullet and collapsed on the road.

Yehuda was wounded at the very beginning of the attack. Together with the others he sprang from the leading truck and took cover behind the wheels. He had lost a good deal of blood and was growing weaker. He crept to the roadside and awaited his end. He became conscious of a barefooted Arab approaching. He closed his eyes and pretended to be dead. The Arab struck him and tried to take off his shirt. Finally he spat in his face and made off. Yehuda lost consciousness.

The three *haverim* still able to do so continued to fire. When they had only fifteen rounds left, a crowd of about a hundred Arabs charged down the hillside towards them. A bullet struck Shalom K. in the head. His last words were "We are lost!" Ha'im remained alone. He crept into a cleft between the rocks and waited for death or a miracle.

At the order *"Inzil"* (Down!) the mob rushed at the

convoy. One Arab kept shouting, *"Jihad! Yalla al Yahud!"* as the others began to stab the bodies and strip them of their clothes. When they had collected all that seemed of any value they set fire to the truck of Massuot Yitzhak. They made off when they heard the explosion of cylinders of cooking gas.

About ten minutes after the Arabs had left the wreckage of the convoy three British police armored cars appeared. The policemen refused to take any of the wounded, who were weak from loss of blood. About twenty minutes later two Red Shield of David ambulances, escorted by Settlement Police in a light truck, came up to collect the dead and the wounded.

Ten people were killed in this ambush and six wounded. Four of the fallen were from Kfar Etzion, one from Massuot Yitzhak, and one from Ein Tsurim; the others were Hagana members from other parts of the country who were attached to the Bloc.

The victims were brought to the Bikkur Holim Hospital mortuary in Jerusalem at 7:00 P.M. The wounded were dispatched to the Hadassah Hospital on Mount Scopus. Late at night, Mrs. Golda Myerson, of the Jewish Agency Executive, came to pay her last respects to the dead.

From the Journal of Kfar Etzion—December 12

Mourning. The sound of weeping is heard in the settlement. Two of our children have lost their fathers; Kfar Etzion's first orphans.

A group of *haverim* have gone out to dig a grave in the rocky ground. They are working in two shifts. The work is proceeding slowly. It is doubtful if they will complete their task before the onset of the Sabbath. . . .

The Arabs of the neighborhood have been warned to leave the fields and to stay in their houses and huts. The inhabitants of Hirbet Zakaria have fled.

The funeral left Jerusalem on its way to Kfar Etzion. Thousands came to honor the victims of the ambush. The Ashkenazi Chief Rabbi Herzog and Rabbi Berman eulogized the dead in front of the hospital. The cortege stopped outside the Yeshurun Synagogue where the Sephardi Chief Rabbi Uziel made a short speech.

At noon the convoy escorted by British police and soldiers brought the dead for burial. The convoy included supply trucks and reinforcements. The escorting soldiers refused to stop to allow *haverim* to salvage the supplies that still remained in the trucks of the ambushed convoy. The police promised to guard the trucks, but the Arabs had already stolen everything of value and set fire to the trucks. The entire Bloc has remained without transport. The commander of the Bloc has requisitioned a light truck that came with the convoy. The driver preferred to leave the truck and to return to Jerusalem.

The bodies were placed in Nveh Ovadia with lighted candles at their heads. Psalms were recited. All the *haverim* marched past the bodies.

The grave-diggers had performed their task. At evening we laid our *haverim* to rest.

We hurried to wash before the Sabbath, *Shabbat Hanukka*. The glow of the Sabbath candles and the knowledge that it was Hanukka seemed to lessen our grief a little. *Kiddush* was recited in a very restrained tone. Only half of the *haverim* were present at the Sabbath meal. The others were on guard duty.

December 13 (Saturday evening)

This morning we received a radio message from Chief Rabbi Dr. Herzog:

> With tears and grief I write these few words of condolence. Be strong and of good courage, for God's deliverance is near. In everything you deem necessary for defense proceed. Build everything necessary and do not heed our Holy Sabbath. Not only is this permitted, but it is incumbent upon you. May the Lord preserve you and hasten your salvation.

After due consultations we resolved to call upon the *haverim* to carry on the work of strengthening the settlement on the Sabbath. Services were held earlier than usual so that we could start work as soon as possible.

The *haverim* set to work with a will. Despite the bad weather the girls also did their share, filling sandbags and stretching barbed wire on the perimeter fence. . . .

The Kibbutz Council met to consider our future plans. We must assume that the present tragedy is not an isolated occurrence, but the beginning of the siege of the Bloc. The following was decided:

> We must regard ourselves as soldiers occupying front line positions. We must mobilize all our resources for fortification and defense, even if the sacrifice of other important interests should be necessary. Our normal routine and all intellectual and cultural activities must be so organized as to neutralize the demoralizing effects of isolation from the rest of the Yishuv. We must consider the possibility of evacuating the mothers and children.

December 14

We have lost another member in tragic circumstances. Late last night two shots were heard from Post Seven.

When the *haverim* rushed to the position they discovered Moshe Friedrich lying in a pool of blood. A weapon on the ground nearby apparently had been accidentally discharged. Once again a funeral procession descended to Abu Rish.

December 17

In our bulletin the following was printed:

> "And there went out fire from the Lord and devoured them (the two sons of Aaron) and they died before the Lord. Then Moses said unto Aaron, This is it that the Lord spoke saying, I will be sanctified in them that come nigh me" (Leviticus 10:2-3).
>
> Rashbam, in his commentary on Leviticus, writes: "Then said Moses to Aaron: Do not mourn, neither shall you weep, nor even desist from your labor, for what I say unto you the Lord has spoken, 'I will be sanctified in them that come nigh me.'"

We are beginning to adapt our lives to a new routine, in keeping with Moses' injunction: "Neither shall you weep, nor even desist from your labor."

People are beginning to talk again at the table, during mealtimes. They are even beginning to smile and sometimes one hears the sound of laughter.

December 18

We learn from non-Jewish sources that the Arabs who attacked the convoy came from Bethlehem and Beth Sahur and from the Beduin tribes of Oubeida and Ta'amra. . . .

A number of Arabs approached the borders of the Bloc in order to till their fields. *Haverim* went out to search them. The representatives of the neighboring village have asked for some sort of agreement. We shall permit them to finish sowing their fields on condition that they come in large groups. When they have finished sowing they must not come near our lands again. . . .

The Seven Days of Mourning have ended. A group of *haverim,* together with the bereaved families, went down to the graveyard to hold a memorial service.

December 21

In view of the danger of the disruption of communications our representatives have submitted a proposal to the Hagana to construct a flying strip. We can use the bulldozer for this purpose, though, unfortunately, its driver is no longer here. Various locations have been suggested. We have asked for an engineer to come here and draw up plans and for a trained operator for the bulldozer.

2 Days of Siege

Hostilities increased in fury throughout the country as the Arabs continued to spurn the resolution of the United Nations' General Assembly. The fact that Great Britain officially announced that the Mandate would terminate in May increased the determination of both the Arabs and the Jews to consolidate their positions and to prepare for the final showdown. Mobilization for the Hagana forces began of all Jewish men and women between the ages of seventeen to twenty-five.

The most vulnerable part of the Jewish defense system was its communications, for the roads linking the Jewish cities and the far-flung distant villages passed in the main through Arab-populated areas. The most exposed were those roads leading to the remote settlements in the Negev, the isolated villages in Galilee, and the highways connecting Jerusalem with the Coastal Plain, and with the few Jewish settlements around the Holy City.

The fate of the December 11 convoy resulted in the suspension of all traffic to and from the Etzion Bloc for a two week period. The Bloc was now under siege and this brought about many changes in the way of life of its inhabitants. Guard duty and work on the defenses gradually replaced the more peaceful tasks of agriculture. At the same time, in spite of the constant state of emergency, the settlers worked hard in order to prevent neglect of their farms.

Another result of the state of siege was the mounting costs of maintaining the villages, as their produce could not be marketed and defense expenditures grew steadily. The settlements were compelled to seek loans to cover the ever-widening gap between income and expenditure. Under pressure of these difficulties, the leaders of the settlements and the representatives in the city met to consider methods of easing the situation and called upon the Jewish national institutions to adopt emergency measures to assist the besieged Bloc.

From a private diary—December 25

A convoy of trucks and passenger cars bringing supplies, fuel, and barbed wire came today. A Field Force platoon, all of whose members are students of the Natural Sciences Faculty at the Hebrew University, also arrived—in addition to the Palmah detachment that arrived in the first week of hostilities. These students are going to train here and will serve as reinforcements for the Bloc.—YISAKHAR

From the account of a Palmah soldier—December 25

This was the period of preparation for what was to come. It was comparatively quiet in the Bloc. "The safest place in the country," we used to say by way of a joke. Nobody knew what fate held in store for us but we got ready, confident of ourselves. Our Palmah platoon numbered twenty odd men and three girls, in addition to two squad commanders and two platoon commanders.

The platoon consisted of *haverim* who had formerly undergone agricultural training at Ramat Rahel and Kiryat Anavim. Most of them were graduates of high schools or trade schools, with a sprinkling of youngsters from the *moshavim,* and a number of Youth Aliya trainees. For the past year, since we enlisted in the Palmah, we had spent varying periods in training around Jerusalem and on route marches in the desert. Even before they had smelled gunpowder the fellows regarded themselves as veterans. Their readiness to accept the most rigorous conditions without any complaining, their rejoicing at every patrol, their cheerful smiles, their utter contempt for all "swank" or show, became characteristic.

Our base was at Revadim. Headquarters was in the corrugated-iron laundry. We were organized in two squads, the command of the platoon being shared by the two platoon commanders.

On the next day after our arrival we made a close inspection of the area. We marched along the valleys and ravines, visited the four villages, inspected the Russian Monastery and Hirbet Zakaria, and then returned to Revadim. A number of our men were already familiar with the area from previous training there.

We did not have a chance to do much training, however. Danny decided that we must occupy Yellow Hill, so we "settled" there. One squad was on guard during the day and another during the night.

From the middle of December we kept the Jerusalem-Hebron road under constant observation. We used to go out in squads of three, under cover of the stone fence near the road, opposite Hirbet Sawir. When a convoy was expected we took up positions by the group of ruins. They were on a high hill commanding most of the road south of Bethlehem down to where it approached the Bloc. Very often we went in vain, for sometimes the convoy expected did not put in an appearance. But when we made out the line of trucks winding their way among the hills, and later, in the twilight, when we followed the headlights feeling their way back to Jerusalem, we were conscious of a profound feeling of satisfaction. Only when we had insured that the convoy had arrived safely did we leave our posts. Then we would return to Revadim to see if a letter or a parcel had come for us, to look at the papers and to read about what was happening in other parts of the country.

When no convoy was expected we would carry on with our routine training—machine guns, first aid, signals. Danny Mass would come round to visit us regularly and to chat with us and encourage us, despite the fact that he was busy organizing the defense of the Bloc. Our admiration for him was boundless; the responsibility that rested upon him was tremendous and in spite of that he lived just like one of us, and was always concerned about the welfare of his men.

Conditions were hard, but we never grumbled. We accepted things as they came, cheerfully. The spirit of comradeship that existed between all of us helped us a lot.—URIEL O.

From the Journal of Kfar Etzion—December 26

The Mukhtar of Bethlehem submitted a complaint to the police that Jews had seized and occupied buildings and other Arab property in Hirbet Zakaria. As a result a police unit accompanied by the owners of the Hirbeh put in an appearance. We told them that the complaint was without foundation.

The British Deputy Police Inspector of the Bethlehem District, who conducted the investigation, called the attention of our representative to the precarious conditions of security in the area and offered the help of the police to evacuate the Bloc.

From a private diary—December 27

We are now living in a state of siege. Orders and instructions all dealing with the defense of the Bloc are being published in rapid succession. A state of alert has been declared and everybody is expected to be ready for any emergency. All the *haverim* keep their personal arms by them and sleep in their clothes. We have been ordered to use as little light as possible during the night. A blackout is observed in all public places.

The defense posts have been reinforced. A roadblock has been constructed and a guard has been stationed at the fork in the feeder road, near the Lone Tree.

December 28

Kfar Etzion's bitter winter has begun. It is getting colder daily. The wind blows fiercely, storms occur regularly. We have frequent mists, covering everything and blotting out everything. It rains occasionally. The ground is covered with heavy clinging mud. We must be specially vigilant on nights like these. . . .

During these dark nights it is difficult to distinguish anything even if it is fairly close. Small wonder that the guards take pot-shots which cause unnecessary alarm in the settlement. . . .

Life in the *kvutza* is determined now by the routine of guard duty. The adult population is divided into three watches which are changed every week. The first watch is on guard during the early hours of the evening; the second till eleven at night. The third watch takes over until daylight, and is also on guard during the day. The members of the first two watches work at their ordinary jobs during the day.

All arrangements regarding work, mealtimes, cultural activities, meetings of the various committees, even family life, must fit in with the demands of defense. The children learn all there is to be known about guard duty, and soon adapt themselves to the hours when their parents are free. They do all they can not to make things difficult for us.—YISAKHAR

From the Journal of Kfar Etzion—December 28

At a meeting of the Kibbutz Council the need for coordinating guard duty with ordinary work was discussed. Constant spells of guard duty have affected work on the farm. The double responsibility has caused fatigue and productivity is decreasing. Defense work is steadily superseding production work. From farmers we are gradually changing into members of a garrison.

From a private diary—January 1, 1948

There are hardly more than a few hundred cubic meters of water in the Kfar Etzion cisterns. All the *kvutzot* are carefully doling out the water that is left. So far the rains have not added to the supply, which is steadily being depleted. We take a shower only once a week. Washing is confined to essentials.

We have been forced to economize with fuel, as it is difficult to obtain and transport it from Jerusalem. Without fuel our generator cannot create electricity and we need electric power for our workshops, the laundry, the searchlights and, above all, to light the perimeter fence. We need it also for the bakery. All work requiring electric current is done now in the evenings. We are using wood for cooking. We are cutting down on lighting in the rooms. The ration of kerosene has also been reduced. . . .

Work is proceeding on the perimeter fence, which we began when the siege started. We have constructed new defense posts and have strengthened the old ones. They have been roofed with tin, to provide protection from the wind and rain. We have constructed a second line of defense by strengthening various structures which were not designed for military purposes.

We are digging communication trenches, but have reached rock in a good many places and cannot get any further without a pneumatic drill. We have been able to dig long, deep trenches only on the east side of the settlement. Elsewhere we are using stone and concrete blocks to cover the approaches to the posts. But they do not give adequate protection.

Our defense plans require large quantities of building materials, tools, and, above all, fortification experts, whom we do not have. Our representatives in the cities are trying to persuade the defense authorities to supply us with what we need to finish the job. At first it was thought that the Solel Boneh contractors would undertake the work, but it turned out that workers did not want to go out to the Bloc because it is cut off. The chances of transporting the materials from the city are becoming more and more slender. For that reason jobs that could be undertaken by the settlers are being delayed. We have the feeling that not everything possible is being done to take advantage of the few weeks that we feel remain to fortify the Bloc.—YISAKHAR

From the Journal of Kfar Etzion—January 1, 1948

We have not yet been supplied with a field telephone and so we have had to devise some other method of maintaining contact between the defense posts and the command post. We have installed an electric alarm system in the form of an illuminated figure on a board in the command post, which indicates the post calling for help. A system of bells gives the reason for the alarm. . . .

Police from Hebron, together with the Mukhtar of Beth Umar paid us a visit to inquire into a complaint that we were interfering with the plowing, that we had begun to cultivate Arab lands, and that we had constructed defense posts on them. After an investigation the police officer dismissed the matter.

From a private diary—January 2

The fact that we are under siege governs our whole life. For days on end no one enters or leaves the Bloc. No representatives of the national or the defense institutions have so far come here to inspect us or to tell us about what is happening in other parts of the country. For days on end we do not even see a newspaper. The news broadcast from Jerusalem from the government controlled radio is ambiguous, when it is not deliberately distorted. Naturally people try to guess and theorize about what is going on. We feel as if we are living forgotten on an island in the heart of enemy territory.

We are waiting for the next convoy. Perhaps someone who can tell us what is happening in the Yishuv will visit us and raise our spirits. From the time when we hear that the convoy is being prepared, to the day it arrives, we are all tense and anxious. From time to time we get reports that the convoy is about to leave. Squads go out to their positions but only too often in vain. And when finally we get news that the convoy has already set out, we are all of us anxious until it reaches us.

When it comes in, what excitement in the farmyard! There is a bustle of loading and unloading. Everybody surrounds the drivers and the escorts to garner snatches of news about what is happening outside. People rush up to get their letters and to take a hurried glance at the newspapers.

When the convoy leaves, once again there is tension and anxiety until we hear that it has arrived safely in Jerusalem.—YISAKHAR

From the Journal of Kfar Etzion—January 4

Yesterday, on *Shabbat,* another convoy came in, escorted by a Hagana unit. It brought fuel, food supplies, and cement. The *kvutza's* representative in the cities also came in for a visit of a few hours to report on developments "outside" and on negotiations with the defense authorities. He told us about a meeting between representatives of the Bloc's settlements and David Ben-Gurion regarding our demands for reinforcements of arms and men. Ben-Gurion was extremely interested in what we had to tell him about the situation and expressed his appreciation of the role the Bloc was playing. He promised to deal with our demands.

From a private diary—January 4

The siege and the state of emergency have confronted us with a number of new Halakhic questions, all pertaining to the observance of the Sabbath: the loading and unloading of the trucks arriving on the Holy Day, the journeys of members on settlement matters, the execution of important defense works, guard duty and training.

There are a number of people here who prefer to stick to the strict letter of Halakha, even where there is room for latitude. On the other hand, there are others who insist that all these tasks and duties must be regarded as religious precepts and therefore do not involve desecration of the Sabbath.

In all problems that we come up against we would like to refer to the decision of the Chief Rabbinate, whose guidance we seek. But a quick decision is generally necessary, and the disruption of communications prevents this. For that reason a Committee for Halakha has been appointed, the members of which are Talmudic scholars who have, in addition, a grasp of the practical considerations involved. This Committee endeavors to solve the problems that arise in the spirit of the general instructions which the Chief Rabbinate has given us.

One opinion expressed during the meetings of the committee is that we shall have to allow a wider latitude in matters of Sabbath observance. Whatever is necessary to protect human life and to insure the safety of the Bloc we shall do on the Sabbath, but beyond that we shall not go. We shall perform our duties, conscious that we are observing a *mitzva,* but we shall make no concession for our own convenience and comfort.

This attitude must inspire all activities in the Bloc, but we must not attempt to interfere in the private life of the non-religious people who are now living with us.—YISAKHAR

3 Two-Way Convoys

Fighting throughout the country continued. According to official figures about four hundred and fifty people were killed and more than a thousand wounded during the month of December alone, mainly on the roads and in the marginal Jewish quarters of Haifa, Tel Aviv, and Jerusalem. The measures that the Mandatory Government took to restore order and security were devoted, for the most part, to restricting the fighting, but not to preventing it.

The villages of the Bloc prepared themselves for the impending storm. Reports had already filtered through of the Arabs' plans to attack them. Work on their defenses proceeded rapidly and agricultural tasks were further curtailed in order to release the necessary labor for defense tasks. Even the domestic services were short of workers.

In Jerusalem the representatives of the Bloc continued to press upon the defense authorities to send more reinforcements to the settlements.

From a private diary—January 4

It has been decided to evacuate the children and mothers to Jerusalem under the escort of British troops. Not only are these non-combatants exposed to unnecessary danger, but they use up valuable food, water, and fuel supplies. They will live in the Ratisbonne Monastery in Jerusalem where we have rented a large hall.

For the past few days the *haverot* have been busy packing the clothes and other belongings of the children. Tension is mounting. The weather is leaden and rainy. We are afraid that the British authorities will go back on their promise to escort the convoy.

January 5

Today, at last, the women and children left. In the morning it was cold and rainy, but at midday it cleared up a little. Two iron-plated vehicles and a number of trucks arrived, escorted by British troops. The womenfolk began to rush around feverishly, loading all the luggage and bundles onto the trucks. Finally we got everything aboard. The children of Kfar Etzion and Massuot Yitzhak and some mothers were crammed into the two armored vehicles. The atmosphere was stuffy, the babies were crying and the mothers bewildered. It was a sad, depressing sight.

Sorrowfully we took our leave of them. We are anxiously awaiting news that they have reached the city safely.

January 7

This afternoon a Hagana convoy of three trucks arrived safely from Jerusalem. Among its passengers was a Field Force platoon—students of the Faculty of Humanities of the Hebrew University who have come to reinforce the Bloc.

On its return journey this convoy took a number of the mothers and children who did not leave yesterday. They traveled in unarmored vehicles. Many of us regretted the lack of caution in permitting them to travel in this fashion. However, we received news from Jerusalem that the trucks had come through without mishap. . . .

The departure of the mothers and children has left an aching void in the village. The family quarters are sad. Everything recalls the life of the families that have now been rent in two. There are no longer those joyful meetings of fathers and mothers and children after the day's work.—YISAKHAR

From a letter of a settler to his family—January 7

For the time being we are grass-widowers. A number of girls have remained behind with us to maintain the various domestic services. The two modernly equipped children's houses, which we built only this year, now stand empty. One is disturbed by the unwonted quiet reigning within. Just imagine Kfar Etzion without its noise, without women, without children! Kfar Etzion, humming with activity, thriving with its stone buildings, its gardens, now has the appearance of a fortified military camp.

Our whole life hinges now on defense. This, coupled with the murder of our comrades, has a deep effect upon us. But do not think that we are down-hearted. From the first day we settled here, we knew where we were going and what we should have to expect. The Hebronites in time of trouble are wont to raze Jewish settlements in their neighborhood. This time, however, they will be destroyed themselves before they succeed in defeating us. It may cost us a lot of casualties, but the settlement will stand firm.—YEHOSHUA S.

From a private diary—January 8

We gave a farewell party for Danny Mass who spent the decisive weeks since the beginning of the siege with us. Now he is being transferred to a command in Jerusalem, and

Uzi N. is to replace him in the Bloc. All those at the party expressed the admiration and friendship they hold for him, and thanked him for his work.

Danny always conveyed the impression of a quiet, modest fellow. He won us over by his smile, by his courage, and by the self-confidence that he displays in everything he does. During the day he would be constantly on the move, from one settlement to the other, supervising the construction of fortifications, inspecting the strategic points, organizing the various military courses. Even on the stormiest nights he would be seen strolling about the settlement compound, wearing shorts and a green muffler, ensuring that nothing is amiss.

Danny was invited to come back as a guest when peace is restored.—YISAKHAR

From the diary of the Bloc's representative in Jerusalem—January 10

Danny and Uzi took part in the meeting at the Regional Field Force Headquarters. The following items were discussed: the convoys, the situation in the Bloc, the flying strip, fortifications, the perimeter fence, defense posts, and the field telephone.

It was decided:

a) To establish a field hospital in Kfar Etzion and to dispatch a surgeon;
b) To dispatch an engineer to inspect the various sites and to determine the location of the flying strip;
c) To investigate the possibility of sending mail and newspapers by plane.

At General Staff Headquarters in Tel Aviv an allocation for defense was approved.

The armaments of the settlements of the Bloc today are as follows:

Kfar Etzion:
- a) Legal: 1 Lewis gun and 33 rifles (of the Settlement Police).
- b) Illegal: 1 light machine gun, 8 sub-machine guns, 12 rifles, 2 two-inch mortars and 200 fragmentation grenades.

Massuot Yitzhak:
- a) Legal: 25 rifles (of the Settlement Police).
- b) Illegal: 1 light machine gun, 8 sub-machine guns, 2 revolvers, 12 rifles, 1 two-inch mortar, 250 scare grenades and 50 fragmentation grenades.

Ein Tsurim:
- a) Legal: 32 rifles (of the Settlement Police).
- b) Illegal: 1 light machine gun, 6 sub-machine guns, 10 rifles, 1 two-inch mortar, 280 scare grenades and 30 fragmentation grenades.

Revadim:
- a) Legal: 20 rifles (of the Settlement Police).
- b) Illegal: 2 light machine guns, 5 sub-machine guns, 4 revolvers, 16 rifles, 1 two-inch mortar, 205 scare grenades and 110 fragmentation grenades.

In addition, there are some one hundred enlisted men in the Bloc, armed with twenty-three Sten-guns, fifteen rifles, 2 two-inch mortars, two Bren-guns and one Schwartzlause heavy machine gun (all illegal).—YOSEF P.

From the account of a member of Kfar Etzion—
January 10

The defense system of the Bloc was based on a perimeter of strongpoints established on the dominating heights surrounding the villages, and on the positions erected around the settlements proper. The hilly terrain offered great possibilities for observation and defense, though this undulating area of more than three miles in diameter created special problems of communications.

Some of the heights had been occupied by the defenders at the very outset of hostilities, while others, it was agreed, were to be occupied in the event of an emergency.

The key to the Bloc was the feeder road that branched off from the Jerusalem-Hebron highway. On either side of this internal road there were two hills that dominated the highway: Hirbet Sawir to the north, on which there was a crumbling ruined village, surrounded by stone fences and an orchard, and Russian Hill to the south. The Russian Monastery stood on Russian Hill and at its foot, near the feeder road, there were several cisterns no longer in use. A tongue extending from the Valley of Brakha, known as Wadi Shahid, separated Russian Hill from Kfar Etzion.

Upward along the feeder road there was a fork near a solitary tree known as the "Lone Tree." The prong to the right continued to Ein Tsurim and Revadim, the left prong to the other two settlements of the Bloc. Near the Lone Tree, east of the road, there was a hill bearing its name, which stood out from the bald ridge stretching between the main road and the settlements. Its location and its excellent field of fire made Lone Tree Hill an important strongpoint.

West of Lone Tree Hill, on the other side of the fork, there was a rise covered with yellow rocks. This was called

Yellow Hill. It was the only site from which all the settlements of the Bloc, Hirbet Zakaria, and most of the strongpoints were visible. A stretch of the highway to the south could also be seen from it. Yellow Hill commanded the internal complex of roads and from its vantage point it was possible to counter any attempt to infiltrate into the area of the Bloc.

The hamlet of Hirbet Zakaria was on the Ein Tsurim-Revadim prong of the road. It consisted of a dozen low, dingy hovels and some stables and sheep pens. In their center was a strong stone mosque, flanked by a clump of tall trees. This strongpoint commanded a length of the feeder road and it stood in the path of any force advancing along this way to Ein Tsurim and Revadim.

Beyond the "Hirbeh" the road split again. To the right, on a hill, was Ein Tsurim. The hill overlooked Hirbet Zakaria and was within sight of Revadim. It was possible to signal from Ein Tsurim to Yellow Hill, Kfar Etzion, and Massuot Yitzhak. To the left, on considerably lower ground, was Revadim. This settlement was situated on the spur of a hill that declined in a north-westerly direction and was enclosed by heights on the other three sides.

Coming back to the first prong in the road, one turned to the left and reached Rock Hill. This hill was given its name because of the immense rocks and boulders with which it was covered. On the south the hillside dropped sharply to Wadi Abu Rish, opposite which rose the Mukhtar's Saddle. On the southeast it bordered with Kfar Etzion and a winding stretch of the road skirted the hill to that settlement. To the west, Rock Hill sloped down gently to Massuot Yitzhak.

Kfar Etzion was located on a rise in the land one mile

south of Massuot. There were gulleys on three sides of the settlement, separating it from the ranges of hills four hundred to six hundred and fifty yards away. These included Russian Hill to the east, and the "Saddles" to the southwest. The latter were a chain of hills more than half a mile from Kfar Etzion which were given their name because of their peculiar formation. The strongholds there commanded almost the whole of the Arab villages of Beth Umar and Saffa, and the path connecting these villages with Kfar Etzion.—DAVID B.D.

From the Journal of Kfar Etzion—January 11

The Mukhtars of Beth Umar paid us a visit to express their regret at the murder of the men in the convoy. They assured us that they had had nothing to do with the attack. They told us that they had come on behalf of the Mayor of Hebron who wanted to come to an agreement with us on non-aggression. We informed them that we were prepared to discuss the proposal.

From the account of an officer of the Students Unit, Mikhmash Battalion, Jerusalem Field Force—January 11

Studies at the Hebrew University in Jerusalem since the beginning of December had been held for only a fortnight in each month, to allow the students to participate in an organized fashion in the Hagana activities. A platoon of "C" Company of the Field Force, which had recently been organized, composed of Natural Science students, was sent to Kfar Etzion in the last week of December for training and guard duty. There were fifty-six men and women in the platoon. It was a heterogeneous unit, comprising ex-soldiers who had served in the British Army, a group of youngsters who had been trained in the Hagana, a number of raw recruits, and some girls. Nevertheless, it was a closely-knit formation. Its officers included Hagana trainees and men who had served in the British and French forces.

The unit tackled its duties with a will. Indeed, this was its most difficult period. The daily program consisted of an eight-hour spell in the strongpoints and three to four hours of training. The irregularity of hours of rest and meals, however, undermined the health of the men.

Billetting and supplies were not well-organized. The men were housed in dilapidated tents and their personal equipment was inadequate. They wore their own light clothes in the rainy and cold weather and it was difficult to stand guard in the windswept defense posts. It was only after the evacuation of the mothers and the children that the buildings that had been rendered vacant in Kfar Etzion were placed at the disposal of the unit.

Relations between the settlers and the enlisted men suffered because of divergent attitudes on many questions. For the settlers the villages were their homes; for the soldiers it was no more than a base to which they had been posted. The settlers endeavored to secure the exemption of as many of their members as possible from guard duty to enable them to carry on their work on the farms. The duties of the unit were of a general nature and for that reason they were reluctant to accept additional guard duty.

On January 7 a convoy brought another platoon of "C" Company, numbering fifty men and women, the majority students of the Faculty of Humanities, and about ten of them youngsters from Jerusalem. The Company Commander also arrived with them. The second platoon was stationed at Massuot Yitzhak and began training, gradually taking over guard and other duties. Despite the improvement in conditions, the health of the men declined. Work on the fortifications and the frequent spells of guard duty weakened them. A considerable number of men were sent back to the city in the return convoys.—YEHOYAKHIN K.

From the letter of a member of Kfar Etzion—January 11

The two platoons of students are taking their duties seriously. We welcomed them cordially and do what we can to make it easier for them to adjust themselves to conditions in the Bloc.

We must, of course, be very tolerant of their "military" habits and ways—such as for instance not to respect civilian property over much. We must accept their rough treatment of the buildings and furniture, of the fruit and forest trees, the flower beds and the stone terraces, with as much equanimity as we can muster. We try to explain the importance of these things to them and forgive them; for this, I suppose, is a feature of life during every war.—DOV

From the Journal of Kfar Etzion—January 12

Information is coming in about the concentration of Arabs not belonging to this district.

Two Syrian officers under the command of Abdul Kader el-Husseini, the head of the Arab forces in the Jerusalem area, are reported to have organized a large training camp at Surif. It is said that about one thousand men are training in the camp. . . .

We have been informed that Arab bands are concentrating at Beth Sahur, apparently with the intention of attacking Kfar Etzion. . . .

A convoy arrived today. It had been attacked several times on the road.

From the report of the Convoy Commander—January 12

The convoy mustered at Ramat Rahel, the kibbutz on the southern outskirts of Jerusalem. It comprised three trucks carrying supplies, one with vegetables, one with coops in which to transport chickens back to Jerusalem, and another with seedlings to be planted in the Bloc. Each of the trucks carried sacks of arms, explosives, etc. One motor car carrying three passengers—including Uzi N., the Bloc Commander—also accompanied us. The convoy was escorted by armed Settlement Police and a detachment of the Field Force. On the outskirts of Jerusalem one truck somehow lost contact with us and returned to the city.

Near Solomon's Pools we encountered a roadblock but were able to negotiate it. We encountered another roadblock about a mile further down the road, but it had been demolished, apparently by the crews of two British Bren-carriers, who were standing by. Fire was opened upon us from rifles and machine guns from the sides of the road as we approached. We returned the fire. We saw the soldiers taking cover in the ditches by the roadside, but they did not take any part in the fight.

On the road we were shot at from an Arab bus traveling along the road, and then again from the hilltops near the road. We returned the fire.

As we were turning into the Bloc we were again fired upon by members of an Arab gang, which had taken up positions behind the stone fences surrounding the orchards of the Russian Monastery. The convoy reached Kfar Etzion safely. We suffered no casualties.—M.M.

From the Journal of Kfar Etzion (Continued)—January 12

One of our units went over to the Monastery to search it. The inhabitants were interrogated regarding the shots fired at the convoy. They claimed to know nothing whatever about it, declaring that they were neutral. An ambush has been posted on the main road. . . .

The attack on the convoy has proved the need for reinforcements. We must establish a strongpoint on Russian Hill to secure our transport. . . .

We have not received any mail or newspapers, as they were on the truck that returned to Jerusalem. Any delay in the mail has a depressing effect on the people here. . . .

With the return convoy we sent two hundred and sixty live chickens to be marketed and two cows to be transferred to the coastal plain.

From the report of the Convoy Commander—January 13

The convoy left at 5:20 A.M. on its return journey to Jerusalem, when it was still dark. It comprised one motor car and four trucks, one of which was loaded with twenty coops of chickens, and another with two cows that added to the difficulties of the journey. The escort was composed of five Settlement Policemen armed with rifles, and ten Field Force soldiers, armed with Sten-guns and hand grenades. There were five drivers and three other passengers.

The trip continued without incident to Solomon's Pools. Then at the turn in the road we encountered a roadblock, and heavy fire was opened upon us. The Convoy Commander and two men of the escort tried to alight to demolish the block, but were forced to return to the trucks owing to the heavy fire. The leading driver was ordered to ram the block, and he succeeded in forcing it. A bullet hit his steering wheel but he continued to force his way through five more roadblocks. The driver of the passenger car was wounded in the leg and his vehicle was trapped in a roadblock. Hanokh Zilberstein, who was traveling in the truck just behind, was hit in the chest and fell onto the road. Zerubaval Ovadia, a Settlement Policeman, jumped down into the ditch to render first aid. He must have been hit as he jumped, as none of the men in the truck heard him cry for help . . .

The crew of the third truck, which was carrying the chickens, abandoned their vehicle after it had been damaged and climbed onto the truck carrying the cows. Two vehicles were left behind: the truck with the chickens, and the motor car.

When the first truck reached the Bethlehem Police Station its men appealed to the constables for help. The latter, however, refused to open the gate for the truck to drive in and it was only after a good deal of talk that the officer in charge allowed them to bring in the wounded men. The British policemen treated the wounded men very considerately and called a doctor from the French hospital. However, the police officer in charge refused to send any of his men to bring in the two missing men and the passengers of the motor car, saying that he must obtain permission from headquarters in Jerusalem. The Convoy Commander asked to be allowed to contact the Settlement Police office in Jerusalem but was told that the Jews had cut the telephone wires.

Only at seven o'clock did the police officer consent to send out a vehicle to the site of the roadblock. The car returned forty minutes later with the motor car passengers. An hour later two armored vehicles with soldiers of the Life Guards arrived and went out to search for the missing men. Upon their return they reported that they had not found any of the men of the convoy and that the remaining truck had been set on fire. The soldiers insisted that the convoy escort get into their cars and go back to Jerusalem, and our men did so. When they had traveled about a mile on the road heavy fire was opened up on them. The British patrol returned the fire and our men also took part in the battle that developed. The patrol accompanied the convoy to the Jewish Agency building.

When the Jewish security authorities in Jerusalem heard of the fate of the convoy they dispatched an ambulance and Settlement Police in an armored car to the scene of the fighting, but they were stopped by constables near the Bethlehem Police Station and not permitted to continue. The police went out to the site and brought back a charred body, which was identified as that of Hanokh Zilberstein of Revadim. The search for the other body continued.—M.M.

From the diary of the Bloc's representative in Jerusalem—January 13

A meeting was held at Headquarters to discuss communications and transport. It was decided that henceforth only heavy trucks with iron-plated drivers' cabins will be used. The escort will travel in Egged or HaMekasher armored buses. These buses will be at our disposal only on Saturdays.—Yosef P.

4 The Attack of January 14

From an account of the Bloc Commander—January 14

The night before the battle a report came in that the road had been blocked and that the Arabs were preparing to launch an attack on the Bloc. We also received information of concentrations of Arab bands in the surrounding hills. It was decided to dispatch a patrol towards the Jerusalem-Hebron road. The unit reached its objective in the early hours of the morning and decided to return at daybreak. After having marched about half-a-mile, the men observed many Arabs moving about on Hirbet Sawir. It seems that the Arabs noticed them too, but mistook them for their own men, as the area was swarming with Arabs.

The commander of the unit resolved to make for Ein Tsurim instead of Kfar Etzion, as had originally been planned. By the time they crossed the ridge, however, and entered the wide valley between Ein Tsurim and Hirbet Elabon, it was daylight and the Arabs identified them. Fire was opened upon them from Hirbet Sawir. The scouts did not reply and fell back in proper formation upon Hirbet Zakaria, under the covering fire of the men who had been posted there.

The scouts joined the men stationed in the Hirbeh and established perimeter positions. They returned the fire of the Arabs who were advancing along the ridge from Sawir.

At first the attackers came up along the southern slope of the ridge, but after they were attacked by a machine gun from Kfar Etzion they crossed over to the north. The movement of Arabs along this ridge towards Lone Tree Hill continued throughout the morning. . . .

It was noon. . . . The Arabs took cover behind the terraces running across the slopes leading up to Hirbet Zakaria. They placed a light machine gun in position on their left, in the middle of the NNE slope of Lone Tree Hill, and prepared for an assault. The machine gun fired without respite, and harassed the defenders a good deal. Yehoshua M. was killed then. A runner was dispatched to one of the settlements to report on the situation. As he was leaving the Hirbeh he was hit in the hand by a bullet, but despite steady sniping succeeded in reaching the settlement. Reinforcements were dispatched to the Hirbeh with ammunition and food.

A few of our men equipped with a machine gun and stationed on Yellow Hill directed fire on the Arabs of Lone Tree Hill, two hundred and fifty to three hundred yards away. One man of the Yellow Hill post was wounded and was moved to Massuot Yitzhak. . . .

Aryei T., commander of the Mobile Force in Revadim, reported that he thought a counter-attack possible. The Bloc Commander was informed and approved of the idea. A small platoon, comprising two squads—one from Revadim and the other from the Palmah unit—armed with two light machine guns, rifles and sub-machine guns, advanced on the Arabs. One squad with a machine gun took up a position in the "Saddle" near the road leading to Ein Tsurim and Revadim facing Lone Tree Hill, about one hundred and fifty yards south-west of the Hirbeh. Under the covering fire of this squad, of whose existence the Arabs, confused by the constant shooting, were apparently at first not aware, the balance of the small force advanced and took up positions on Lone Tree Hill. The Arabs had been concentrating on the Hirbeh and had left their left flank unprotected. The counter-attack force could hear their cries of "*Aleihum*" and "*Jihad*" quite clearly. . . .

The detachment that had reached Lone Tree Hill was joined by the covering squad. From their position they could see the machine gun of the Arab force to the east firing away. It was stationed in a small isolated house on the slope west of Hirbet Sawir. There were about fifty Arabs assembled nearby, eating oranges as they waited for orders to advance upon the Hirbeh. Our men opened fire with all their weapons upon the machine gun squad and the concentration near it, hitting at least twenty-five of the Arabs.

Immediately afterwards the platoon stormed the enemy positions on Lone Tree Hill, and those Arabs who were not hit, beat a hasty retreat towards their command post in the orchard on Hirbet Sawir.

Throughout the fighting the force defending Hirbet Zakaria assisted the platoon in its counter-attack by giving it covering fire and keeping the Arabs pinned down.

A little later, the counter-attacking force discovered about one hundred Arabs some sixty yards away from Hirbet Zakaria preparing for an attack upon this strongpoint under cover of the terrace. It concentrated all its fire power upon these Arabs from a range of no more than two hundred yards. It was clear that the Arabs did not know where the fire was coming from and retreated in panic up the wadi, towards the solitary house at Hirbet Sawir, leaving behind at least twenty to twenty-five dead. Some of the dead and wounded were carried off by their comrades.

The counter-attacking force then advanced on Hirbet Sawir under its own covering fire, with the support of the detachment in Hirbet Zakaria. But, seeing the Arabs getting ready to counter-attack, the men crawled back. When the Arabs did charge they found the positions empty. Our men were about two hundred yards away from them, and lay there for about an hour and a half holding their fire. . . .

From an account of a member of Revadim—January 14

At two in the afternoon the call "Striking Force, all out!" reverberated in the Revadim compound. Within a matter of minutes we were marching in column formation, following Ya'ir up the hill. Bullets were whistling overhead as we advanced, but the terrain concealed us from the enemy. . . .

The command rang out, "Prepare to charge!" The enemy was nowhere in sight, but we got ready to engage him. As we reached a high fold in the ground fire was opened up on us by a large number of Arabs directly ahead. We returned the fire and charged at them. The enemy began to retreat in great disorder. We continued to pursue him, until suddenly, heavy fire was directed at us and we hit the ground. We saw that the Arabs were preparing to flank us and once again we charged at them. This time, however, we were caught in a crossfire. Ya'ir realized this at once and shouted with all the force he could muster, "Retreat!" He continued to urge the men to withdraw, until he fell, fatally wounded.
—Eliyahu R.

From an account of the Bloc Commander (Continued)

By this time the counter-attacking force numbered no more than twelve men. One squad commander had been shot dead during the withdrawal prior to the Arab attack, one machine-gunner had been killed, two others were severely wounded, another had been wounded lightly, while a medical orderly who served as a reserve machine-gunner, had sustained a wound in the leg. The orderly bandaged two of the wounded and took them out of the line of fire, besides taking their arms and ammunition back with him. It was only when he reached the dressing station that he revealed that he had been wounded.

No Jewish arms had been left in the field. All our dead and wounded, together with their arms and ammunition, were brought back under fire to the field dressing station under the Lone Tree. The counter-attacking force concluded its task at half-past five, after a battle lasting two hours. Under cover of the dark our men withdrew to the Hirbeh. The wounded were removed to Revadim. . . .

From the report of the District Commander—January 14

On January 14 at about 7:00 A.M., we saw a group of Arabs advancing from south of the Russian Monastery. Dozens of Arabs could also be seen making for Kfar Etzion from the direction of Beth Umar. The alert was sounded and all men took up their positions.

Loaded trucks were also pulling up to Hirbet Marina, near the Government Experiment Station, from the direction of Hebron, and their passengers alighted. There, as we later learned, a transport park, a clearance station for the wounded, and a withdrawal point had been established.

Shortly afterwards the first shots were fired on Kfar Etzion from the south.

A squad of men of the Field Force, who had been stationed on the Mukhtar's Saddle since early morning, returned the fire. Our men, however, were in danger of being cut off and were ordered to retreat under covering fire from Kfar Etzion. Their retreat was very hazardous, for the Arabs had taken up positions on the slopes and were keeping up heavy fire. It was only at noon that the squad succeeded in reaching the settlement.

Meantime, at 10:15 A.M. we received a report of a large concentration of hundreds of Arabs in the Valley of Brakha. Another mob, also numbering hundreds, remained in the shelter of a hill, apparently waiting for their chance to loot when the fighting was over. At about 11 o'clock the Arabs began to advance from the direction of the Valley of Brakha towards Wadi Piretrum, immediately south of Kfar Etzion. Here they were greeted with heavy fire from a machine gun and a mortar and, after suffering a number of casualties, hastily retreated. They tried their luck again and again but the fire from our positions forced them to retreat. All the time the settlement was under concentrated fire from three directions. After the attack from the wadi failed, a few dozen Arabs crossed over to Wadi Abu Rish by way of the Saddle. Here, too, their advance was soon stopped by fire from our positions.—YA'AKOV A.

From an account of the Bloc Commander (Continued)

Throughout the day the Arabs in this sector made sporadic attempts to advance, but retreated after encountering resistance. When it became dark they retired to Hirbet Marina and the transport park, from where trucks took them back to their villages. Crowded trucks traveled back to Hebron. They left no wounded or dead behind.

We can assume that the Arabs (attacking from the south) sustained about fifteen casualties caused by a mortar shell that hit a group of them in the Valley of Brakha and our rifle fire at the Mukhtar's Saddle.—(Abridged from *Ma'arakhot,* March, 1948)

From the Journal of Kfar Etzion—January 14

When the shooting died down after dark it was revealed that the Bloc suffered three dead and many wounded. Nine of our wounded, some of them in a serious condition, were brought in from various places to the Kfar Etzion clinic. Their wounds were dressed by the local doctor, but in the absence of the necessary instruments and equipment he was unable to operate.

Headquarters in Jerusalem was requested to arrange with the British Army authorities for the removal of the wounded. . . .

A number of our men went out to the battlefield to see what booty they could pick up. They brought back three ancient rifles. . . .

The battle is over but none of us doubt that they will come back again. Reports reaching us confirm this. Our guards are vigilant, and the strongpoints have been reinforced. Girls serving in the Field Force also do guard duty, in order to give the *haverim* the chance to rest.

From a private diary—January 14

The tension and vigilance of the day have not abated. The strain is beginning to tell. The eyes close involuntarily and the tired body craves for sleep. But one must remain alert and keep a close watch in one's sector until guard duty is over.

A number of miracles happened today, but how long can we hold out in this fashion? Where will our reinforcements come from? We are a tiny island in a stormy sea of Arabs.

January 15

During the morning we heard the deep purr of an airplane engine, and soon we observed a plane circling above the Bloc.

Now I remember that yesterday during the battle when I was stationed on the roof of Nveh Ovadia I saw a plane flying overhead. I thought it was a British aircraft out on reconnaissance.

Today the plane flew low over the farmyard—so low indeed that we could see the pilot and observer clearly—and then dropped a parcel that fell somewhere in the wood. The *haverim* rushed to get it. The plane circled again and dropped another parcel and then others in quick succession. Then he dropped a note attached to a two-piaster piece asking us to signal to him if the battle was still in progress. The *haverim* scattered over a wide area searching for the ammunition and dressings which fell out of one of the packages.

Have we really got planes helping us in this war?

A larger plane suddenly put in an appearance at a higher altitude and our little plane made off without delay.

From the radio we learned that the larger aircraft was an R.A.F. plane, which, on the pretext that it had been fired upon, was trying to find out what our little plane was up to. The report stated that our pilot had been searched on landing in Tel Aviv but that nothing suspicious had been found on him. The name of the pilot was Weizmann. On the basis of this the Arabs reported that Dr. Weizmann had flown over Kfar Etzion—YISAKHAR

From the Journal of Kfar Etzion—January 15

This morning Inspector Dougan paid us a visit. He transmitted the request of the Arabs to be permitted to remove their dead from the battleground. According to them eight Arabs were killed and three are missing. They also admitted that twenty-four of their men had been seriously wounded.

Walking around the farmyard he found a piece of an American ammunition box, from the consignment that had been dropped to us earlier in the morning. He gave us a friendly warning that such things should not be found in the area. He told us that on the day preceding the attack an Arab from Bethlehem, whose name he did not know, appeared in the Hebron marketplace, and in a fiery speech declared that no Jewish settlement must remain within the Arab district of Hebron. A large number of the younger Arabs gathered together and began to organize themselves for the planned attack. A large Arab gang, composed of members of a Beduin tribe, were billeted in Artas and Beth Sahur. Many of them were ex-soldiers and equipped with modern weapons. Villagers from Beth Fajjar, Beth Umar, Surif, Nahalin, Al Hadar, Bethlehem, Hebron, and the Ta'amra tribe, as well as from Artas and Beth Sahur also took part in the attack. The dead included villagers from the entire district.

Inspector Dougan declared that he himself was convinced that the losses suffered by the Arabs were far in excess of the number they acknowledged. The Arabs of Beth Sahur and the Ta'amra tribe would never leave one of their dead compatriots on the field, even if they risked their lives in carrying them off. They had asked for accommodation for the wounded in the hospital, where, however, there was no room. The villages of the district were full of wounded Arabs. In the morning ambulances had made a round of the villages to transfer the wounded.

Dougan's estimate was that about one thousand Arabs had participated in the battle, but the attack, in his opinion, had not been well-organized. It was a mob operation. The Arabs in the district were poorly armed and equipped. With the exception of the transport arrangements, the entire attack had suffered from bad organization. Some of the wounded had had to make their way home on foot, even as far as Beersheba.

Dougan had only learned of the attack at noon, when an Arab police constable told him of shooting in the Kfar Etzion area. He had been unaware, however, that it was of serious proportions. At noon, Arabs had danced in the streets of Hebron at the news that Kfar Etzion and Revadim had been wiped out. He had immediately contacted Jerusalem, where the report that Kfar Etzion was being attacked was confirmed, but was informed that the Arabs had not dared to come close to the settlement. He had also contacted the British forces stationed in Halhul, who were standing by, and asked them to be ready to help in case of need. Practically throughout the battle Englishmen dressed in Arab clothes had been present and had transmitted reports to their headquarters in Jerusalem.

When he had learned of the heavy losses sustained by the Arabs he had decided not to interfere so that the Arabs would learn a lesson.

At about half-past four in the afternoon he had gone out

to the road, together with a number of Arab notables, and had insisted upon a cease fire, threatening otherwise to call in the troops. He had done so because a British brigadier had been held up by a roadblock.

Today, eleven bodies were found in the area. One of the commanders of the band, Ibrahim, is reported missing. . . .

This morning, Colonel Oliver of the British Army paid us a visit, accompanied by ambulances and military vehicles. His job was to ensure the removal of all bodies from the neighborhood. The body of Yehoshua Marx was taken to Jerusalem in one of these ambulances. The wounded were also removed.

In the afternoon the British ambulance driver who carried the wounded to Jerusalem put in an appearance. Me'ir has established good relations with this corporal, and the latter agreed to take him to Jerusalem for an hour to deliver regards to the girls in the Ratisbonne Monastery. They were thrilled to hear about the course of the battle. The soldier promised to pay us another visit on his way down to the units stationed in the Hebron area, to bring us fuel and to deliver letters to Jerusalem.

From the summary of the District Commander—
January 15

The battle was the biggest and fiercest fought in the country since the outbreak of hostilities. This was the first time such a large Arab force, about one thousand strong, was mustered to launch an attack upon a bloc of settlements. . . .

The planning of the attack indicates a knowledge of military tactics. The preparatory work and the organization of the various services prove military experience. It is very likely that the attack was directed by foreign officers working in the headquarters of Abdul Kader el-Husseini.—YA'AKOV A.

5 The Thirty-Five

From the diary of the Bloc's representative in Jerusalem—January 15

All the morning papers are full of the Etzion Bloc victory. . . . Radio messages from Kfar Etzion during the attack repeatedly complained of the lack of batteries. The transmitting station, however, operated without interruption. Contact is weaker at the moment. We have obtained two batteries for the village. . . .

A detachment has been prepared to reinforce the Bloc. It is made up of two squads of the Field Force and two of the Palmah—forty men in all. Danny Mass is in command. Their arms include four Bren-guns, sixteen rifles, fifteen sub-machine guns and seventy hand-grenades. They are taking three thousand rounds of rifle ammunition for the Bloc. They will proceed by way of mountain trails, as the road to the settlements is blocked.—YOSEF P.

From a restricted Hagana report—January 16

On Wednesday night, January 14, the detachment started out from Jerusalem via Ein Karem. All the men carried heavy packs consisting of first-aid equipment, bottles of plasma, arms and ammunition for the Bloc. They were delayed by having to climb stone fences and other obstacles. They were picked out by searchlights while passing Arab hill villages and were shot at. With the night almost over they found that they had made little progress and realized that the enemy might easily locate them. It was resolved to withdraw by the shortest route to Jerusalem.

On Thursday morning they were back in the city. They were given a few hours in which to rest, but the order to get to the Etzion Bloc at all costs remained unchanged. Zero hour for their departure was 5:00 P.M. A new route was worked out. They were to travel in an armored car to Hartuv, from where they were to slip through the hills to the Etzion Bloc.

Near Hartuv there was a police station manned by British police constables and a unit of the Arab legion. To bypass the station, the detachment had to make a detour which added about five miles to its route. It was 11:00 P.M. when they were finally ready to set out. Raphael, the Commander of Hartuv, and a number of the men stationed there advised them to postpone their march to the following night. They argued that even if the detachment encountered no obstacles and did three miles an hour, it would not reach its objective before daylight. Raphael insisted that Danny Mass contact Jerusalem. He tried to do so, but without success. Danny declared that whatever happened they must reach the Etzion Bloc that night. He relied on the assurance given him by the Officer Commanding the Jerusalem Region that if for any reason they must delay their departure a plane would signal them. Two men of the detachment had no arms. Danny asked the local commander to supply them with arms but the latter was unable to comply, as Hartuv itself was under-equipped. The two men were left behind in Hartuv.

The Commander of Hartuv and a number of his men accompanied the detachment, which now numbered thirty-eight men, down the hillside, along the wadi facing Tsorah. They marched round the fields of Hartuv, and then turned left through the wadi until they came to the railway bridge. The men from Hartuv left them at the big fig tree. The detachment proceeded down the wadi. On the track between Beth Shemesh and Dir Abban one of the men sprained his ankle, and was sent back to Hartuv accompanied by two of the detachment. During the morning, Raphael recalls, one of our planes flew over Hartuv but he is not certain if it gave a signal.

On Friday morning at about ten an Arab informer reported that fifty Jews, including one girl, had been killed in battle in the vicinity of the village of Beth Natif. The Arab further reported that the unit had marked out their route from Hartuv, apparently with a line of flour. Raphael assumed that there had been a leakage of dynamite from the packs of one of the men of the detachment. However, he did not believe the report, as during the morning contact between Jerusalem and the Etzion Bloc had been resumed, which he attributed to the fact that the batteries brought by the detachment had reached the Bloc.

From the Journal of Kfar Etzion—January 16

We held the Sabbath evening service in Nveh Ovadia. The bullet holes in the doors and walls reminded us of the recent battle. We were in a quiet mood but our hearts were full of thanksgiving. After *Lekha Dodi,* Yosef D., who acted as cantor, read Psalm 18: "A Psalm of David, the words of this song on the day that the Lord delivered him from the hands of all his enemies."

The commanders of the Bloc are very worried because the detachment has not arrived.

January 17

Last night the guards were given orders not to open fire if they saw a group of men approaching. The searchlight operator was ordered to signal towards the north and west. We lit a beacon on Yellow Hill. Palmah patrols went out at night on reconnaissance in the vicinity. They brought back no news.

Just before dawn a scouting party made up of settlers and enlisted men combed the hills nearby, searching for the detachment.

In the afternoon one of our planes flew over the farmyard and the pilot dropped notes instructing us to spread out mattresses so that he could drop batteries for the transmitter. We did so, but the batteries were smashed by the force of the fall. The pilot informed us that he was continuing to search for the missing detachment, but so far had found nothing.

Two British soldiers who had brought fuel were in the settlement at the time. They told us that Arabs employed in their camp in Jerusalem were speaking of fifty Jews who had been killed in the Judean Mountains. We transmitted this information to Regional Headquarters.

Later on Headquarters informed us that according to Arab sources bodies of Jews have been found in the area between Jabba and Surif.

This evening the Jerusalem radio reported the killing of all men of a detachment sent to reinforce the Etzion Bloc.

From a report by an Israel Army Officer

[When we returned to the Hartuv area with our troops, in November, 1948, we interrogated every Arab we had taken prisoner in our efforts to solve the riddle. On the basis of their replies we have constructed the following sequence of events:

The thirty-five men left Hartuv for the Etzion Bloc via the wadi that runs to the west of Dir Abban. From there they continued along the wadi that leads northwest from Surif. At dawn they came across an Arab shepherd whom they asked to guide them. The shepherd raised the alarm among a training school for local Arab fighters. The latter went out *en masse* and at about 9:00 A.M. the battle began, continuing till about noon. Our men made desperate efforts throughout to break through to the Bloc, which was only three miles away. According to the Arab prisoners there were six frontal assaults on the detachment. All of these were repulsed.

When the detachment's ammunition ran out the Arabs launched their seventh attack. One of the men of the detachment rose at the critical moment and began to throw grenades. The Arabs replied with murderous fire and then attacked again, thinking apparently that they had put an end to all resistance. The solitary fighter, whom the Arabs describe as being tall and dark, continued to throw grenades. According to the Arabs he was found dead with a stone in his hand.]

From the Journal of Kfar Etzion—January 18

On Sunday morning a number of British half-tracks arrived together with the Police Inspector, who informed us that in the evening the bodies of the thirty-five men of the detachment would be brought to Kfar Etzion. A little earlier Regional Headquarters had informed us that the men would be buried here. We began to dig the common grave on a slope of Abu Rish. After nightfall, three trucks covered with tarpaulins, escorted by half-tracks and a military guard, entered the farmyard. The Police Inspector once again put in an appearance and asked all women to go indoors. When we removed the canvas tarpaulins we saw the bodies lying in pools of blood. It was clear that they had been mutilated. Not all of the men were able to overcome their initial shock at the sight and to help remove the bodies from the trucks. We asked the troops to dim their lights and carried on in the darkness.

The corpses were wrapped in cloth and in sheets and were carried into Nveh Ovadia on stretchers. A number of them still bore bandages proving that in the course of the battle the orderly had dressed their wounds.

Throughout this scene the British soldiers stood rooted to the ground. It seemed as if they were making an effort to master their feelings. A guard of honor, of settlers and enlisted men, was posted by the dead bodies. Candles were lit and *haverim* recited Psalms throughout the night.

When all the bodies had been removed to Nveh Ovadia the Police Inspector asked if he could help in any way during the next day. We requested the assistance of the military in enabling the parents and relatives to attend the funeral.

From a private diary—January 19

The convoy bringing the relatives to the funeral arrived in the morning from Jerusalem. They were silent. It was clear that they were making every effort to restrain their grief out of respect for the feelings of the settlers.

Among them were a man and woman, very subdued, who gathered the mourners together and quietly urged them to restrain themselves at this hour. The woman walked among the houses as if seeking some tangible evidence of the work of her son, Danny, who had spent some weeks here and had done much to strengthen the settlement's defenses. "For years now," she told the other bereaved mothers, "I have known that Danny belonged to the Palmah. I knew of the operations in which he participated and I was ready for this. All these years, in which he would come home at intervals for a few days' leave, have been a kind of gift to us."

In the meanwhile, the Hagana men, together with the members of the Jerusalem *Hevra Kadisha,* headed by Rabbi Levin, who had come in the convoy, were engaged in wrapping the men in their burial shrouds. They were laid out in the hall; by the side of each was a small board bearing his name. Candles were lit at their heads. Rabbi Levin recited Psalms and then the Memorial Prayer for the dead. Parents, wives, brothers and sisters stood silently weeping.

An airplane circled overhead and dropped four stretchers for the funeral. There were not enough in the Bloc.

Twice the procession descended the slope of Abu Rish to where the huge grave gaped in a wood of young pines. The pall-bearers, enlisted men, settlers, relatives, plodded along without a word. One woman with noble features walked alongside the stretcher, quietly supporting the head of her son.

Partitions of stone and wood separated the bodies in the common grave, which were then covered with boards and heavy stones to protect them from wild animals. . . .

The troops posted a guard equipped with half-tracks and light machine guns between the graveyard and the rocks. Our men secured the graveyard from the direction of the

Mukhtar's Saddle. That day for the first time our illegal arms were taken out under the eyes of the authorities.

Avraham H., who represented the Regional Command, spoke briefly. Volleys were fired in honor of the fallen men, one of the settlers read Psalm 94 and then *Kaddish* was recited by one of the mourners.

The sun was already sinking and the mourners had to return. Settlers and enlisted men remained in the graveyard to cover the graves.—YISAKHAR

From an account of the District Commander—January 19

After the funeral a British police officer told us how the bodies had been found.

On Saturday he had received a report from Police Headquarters that all the men of a Jewish detachment had fallen in a battle near the village of Surif. After receiving this report and on the basis of information we had given him, he set out for Surif, where he called the Mukhtars and notables of the village together for interrogation. The Arabs, however, claimed to know nothing at all about the matter. When it became clear that neither pressure nor persuasion would prove of any avail the officer returned to Hebron.

On Sunday he was again ordered to find the bodies at all costs. He returned to Surif accompanied by a platoon of British troops, but once again, despite his threats and exhortations, his efforts were fruitless.

Finally, he decided to use other tactics. "What you have done to the Jews," he told the headmen, "has been well done, for they were your enemies. But remember that the souls belong to Allah and you must give up the bodies so that they can be buried." After a short pause an Arab boy appeared and said to the officer, "Come! I will show you where the bodies lie." The lad led him to the valley between Surif and Jabba, where the thirty-five bodies lay scattered. The villagers refused to carry them on their camels to the army trucks and finally the British soldiers had to do so themselves with the aid of stretchers.—YA'AKOV A.

From a private diary (Continued)

Yosef has come from Jerusalem for a short visit to discuss important issues. He has reported that the loss of the thirty-five men of the detachment sent to reinforce us has aroused deep concern in the Yishuv. In Jerusalem, from which most of the men came, the question is being asked, whether it is worthwhile defending an isolated bloc, the defense of which ties down a large body of troops and requires the sacrifice of so many men. It becomes clear as the result of the recent battles that the Bloc must rely entirely on its own resources, while any attempt to reinforce it by means of small forces infiltrating through enemy territory must fail. The time has come for us to change our tactics in the conduct of this campaign. In any case we shall eventually, for political reasons, have to evacuate the settlements.

These issues were discussed by the defense authorities in Jerusalem. Rumors of these discussions have reached the ears of the womenfolk of Kfar Etzion, living in the Ratisbonne Monastery in Jerusalem, and have increased their anxiety. A number of them have resolved to ask for the evacuation of the Bloc. However there is strong opposition to such a step.

Leading members of the *kvutza* and the security people have been shocked by these reports. We ourselves never believed that the situation was serious enough to warrant the evacuation of the Bloc. Yosef was requested to inform the *haverot* that we will not request evacuation. At most we can try to explain our difficulties to the responsible authorities and get them to pay more attention to them. Our own conduct must be governed by their decision.—YISAKHAR.

Two articles have been published in the Tel Aviv *Ha-Aretz* which express the conflicting, current opinions within the Yishuv regarding the Etzion Bloc.

The first one says:

> The nature and dimensions of the campaign in which the Yishuv is at present engaged are now becoming clearer in the light of the dramatic battles being fought in the Hebron Hills and the Etzion Bloc. What is being waged there is not a single engagement but a series of battles over a wide area.
>
> The difficulties of the four Jewish settlements in the Bloc, situated as they are in the heart of a purely Arab district, are patent even to the layman. The Bloc is fully capable of conducting its own defense; the difficulty, however, is that of communications. The situation in this respect is aggravated by the fact that officially the Hagana is an illegal force and the British forces—who took no part in the major battle of January 14—will not permit it to use the roads.
>
> From the military point of view the maintenance of these four isolated settlements, completely surrounded as they are by the enemy, is not justified. There is only a psychological reason for not evacuating the settlers and the auxiliary forces. The national institutions of the Yishuv must now decide—after careful consideration of all aspects of the struggle we are now facing—whether we must pay the high price demanded for the occupation of these four settlements by the pick of our forces.

The other article states *inter alia:*

> Were this a normal war, the shortening of the Yishuv's lines of defense would be a primary necessity. It would thus be able to economize in manpower and armaments. Such a policy, however, would call for the evacuation of settlements in Upper Galilee, in the Kfar Etzion area and in the Negev, as neither symbolism nor sentiment would justify the danger and the defense forces they call for.
>
> But this is not a normal war. And if there may be adequate reason for a withdrawal from the Negev, there is none for the evacuation of the Kfar Etzion area. Above all this Bloc, together with the Motza-Kiryat Anavim Bloc, constitutes the outer defenses of Jewish Jerusalem.

From letters written by settlers—January 19

From the military point of view we dare not evacuate the Bloc. This would release enemy forces for action against Jerusalem. As long as we stay here they are tied down. Obviously we cannot decide the issue.

In the meanwhile, we are making good use of the lull to strengthen our defenses, and it will not be easy to get us out of here. The normal work in the forest, in the orchards, and elsewhere is left undone. We have not got sufficient men for both work and guard duty. Nor are there enough girls to do all the work that is necessary.—AVRAHAM F.

The prevailing opinion here is that only the national institutions can decide whether the Bloc is or is not to be evacuated. Can we decide to leave while others remain? We cannot oppose discussion of the question but we must be very careful in making decisions.

The Kibbutz Council discussed the question fully, and finally decided that we have no right to ask for the evacuation of Kfar Etzion or of the people here. We must submit a detailed memorandum to our authorities on the problems of defense, communications, water, and manpower facing the settlement. They must make their decisions on the basis of this memorandum.—SHALOM G.

6 Entrenchment

The attack on the Etzion Bloc marked a new development in Arab fighting tactics throughout the country. Many other Jewish settlements were singled out for mass attack, especially the isolated ones in Upper Galilee that were attacked by bands operating from Syria. These assaults, however, were also repulsed.

The Jerusalem front continued to be the most complex and bore the heaviest brunt of the fighting. As there were few Jewish settlements around the Holy City, its Jewish community had to be supplied by convoys from the coastal plain; their forty-five mile route wound through steep, hilly terrain in which the Arabs could deploy their ambushes without difficulty.

Sniping, bombing, attacks, and hit-and-run raids went on in all parts of the city. The siege of the Jewish Quarter, enclosed within the historic walls of the Old City, posed a special problem, and continually strained the manpower and resources of the Regional Command. To the north of the city, on the road to Nablus, there were two Jewish settlements, Nveh Ya'akov and Atarot, whose problems of supply were not very different from those of the Etzion Bloc.

It is against this background that the siege of the Etzion Bloc must be viewed. Jerusalem, which was the immediate hinterland of the four beleaguered settlements and their source for supplies and manpower, was itself engaged in a massive struggle.

The siege of the Bloc steadily tightened. Because of the increasing danger of ambush along its supply line from Jerusalem, the Jewish authorities endeavored to arrange for escorts of British troops to accompany the convoys.

The slender flow of supplies from Tel Aviv continued without interruption. The parachuting, from time to time, of ammunition, medical supplies, and newspapers to the besieged defenders, helped to keep morale high.

From the account of a Field Force officer—January 20

The attack launched on Kfar Etzion was analyzed at a meeting of commanders held after the attack of January 14. In view of the difficulty of maintaining rapid communications between the settlements and strongpoints of the Bloc, it was decided to split up the reserves and to place larger detachments, capable of holding out independently for a longer time, in the strongpoints.

The Student Company was split up as follows: two squads were stationed in Hirbet Zakaria, a third squad on Yellow Hill, a fourth on Lone Tree Hill, a fifth at Massuot Yitzhak to hold the Mukhtar's Saddle, and a sixth to hold Russian Hill. The Command Post of the company remained at Kfar Etzion.

The company was issued with several additional machine guns. Practically every soldier was issued with personal arms. The ammunition store was augmented. One squad was trained in the use of the Schwartzlause and the Browning. Another underwent preliminary mortar training. The units received field training on a squad level. Every day one squad was kept busy at fortifying the strongpoints, digging defense posts and trenches, and erecting barbed-wire fences. Stone fences which may have proved of assistance to the enemy were destroyed. A detail of men was assigned to Bloc Headquarters for defense works, such as laying mine fields, levelling the flying field and laying telephone lines between the settlements and the strongpoints. A radio expert examined the radio installations. From time to time squads of students provided a guard for settlers at work in the orchards. Patrols of the entire neighborhood were carried out by our men, night and day.

Once initial precautions had been taken and Hirbet Zakaria fortified, the men began to make the six stone buildings there habitable. The students attached great importance to this work, though veterans in the district said that it was better to live in a clean tent than in a filthy and flee-ridden stone house. But after the big tent that had been pitched on a protected site was blown over, it was decided to move into the houses. We were all grateful to one of our men who donned a rubber coat and fumigated the rooms with sulphur, sprayed the walls with DDT and then whitewashed them.

We had difficulty in getting our supplies. At first rations were brought from Kfar Etzion on donkey-back or with the wagon. The food, however, was always cold, tasteless, and insufficient. Finally we got our rations from Revadim and Ein Tsurim, which were nearer.

One of the important functions of the unit stationed on Russian Hill was to watch enemy traffic on the Jerusalem-Hebron highway. The commanding position of this height made it a good observation post. The squad pitched a tent, set up defenses around it, and then dug other posts and communications trenches. The surrounding area was mined. Our men began to pay visits to the Monastery, where they were courteously received by the two monks and the lessees.

Huts were erected on Yellow Hill and Lone Tree Hill to house the men stationed there.—YEHOYAKHIN K.

From the diary of the Bloc's representative in Jerusalem—January 20

We, the few *haverim* assigned to Jerusalem, attend to the practical work involved in supplying the Bloc. We must procure the supplies, organize convoys and mobilize the necessary trucks and drivers. Owing to the danger on the road we have been forced to pay large sums of money to the truck owners, and especially to the drivers. Since the heavy attack upon the convoy on January 13, when a number of drivers were wounded, we can no longer get the trucks or the drivers for any price. The security authorities are now compelled to requisition vehicles for service with the convoys. . . .

Yesterday we received a radiogram from General Staff Headquarters in Tel Aviv that they are planning to drop a large quantity of supplies for the Etzion Bloc from planes. Medical supplies will be included. It is proposed to supply us with ten tons of supplies over a period of four days. A surgeon, a surgical nurse, and equipment for a hospital are to be dispatched to the Bloc. . . .

We have discussed the matter of reinforcements for the Bloc with the Regional Commander. We have proposed the creation of a transport unit to serve all settlements in the Jerusalem area, the unit to comprise six or seven armored trucks and a roadblock buster, and to be equipped with a radio. A strong Hagana escort under the command of an experienced officer must be attached to it.

We have also applied for recognition of the settlers as members of a military unit. We hope in this way to solve the problem of maintenance. Such recognition would enable our people to devote themselves entirely to work on fortifications and defense.—Yosef P.

From a letter of the Kfar Etzion Secretariat to the settlement's representatives in Tel Aviv and Jerusalem—January 20

We have hardly done anything on the farm this week. The arrival of the convoy, scouting parties, the attack, guard duty, and the construction of new defenses have all kept us busy. . . .

It is important for us to level the fig orchard stretch immediately, and transform it into an air strip. We are awaiting the arrival of an engineer and a driver to operate the bulldozer. The importance of an air strip was proved in the week following the attack, when we found it impossible to transfer the wounded.

We have decided to dig a channel around the farmyard, to conduct rainwater to the reservoirs. We shall have to use up all our stocks of cement. The job is proceeding slowly because of the shortage of workers; other jobs are also being held up for the same reason. The stock of building timber is very low. . . .

The Arabs have occupied many strongpoints in the neighborhood, including one in Beth Fajjar. Within the next few days the neighboring British Forces are expected to evacuate their camps, leaving behind only one company.

From the diary of the Bloc's representative in Jerusalem—January 20

We have transmitted to the Regional Command in Jerusalem a list of the equipment and supplies we require for a month. The list will be dispatched to Tel Aviv, where arrangements will be made to parachute the material to the Bloc.—Yosef P.

From a letter of the representative of Massuot Yitzhak in Jerusalem—January 21

Representatives of the Bloc had another meeting with David Ben-Gurion, when he was in Jerusalem, in order to discuss urgent security and economic problems. We insisted that the fortification of the Bloc should be delayed no longer and not be executed piecemeal, as at present. The Arabs are not marking time and the situation here is very serious. We asked for immediate and substantial reinforcements of both men and equipment.

One of those present at the meeting told us later that our insistence made a strong impression.

Ben-Gurion replied that so far we had received whatever it was possible to send. For the time being Headquarters could not promise anything. He undertook, however, to expedite the fulfillment of our demands. . . .

We are organizing a convoy and have asked for a military escort. Negotiations are proceeding with the authorities.

From the Journal of Kfar Etzion—January 22

We received by air 2,806 rounds of British rifle ammunition, 1,275 rounds for the Italian carbines, 2,400 rounds of German ammunition, 150 Mills bombs and detonators.

1,500 rounds of ammunition and 30 hand grenades were damaged.

We also received cigarettes, conserves, sugar and other foodstuffs, and ten aerial photographs of the neighborhood.

We asked for supplies of sandbags, barbed wire, explosives, and mines.

From the diary of the Bloc's representative in Jerusalem—January 24

We were organizing a convoy with an exclusively Jewish escort, but at 5:00 P.M. yesterday, the Regional Commander informed us that he refused to allow a convoy escorted only by Jews to leave for the Bloc.

Once again we applied to the British Forces asking for an escort for the following day, as the trucks were already loaded. At 8:30 P.M. we were informed that the convoy would leave at nine in the morning, and that the trucks must be readied during the night.

At nine on Saturday morning the convoy left escorted by the military. It comprised four eight-ton trucks carrying supplies and a tanker with five cubic meters of fuel. Among the supplies there were telephones and exchanges for all the strongpoints and defense posts in the Bloc.—YOSEF P.

From the Journal of Kfar Etzion—January 24

The arrival of the convoy was greeted with general rejoicing. The big trucks were loaded high with supplies and this time they also brought building materials. The attitude of the men of the escort was very courteous, especially that of the officer in command. . . .

There has been some rain. We are praying that the cisterns be filled.

January 25

Life is continuing here as usual. Every day we have public prayers. We have study circles in Talmud, Mishna, Maimonides, and the weekly Portion of the Torah. The reading room is looked after carefully, and many *haverim* use it during the day.

The twenty-one women cannot cope with all the work they have to do, as the kitchen and the laundry have to provide for the dozens of enlisted men too. The girls also do their share of guard duty, which prevents them from working overtime. A number of *haverim* are therefore being employed in the domestic services. The rest are working in the dairy, in the poultry run, on the building of fortifications, and, of course, there is always guard duty. The enlisted men guard the strongpoints and so do not undertake guard duty in the settlements.

January 26

Today is *Hamisha Asar B'Shevat,* the Jewish Arbor Day. This afternoon members of the kvutza gathered at the gate to plant a wood in memory of the fifty-one defenders of the Bloc who have fallen.

The ceremony began with the reading of the traditional prayer for the planting of trees.

The honor of planting the first saplings was given to the new immigrants. This was the first opportunity they have had for planting trees in this country. One of the *haverim* spoke about the fallen. Then the Scroll of Planting composed four years ago by the late Shalom Karniel was read.

The strains of *HaTikva* resounded among the hills. It echoed the will and the faith that the mountains of Hebron would be resettled and that the waste places would be rebuilt.

From the Journal of Ein Tsurim—January 26

Life is being influenced to an increasing extent by our military responsibilities. Most of the *haverim* are employed in the construction of various fortifications. We are building defense posts, the bungalows are being reinforced, and we are trying to dig into the rock. At first we made primitive booby traps—cans containing grenades, which were ignited on removal, were tied to the perimeter fences. Later, however, we replaced them by mines of our own manufacture.

All members of the settlements, both men and women, are now included in the intensive training program. Everyone has been given personal arms. From time to time the alert is sounded to test the preparedness of the *haverim*. We all take turn at guard duty.

Our relations with the enlisted men are very good. We have a high opinion of the Palmah boys who are here with us. Their soldierly skill, their high spirits and their constant vigilance have taught us a good deal. . . .

We are beginning to dig pits in the orchards and have already planted two thousand fruit trees. We have also built a third bungalow.

From a letter of a member of Revadim—
January 26

The general mood in the kibbutz is encouraging. The *haverim* are now more composed and have become reconciled to the tragedy, to the graves down below on the road to the crags. Something binds us with a bitter grief to those who have departed. From time to time one of us remembers some one who is no longer here. . . .

No work is being done outside the farmyard. We are all concentrating on building fortifications, some of them inside the farmyard, and some of them further removed. The girls are busy in the kitchen or on guard duty. We are waiting for new people to come and cheer us up, so that we can respond to life again.—NAOMI D.

From the Journal of Kfar Etzion—January 27

The supply situation has improved a good deal after last Saturday's convoy. . . .

Yesterday and today planes flew over the Bloc and dropped supplies, ammunition, and newspapers. For the first time a number of letters have come from Tel Aviv.

On Saturday and Sunday there was some rain and the level of the water in the cisterns rose. In Kfar Etzion we now have about sixteen hundred cubic meters of water.

From a private letter—January 30

The complex of fortifications is being expanded and improved throughout the entire Bloc. Most of the work is being executed according to the plans drawn up by Danny, and upon the basis of the experience gained during the attack a fortnight ago. One of the jokes going the rounds of the settlement is that the Bloc should now be renamed "Etziongrad."

The field telephone has been installed, linking up the Bloc Command Post in Kfar Etzion with all the settlements and strongpoints.

Each settlement also has a small transmitting-receiving set. In case of emergency it is possible to use each of these sets for communicating with Jerusalem—this in addition to the transmitting station linking up the Bloc with Regional Headquarters in Jerusalem and General Staff Headquarters in Tel Aviv. It is also possible to signal Jerusalem from Massuot by means of helio.—Dov

From the diary of the Bloc's representative in Jerusalem—February 1-2

We have been informed that the British Army is prepared to escort a weekly convoy to the Bloc carrying no more than ten tons of supplies. Reinforcements may not be transported in these convoys.

We have been instructed by the authorities to prepare a convoy to leave tomorrow for the Bloc. We could not get trucks until the late hours of the night. We succeeded in getting hold of two trucks only after a good deal of running around in various offices. We worked until 1:30 A.M. As we were working we heard the sound of a tremendous explosion, which, it turned out, came from the *Jerusalem Post* building on HaSollel Street. The building had been blown up, and there is a strong suspicion that it was done by some Englishmen.

Early in the morning we got hold of a few other trucks onto which we loaded barbed wire, pipes, medical equipment for the operating room, and supplies.

The convoy set out at 9:00 A.M. When we reached the British Protected Area, near the Jewish Agency building, we were stopped and soldiers made a close search with magnetic instruments. Nothing was found. The soldiers detained Gershon of Ein Tsurim near whom, they said, they had found a grenade. We hope to have him released during the day.

The British Lieutenant-Colonel refused to permit the transport of cement, timber, corrugated iron, and pipes. He declared that the settlers in the Bloc do not require any new buildings at present. He repeated a number of times his offer to help us to evacuate the Bloc. He was convinced, he said, that the settlers wanted to leave the Bloc, but that the Jewish Agency was bringing pressure to bear upon them for political reasons. He stressed that he would permit the transport of supplies and fuel only. He would not allow other people to go out. A number of men could travel with each truck but they must promise to come back with the returning convoy.

As a result only one truck, carrying medical equipment and a small quantity of supplies, set out. Dr. Alkalai went in this truck to organize the hospital.

This attitude on the part of the British Army means a tightening of the siege. Throughout the day the Jewish Agency representatives tried to persuade the military to change their attitude, but it was useless. Finally we had to unload the trucks that remained in the city.—YOSEF P.

From a private diary—February 2

When the truck that reached Kfar Etzion was being unloaded, a number of cylinders of oxygen, which are needed for work in the metal workshop, were taken off. The British officer became very angry when he saw the cylinders and declared that the Jews had deceived him and, despite their promise, had smuggled in military supplies. He refused to believe that we need oxygen for the normal operations of the workshop.

It has been decided to transfer part of our dairy cattle to one of our settlements in the coastal plain. We do not grow enough forage for our cows, and we cannot depend on the convoys for additional fodder. We shall send the cows with the return convoys.—YISAKHAR

From a private letter—February 2

The latest joke following the arrival of the surgeon is: Previously you had some hope of getting to Jerusalem—if you were wounded. Today even that chance has vanished! . . . We are steadily manufacturing mines. Just now—9:30 P.M.—the first shift has gone off duty and has been replaced by the second. Most of the work must be done at night when the generator is supplying current to light up the perimeter fence. We do not rest even on the Sabbath.

We went before noon to lay mines in the various fields. Some of us continued until nightfall. All for defense!—AVRAHAM SH.

From a private diary—February 3

Avraham, always so restrained and quiet, is entirely absorbed in the manufacture of mines. For this purpose he requires a variety of materials, and where is he to get hold of them? The machines and the tools necessary for work of this kind are not available here. Necessity, however, is the mother of invention, and Avraham finds a way. He has collected the tools we have and has adapted them to his purpose. He has given orders to collect all empty cans, cartridges, nails, and pieces of iron. We still have a supply of explosives from the time we worked the quarry and it has been requisitioned for this purpose. Detonators are sent from the city.

With a perseverance beyond all praise he conducted his experiments, until he succeeded in contriving a workable mechanism made up of a sharpened nail and of a spring made of steel wire and ignited by a detonator. Having succeeded in manufacturing the first workable mine, he has been at work together with his staff until the late hours of the night. Slowly they are progressing from scare-mines to the manufacture of fragmentation ones. These, also, are gradually improving. Alex, David, and their assistants go out at night to lay mine fields near the strongpoints.—YISAKHAR

From the diary of the Bloc's representative in Jerusalem—February 4

We have discussed at Headquarters the chances of organizing another convoy to the Bloc. The Jewish Agency Liaison Officers are of the opinion that we must maintain our contacts with the British Army, which is prepared to escort supply convoys. We must not organize our own escorts.

At the same time it is clear that we cannot rest content with the supplies they are prepared to allow us. We must transport building materials, which are vital for the building of fortifications, and for cementing the area near the cisterns, so that we can conserve a larger volume of water.

It was finally resolved that if we do not get a satisfactory answer from the British military authorities in the course of the next few days, we shall organize a convoy of our own at the beginning of the week. The three armored cars which have been allocated for internal transport within the Bloc will be sent together with the convoy.

The composition of this convoy has been decided and we are already at work organizing it. It will include three trucks carrying building materials, corrugated iron, timber, and pipes; one truck of cement; a fuel tanker; and three armored cars for internal transport. The escort will include three sappers to remove roadblocks.

A special Liaison Officer has been appointed to negotiate with the military in the event of a search being made. A labor unit is to be organized to undertake quick loading and unloading. A stock of gasoline is to be got ready for the three armored cars that will remain in the Bloc.

In this convoy we shall be able to transfer to the Bloc the eighty people who have been waiting in Jerusalem for the opportunity to proceed to the Bloc.—YOSEF P.

From a letter of the representative of Kfar Etzion in Tel Aviv—February 4

One of the things which we regard as particularly important is the establishment of direct contact between the Bloc and the General Staff in Tel Aviv. The Jerusalem Command itself is short of men and equipment and can't possibly meet our demands. The air link to be established can help to solve the problem of supply.

We were received by Yisrael Galili, Chief of National Headquarters, who agreed to allow us to appoint a representative to work with the General Staff in all matters affecting the Bloc. This does not mean that we have achieved our main objective, but technically it is of the utmost importance because it gives us direct access to the High Command. . . .

No one has decided finally who is to be responsible for our maintenance. Though there is still a certain amount of confusion among the people of the Settlement Department and the security authorities, there is, of course, no doubt whatever that we shall come under the authority of the latter and be considered as a military camp. The question of the support of the women and children now in Jerusalem will then have to be dealt with.

Eliezer Kaplan, Treasurer of the Jewish Agency, has made a new suggestion. He agrees that the Etzion Bloc has become a military camp and can no longer carry on normal agricultural activities. He suggests therefore that *haverim* whose families in the city must be supported should not be stationed in the settlement, and that they should be transferred elsewhere, where they will be able to provide for their dependents.

Most of the men of our *kvutza* have wives and children, so that if Kaplan's suggestions were accepted, it would mean a breaking-up of the settlement. The problem is not so serious for Massuot Yitzhak, and does not exist at all for the other two *kvutzot,* where there are only a few married couples and no children.

We have decided to oppose any such solution, which merely evades the problem but does not solve it. If settlements are to be defended some arrangements must be made for the support of their members. The Settlement Department of the Jewish Agency is also opposed to any such step. It is considering various forms of employment which could be maintained even under conditions of siege, and could solve the question of the maintenance of the Bloc.—NATAN SH.

From a private letter—February 5

I waver between good and bad moods. I try to control my feelings by talking to different *haverim,* hoping to hear a more optimistic view of the situation.

I often wonder whether my own or any one else's feelings about the future have any significance. What importance has any individual in the struggle being waged here? The establishment of the State will determine the destiny of our people for generations to come. My own feelings are not important, but how Ruhama'le will feel in another ten or twenty years, and how thousands of other Jewish children for whose sake we are fighting now will feel, that is important.

We are experiencing long hours of boredom, and feel despondent and anxious about what fate holds in store for us and for our dear ones. Every one of us is occupied with the same thoughts. I can see the worry reflected in other eyes. The only thing we can do, however, is to try to understand the situation.

No one can tell what the future will bring. When will we again have a normal family life? No one knows, the more's the pity. Many Jewish villages throughout the country needn't worry at all. It is a caprice of fortune. It's no use for us to try and rebel against our fate. We witnessed the same game of chance several years ago. We succeeded in reaching the shores of this country while our brothers and sisters were led to the gas chambers. They certainly had the same thoughts about us: "They are happy. They do not know what the crematorium and the camp are like!"

Fate has decreed that we settlers of the Bloc should be placed in a dilemma from which there seems no way out. A Jew at all times must have faith in the future and in Divine intercession.—BEN ZION G.

7 Defying the Siege

From the letters of settlers—February 6

The men are continuing to work on the construction of defense posts and various installations. . . .

We waited many weeks for the arrival of an airfield engineer and the bulldozer operator. We had a lot of promises but nothing more. Then a number of youngsters from the Palmah detachment, who come from settlements and know how to work with tractors, attempted to operate the bulldozer and were able to do so. The flying strip has been laid out on the road near the turning at the Lone Tree. Rocks were uprooted, holes filled in and the stretch on both sides of the road was widened and leveled to permit aircraft to land. . . .

The domestic services are working efficiently. Food is adequate. There are no vegetables but the quality of the food has not declined. We have received supplies of frozen fish, canned meat, sardines, and salami. We produce our own milk and eggs and slaughter chickens for the Sabbath. . . .

The saplings for the forest have been distributed among the settlements and have already been planted. We have begun late with the pruning of the trees, and it is doubtful whether we shall manage to prune the vineyard. At present we are working in the orchards on our hill. We shall start on the other orchards when we finish here. . . .

So far about twelve inches have fallen, approximately half the rainfall for the season. The cisterns are almost full.

From an announcement posted on the Kfar Etzion bulletin board—February 6

The large number of members attending the lectures held during the course of the week offers good prospects for further cultural activity. Next week we hope to arrange lectures on the following subjects: The soil of Palestine—Shalom G.; Blood transfusions—Dr. Alkalai; The Negev —Yehoshua L.

But attendance at lectures cannot be regarded as regular study. Every member must set aside a definite time for Torah. We are organizing study circles in which *haverim* and *haverot* can participate regularly.

The first group will meet twice a week and will study the Book of Judges under the direction of Yehoshua L. The second group will also meet twice a week for Bible study, under the direction of Shmuel A. The book will be chosen by the participants.

Another regular lesson will also be held devoted to the study of source works and problems of Judaism. So far as it is possible, we have ensured that members of the same study circles do the same spell of guard duty.

From a private diary—February 8

It was Saturday yesterday. The weather was fine and many *haverim* went for a stroll. At three in the afternoon we heard the drone of a plane. The *haverim* gathered by the fence waiting for the parachute. But the plane circled without dropping anything. Then it approached the landing strip, flying low, and rising again as if seeking a suitable place to land. We watched its efforts anxiously. Would it succeed? Then it flew over the strip again, flying low, and then suddenly it was taxiing. We ran to the strip with shouts of joy.

We came closer to the plane and looked at it doubtfully. Could this little canvas bird bear all our hopes and longing? It seemed so slight and delicate, with only two seats in the cockpit, and room in the fuselage for no more than two hundred and fifty pounds of freight.

One of the *haverim* recited the *Shehehiyanu* blessing. The pilot got out of the plane, inspected the strip, and gave us instructions on how to improve it and how to fix a windbag.

We led the pilot to Kfar Etzion in a triumphant procession. We gave him leftovers from yesterday, *tsholent,* and noodle pudding. Then we wished each other success over a drink.

The excitement of the *haverim* seemed to infect the pilot. He began to understand the encouragement he brought to the besieged settlers and fighters. According to him spirits are higher here than in the beleaguered Negev settlements which he had also visited. Now, the pilot told us, it will be possible to fly in the necessary experts, and also a bulldozer driver, to extend and improve the strip.

A new phase in the life of the Bloc has begun. The land siege continues, but now we shall have a living contact with the Yishuv—by air. If nothing unexpected happens the representatives of the *kvutzot* in the cities will come for consultations about the state of security in the Bloc. We hope that leaders of the various national institutions will also visit us to study our needs and the general situation. Now it will be possible to transport arms and ammunition, medical, and other equipment. We can receive letters and newspapers, while our letters can be taken out regularly.—YISAKHAR.

From the Journal of Kfar Etzion—February 9

On Saturday morning at half-past ten, two Arabs herding cattle approached the Russian Hill area. Our lookouts opened fire, seized one of the herdsmen, and impounded the cattle in our farmyard. The other Arab, who had been hit, brought British troops who came in vehicles and half-tracks which they parked outside the gate, as we refused to allow them to enter the farm compound. The officers came in and asked for a detailed report of what had taken place. They threatened to stage a search. The interrogation lasted for about an hour. We agreed to let the herdsman and the cattle go, warning the Arab not to come near our lands again.

In the evening Jerusalem Radio reported that one Arab had been "severely" wounded, another "kidnapped" and twenty-five head of cattle "stolen."

When the troops arrived the plane was standing on the landing-strip and we thought at first that they had come because of it. The officers inquired about it, but they had no authority to do anything on the spot.

Spirits were high on Saturday. After the service we gathered in Nveh Ovadia to hold a "vocal newspaper." The articles and sketches read by the *haverim* dealt with the problems confronting us. The program of lessons and study circles was kept up. . . .

A meeting was called to discuss Eliezer Kaplan's proposals. By general consent we resolved to refuse to discuss any proposal that did not solve the vital problems of the *kvutza.* We have sent on this resolution to our representative in Tel Aviv. . . .

Me'ir F.'s English friends continue to visit us, bringing with them substantial quantities of fuel. The visits of their ambulance have already become a regular feature. The fuel they sell us is worth its weight in gold as the convoys from Jerusalem do not supply us with sufficient quantities for our needs. There is now an additional need for fuel—for the bulldozer that is widening the flying strip. . . .

In the last few days we have been conducting negotiations regarding the purchase of arms in our neighborhood. We had a good chance of closing the deal but we did not have enough money. We sent a message to our representatives in Tel Aviv who raised five hundred pounds from the Executive of HaPoel HaMizrahi. The money was dropped to us in a special bag from a plane. Unfortunately, the deal fell through.

From the diary of the Bloc's representative in Jerusalem—February 9

An armored vehicle assigned to the Bloc has been received in Jerusalem.

The British army authorities do not allow us more than a weekly two-truck convoy. We have submitted a memorandum in which it has been explained that the corrugated iron, timber, and cement are required for the construction of rainfall catchment areas for the reservoirs. We need fodder and fuel and for that reason we cannot rest content with such a small convoy. Just before evening we received news that the Army was ready to escort a convoy of three trucks carrying whatever material we chose.

February 10

At 10:15 A.M. the convoy, comprising three trucks and escorted by British troops, set out. It was carefully examined by the Military Police in the "Protected Area" near the Jewish Agency Buildings.

Just before evening the convoy returned to Jerusalem. One truck was loaded with a variety of goods and another with two cows and two calves from Kfar Etzion. The third truck, carrying the cows of Massuot Yitzhak, was left behind, as the troops refused to wait for it.

The calves have been sold, while the cows will be transferred to Kvutzat Yavne.—YOSEF P.

From the Journal of Kfar Etzion—February 13

The bulldozer operator, for whom we have been waiting for so long, has come at last. When the ground dries we shall get busy widening the air strip. . . .

Police officers from the Bethlehem Station, accompanied by Army officers, paid us a visit in connection with an old land dispute. They told us that thousands of Arabs from the neighboring villages took part in the attack of January 14. According to them, not very many men remained in Bethlehem on that day. Most of them had gone out to the battlefield. The policemen dropped a hint that the Arabs are preparing another "surprise" for us. . . .

The daily press continues to write about the general attack against the Yishuv which the Arabs have proclaimed for February 15. It is feared that they intend cutting off the more isolated areas, in order to separate the various parts of the Yishuv. According to some reports the Arabs are planning to use heavier weapons, including artillery. . . .

Ben Gurion addressed the meeting of the Mapai Council

held a few days ago, on the progress of the war. He touched upon the part played by the settlements in the Jerusalem district saying, "These outposts provide major support for the city and strengthen its defenses."

From the diary of a Humanities student stationed at Massuot Yitzhak—February 13

The wintry weather is very depressing. Strong storm winds blow across the bare hills and a mist covers the hills of Hebron. The sun, for the few hours it is visible, is pale and weak, without any warmth. Isolation adds to the melancholy atmosphere.

Our squad has just returned from night exercises. We went a long way. We patrolled the hills surrounding the Bloc. At one spot we staged an attack and a defensive operation. We crawled across a five-hundred-yard stretch of rocks and thorns, but we finished without mishap.—MENAHEM TSVI K.

From the account of a girl student stationed at Hirbet Zakaria—February 13

We finished the fortifications and decorated our quarters. The old desire for cultural life awoke in us again. We became friendly with the people of Revadim and together with them organized parties on Friday nights. They brought the refreshments and the good voices and we, an accordion and the party spirit. Now and then Palmah men dropped in, sometimes with a bottle of something to drink. On Saturday nights we had a concert of gramophone records. From time to time our men lectured in Revadim and the other settlements, on subjects connected with the natural sciences and the humanities. Once a week we had a study day. We organized study circles for physics, chemistry, and agriculture.

We formed deeper friendships than any we had known during our studies in Jerusalem. We felt like a single unit, united by feelings of companionship. Even the men of our detachment who had not been students and whom we had not known before we came to the Bloc mixed well, and took part in all our activities.

The great moment of our lives in the Bloc was the day the mail and the newspapers came. Whoever was lucky enough to get a letter moved off into some corner to read it again and again, with his heart full of longing for the members of his family and his friends who seemed so far away.

We opened the newspapers in fear and trembling. Only too often the black borders informed us of the death of friends in action.—RINA K.

From the Journal of Kfar Etzion—February 14

A large number of people take part in the *Oneg Shabbat* gatherings. We sing Hassidic songs at the *seudah shlishit.* One song that is sung with a special fervor—the melody was brought here from the DP camps in Europe—consists of verses from Psalm 119:

> Remember the word unto Thy servant
> Upon which Thou hast caused me to hope.
> This is my comfort in my affliction,
> For Thy word has quickened me.
> The proud have had me greatly in derision,
> Yet I have not declined from Thy law.

One of our *haverim* has called it "The Anthem of Kfar Etzion under Siege."

From a private diary—February 14

The Committee for Halakha meets from time to time to consider the various religious questions that arise. Almost invariably there are some who insist that the *mitzvot* must be observed under all conditions. On the other hand, it is realized that we are living in a state of emergency, both for ourselves and for the Yishuv, and that Halakhic provisions are made for such a period, to ensure the saving of lives and the security of the community.

The nature of the questions varies. At one time religious scruples impelled us to ask whether it was right to take offensive action against the enemy, but the mass Arab attacks upon our convoys and the Bloc, and their cruel treatment of our dead suppressed any such thoughts.

The most important questions which the Committee for Halakha have to deal with concern the holiness of the Sabbath. In this emergency period, work on fortifications and the air strip, and the manufacture and planting of mines must continue. All these works are essential for the preservation of the Bloc's defenders. The problem that concerns us is how to perform these tasks on the Sabbath while still remaining conscious of its holiness. So we try to have a rich cultural program on the Sabbath, the major part of it consisting of the meetings of the study groups. Festive prayer service and the *zemirot* at the decorated tables also help to create a Sabbath atmosphere.—YISAKHAR

From a letter to the representatives of Kfar Etzion in Tel Aviv and Jerusalem—February 17

I do not know what stage the discussions of the national institutions have reached and whether they have decided in favor of evacuation or are thinking of maintaining the Bloc.

It seems that if anything is to be done, we must constantly prod them. It is quite clear now that in the present emergency the main thing is to hold on, to do all we can to insure that we are not swept away in the storm. At the same time we must not forget for a single moment that while the entire Yishuv will return to its normal way of life after the war, the situation will be entirely different for us who will have to live under Arab rule. If we do not succeed in consolidating our position in the transitional period, we shall have little prospect of remaining here when peace is restored. We cannot, therefore, rest content with what the national institutions are saying and doing. We must insist that they help us now to lay the foundations for our future, despite the fact that they are absorbed in other vital problems. It seems from your letters that there has been no progress in this matter.

Of course it is highly desirable at present to maintain a settlement here capable of diverting large enemy forces from other fronts. This, however, has no direct bearing upon our own future. All of us want the *kvutza* to remain here, but if the institutions are really contemplating evacuation should the situation become more difficult, they must let us know beforehand. Of course, if the institutions say so, the *haverim* who are fit enough to defend the place will remain. They are in the same position as other men liable for service who could be sent here. This, however, has nothing to do with the *kvutza*.

You may perhaps think that our isolation and the loneliness of the past few weeks have brought us round to this way of thinking, and that you, who live under more favorable conditions, must encourage us not to be so pessimistic. In fact, however, I am not thinking fresh thoughts. I just see more clearly that the time is coming when *all* roads will be blocked for us. Previously there might have been many possibilities of insuring our future economically; today the prospects are shrinking and we are no longer masters of the situation.

I believe that only if the Arabs reconcile themselves to the establishment of the State—their acceptance of this would be a miracle in itself—is there any chance for us to remain here as a settlement. I do not wish to rely entirely upon that miracle.—YA'AKOV A.

From a letter of a havera *in Jerusalem—*
February 19

Only six weeks have passed since we left home, but it seems to be years. Only about fifteen miles separate us but it seems far, far away. In peacetime our *haverim* were not afraid of chasing Arab bus Number 23 right down to Bethlehem. Today the very idea makes me shudder. We all long to travel along it as we used to, to be together with you and to talk about everything. We hope and pray that with God's help we shall yet do so. In the meantime, seeing that that is impossible, we must confine ourselves to letter-writing.

Life here is fairly well organized, when compared with life in the country. From time to time one of the children falls sick, but that's not more than usual. The building in which we are staying is not suitable for the accommodation of a large number of children. The place resembles a transit camp: it is too big, too public. One has the feeling of living under a searchlight, which adds to the difficulties of the people working here. I hope that before long we shall be able to find some solution to these difficulties. . . .

Very often when we are discussing things we say that we

shall overcome all these difficulties, too, with God's help. The State which our people, the DP's and the "illegal" immigrants need so badly will be established. Even those who live in happier conditions need it. We pray that we shall see it.—SHOSHANA K.

From the diary of the Bloc's representative in Jerusalem—February 19

In talks with members of the Jerusalem Command it has been stated that we must hold the Bloc at all costs in order to divert enemy forces and to prevent them from advancing upon Jerusalem. The defense of the Bloc will also divert the enemy from the Negev front. The Bloc is tying down Arab forces from Bethlehem to Hebron, and even from the Beersheba District. In the opinion of Staff Officers the number of men in the Bloc and the equipment they have is not inadequate. We must hold out for a few weeks more until the situation changes in our favor. They say that perhaps our forces can withdraw from Hartuv and Beth HaArava but we dare not give up the Etzion Bloc and Atarot. On the other hand we have heard that the impression was gained from talks with responsible leaders that a withdrawal from the Bloc might be considered. It has been decided to discuss this matter thoroughly with the Regional Commander.

Headquarters has decided to dispatch a convoy on Saturday. We shall provide our own escort. We have been instructed to prepare a list of returning settlers and of the members of the youth group who are being transferred to Revadim. The men will travel in three armored cars which are to remain in the Bloc. The convoy will be escorted to Solomon's Pools by three armored cars from Jerusalem. If we can't arrange the transport of supplies with the help of the British until then, we shall have to include a number of trucks in the convoy.

The Liaison Officers argue that organization of an independent convoy will result in a rupture of relations with the Army.

At half-past six in the evening we were told definitely that the Army would be prepared to escort a convoy of three trucks of supplies tomorrow morning. In the evening the Hagana requisitioned three trucks for this purpose. During the night we loaded about ten tons of supplies outside the "HaMashbir" stores.

February 20

At eight-fifteen in the morning a high-ranking police officer accompanied by Mr. Bergman of the Government District Office, came to examine the trucks going out to the Bloc. The trucks were brought to the Protected Area in "Bevingrad." The search lasted till about ten o'clock, and when it was completed the escort was ordered to accompany the convoy.

On the return journey several cows of Kfar Etzion were brought back. The truck with the cows of Massuot Yitzhak, which remained behind last time, also returned. The cattle were transferred from Jerusalem to Kvutzat Yavne.—YOSEF P.

From a private letter—February 20

The press has written a good deal about the countrywide Arab offensive that was supposed to have been launched on February 15. It is February 20 already and though the enemy have intensified their operations in Yemin Moshe and

Tirat Tsvi, their decisive defeats there indicate that there is no reason to be afraid. Even if we should suffer casualties, we need not despair.

For the time being it is comparatively quiet in our neighborhood, and there are signs that the Arabs are afraid of us.

We have extended our cordon of defense and have occupied new strongpoints. We have developed a defense-belt several miles in depth, within which we could not be taken by surprise. The surroundings have been closely mined and we are laying more and more mines every day.

Kfar Etzion is not threatened by any attack in the immediate future. However, something unexpected may crop up and change the situation fundamentally.—BEN ZION G.

From the Journal of Kfar Etzion—February 20

It is spring weather. The plowmen went out to the Mukhtar's Saddle today. . . .

After a long interval two planes landed here today. The pilots were given a very hearty reception.

From the diary of the Bloc's representative in Jerusalem—February 20

We have had a meeting with the Jerusalem Regional Commander and asked for reinforcements. Since the attack in January we have not been getting equipment on the required scale. The Regional Commander promised to meet our demands as soon as possible. It has been decided to dispatch a convoy escorted by Hagana forces and to transport all the necessary material, and the reinforcements and settlers who have been waiting in Jerusalem. Arms and ammunition are to be delivered by air. Every effort is to be made to improve the air strip. Five tons of barbed wire have been allocated for the reinforcement of the Bloc. Other materials necessary for fortifications and mine fields have been promised.

The convoy is being prepared. The drivers of the trucks and the armored cars have held maneuvers on similar hilly roads. We finished loading five trucks on Friday night, close to midnight.

February 21

At 4:30 A.M., we left the city for Ramat Rahel. The twelve trucks of the convoy were already parked on the road. At 6:30 A.M. a reconnaissance plane appeared overhead. It returned at 7:20 A.M. and the starting signal was given. Everything was ready and ten minutes later we were on our way. The convoy was led by the roadblock buster, followed by a radio car and two trucks loaded with supplies. An armored car, carrying the reinforcements, was fifth in the convoy. Then came a truck carrying barbed wire and another with fuel, beds, and mattresses; a truck carrying the belongings of the reinforcements; another armored car with men equipped with an "Avinoam" radio; an armored car with the men of the escort detachment; and another roadblock buster, also carrying men. At the end of the convoy was a small armored car with other men of the escort. With the exception of the trucks, all armored cars in the convoy were in radio communication with each other and with the Commander of the convoy. The command car was in communication with the base at Ramat Rahel, with the pilot of the plane and with the Etzion Bloc Command. We traveled fast, entered the Bloc at 8:37 A.M. and left at

9:13 A.M. At ten o'clock the convoy was already back at Ramat Rahel. We were overjoyed at our success.

The convoy transported one hundred bales of barbed wire, four hundred iron pegs, and two hundred six-foot iron posts. One armored car and a roadblock buster remained behind for the Bloc Command.—YOSEF P.

From a private diary—February 21

The great event of the day was the success of the convoy, which arrived here after we had gone through a long period of isolation. The organization of the convoy was excellent. Settlers who served in the Jewish Brigade during the war said that the experience gained at that time was apparent in the organization. It did much to increase confidence in the Yishuv's ability.

A number of planes also landed here during the day. Three aircraft were together on the air strip for a short time. They brought a quantity of arms, including a three-inch mortar, two two-inch mortars and two Breda machine guns.

Who would have thought that our military power had made such strides?—YISAKHAR

From the Journal of Kfar Etzion—February 21

The *haverim* are engaged in a great deal of cultural activity. There are study circles for Torah, the Prophets, Talmud, and Maimonides *(Laws of Martyrdom,* and *Laws of Kings and Their Wars).*

Lectures are held in the intervals between work and guard duty by members of the *kvutza* and people at present in the Bloc.

The Dramatic Circle is preparing a program for Tel Hai

Day, commemorating the heroic stand of Yosef Trumpeldor and his comrades against the Arab bands at Tel Hai twenty-seven years ago. It is also preparing a program for Purim.

At 11 o'clock this morning we held a Vocal Newspaper devoted to current affairs. Among the "articles" we heard were:

1. Current Spiritual Affairs by Yehoshua L.;
2. Problems Involving Defense and the Saving of Lives on the Sabbath by Tsvi T.;
3. The Sabbath in the Wars of the Hasmoneans (a reading from the Book of Maccabees).

From a notice on the bulletin board—February 21

A gathering in memory of Yosef Trumpeldor and his comrades and of the detachment of thirty-five sent to reinforce the Bloc, will be held in Nveh Ovadia on 12th Adar Aleph (February 21), at 3:00 P.M.

The Program

1. Opening Address—Yosef D.
2. In Memoriam: Yosef Trumpeldor—Yehoshua L.;
3. "See Oh Soil," (S. Tchernihowsky)—Dov Kl.;
4. The Thirty-Five—Ya'akov A.;
5. The Ballad of the Thirty-Five—Sha'ul R.;
6. Massada (Yitzhak Lamdan): Tableau—The Dramatic Troupe;
7. "Wertheimer"—a one-act play by Yehoshua Bar-Yosef: presented by the Dramatic Troupe.

From a private diary—February 22

Two dreadful accidents occurred today. In the morning Naomi Druzdik, of Revadim, went out to the air strip after an Auster had landed, to speak to the pilot. As she came close to the plane the propeller suddenly began spinning around and Naomi was struck in the head. Apparently, the pilot had not noticed her approaching. Naomi was rushed to the hospital in Kfar Etzion, but there was little that Dr. Alkalai could do for her. An hour later she was dead.

In the afternoon, after the plane had already left, a loud explosion was heard from the direction of the carpentry shop, where anti-vehicle mines were being manufactured by two Palmah men. A mine had exploded. The building was in ruins and after the rubble was cleared the two men were removed—Yehuda Me'irov was suffering from severe burns, Shimon Zilberman was dead. The former was treated for his wounds, and a plane was summoned from Tel Aviv to remove him. But he, too, was beyond help, and died that evening in a Tel Aviv hospital.

Two more graves were dug that day in the Bloc, one in the cemetery of Revadim, the other in that of Kfar Etzion. —YISAKHAR

From the diary of the Bloc's representative in Jerusalem—February 22

Yigael Yadin, of the General Staff, flew to the Bloc on Saturday. He inspected the strongpoints and discussed defense matters with the commanders. He left an hour later.

Mr. Bergman has informed us that the Army is refusing to provide an escort for our convoy as we sent one independently on Saturday.—YOSEF P.

From the Journal of Kfar Etzion—February 22

The following cable has been transmitted to Jerusalem:

Of the one hundred and sixty men sent to reinforce the Bloc only one hundred and ten remain. What are we to do to make up the difference?

Why has the fortifications engineer not arrived? Valuable days are being wasted.

8 The General Meeting

Three months remained before the total evacuation of Palestine by the British. The Jewish authorities were registering the twenty-six to thirty-five-year old age groups for military service. Training camps were established throughout the country to build up the military strength for the defense of the Jewish State to be.

The Arab attacks on the roads to the Negev, to Galilee and to Jerusalem, increased in vigor. Jerusalem continued to be the city most exposed to gun fire and bombs. The worst outrage in the Holy City was the explosion in Ben-Yehuda Street, in the heart of the business center, in which fifty Jews were killed and one hundred and thirty wounded, for which members of the British security forces were held responsible.

The financial position of Kfar Etzion was steadily deteriorating. The settlers could not work their farms or market their limited produce, while the costs of maintaining the settlement mounted. The Jewish authorities had not yet agreed who was to support the settlers—the Settlement Department of the Jewish Agency, which traditionally aided the settlements to establish and maintain themselves, or the defense authorities, who were responsible for the growing military establishment. Not only the inhabitants of Kfar

Etzion, but their wives and children as well, in Jerusalem, were feeling the economic pinch.

So when the proposal was advanced by the settlement authorities to transfer a number of men to the coastal plain to support the women and children, it aroused intense arguments. The heated debates reflected the anxiety of the haverim *about the future. That the Etzion Bloc was to be included in the proposed Arab State, according to the Palestine Partition Plan, was of particular concern to the settlers. The various points of view were given formal expression in the convention of the supreme body of the* kvutza—*the General Meeting.*

From the Journal of Kfar Etzion—February 24

Natan has arrived from Tel Aviv to report on the proposal of the Jewish Agency Settlement Department to transfer the married men elsewhere—either to some other collective settlement or a labor camp. They will be replaced by enlisted men whose maintenance will be cheaper. The womenfolk and children in Jerusalem will join their husbands and fathers. We decided to put it on the agenda of the General Meeting, as no other solution has been advanced to the problem of supporting the women and children now in Jerusalem.

From the Journal of Kfar Etzion—February 24-26

The Kibbutz Council submitted the following agenda for discussion at the General Meeting:

a. The Settlement Department's proposal;
b. That the *kvutza* must remain in the Bloc at all costs;
c. Election of a committee to draft the resolutions passed by the Meeting.

Hanokh H. opened the discussion on the Settlement Department's proposal to transfer the fathers of families. He said: The total or even partial evacuation of the Bloc is not being proposed. The defense authorities are doing all they can to strengthen our defenses. We may assume, on the basis of the strength of the last Arab assault, and the forces the enemy can muster in the near future, that the Bloc's defenses are adequate. The national institutions are planning a large-scale fortification program and also the reinforcement of the Bloc to enable it to withstand any future Arab attack.

In keeping with the Settlement Department's proposal, it might be advisable to transfer a number of our members —not more than half at most—to some other settlement. I myself do not believe that the proposed plan is workable, involving, as it does, the transfer of *all* fathers of families. Many of them perform important roles in the settlement. What we can do is to send a limited work group on a temporary basis to some other settlement, and its earnings will help maintain the women and children. We must ensure the defense of this district and we must maintain the *kvutza* as a single unit.

NATAN SH.: We are faced with two problems, one military—the defense of the area; the other national—our capacity to hold out here, politically and economically.

We must not confuse these two problems. The military problem is the one we have to deal with at present. We are in the "heart" of an Arab-populated region, isolated from the entire Yishuv, and separated from our families. Should *haverim* here take the floor and say that they cannot hold out much longer under these conditions, that the strain is beginning to tell on them, or advance some other reason for leaving this place, we must understand these people and try to have them transferred elsewhere.

But, if everyone agrees that if ordered to remain and defend this place, we will do so—why tie up the present problem of security with the problem that may come up in the future of maintaining a settlement in this area? Who can predict whether or not we can maintain a Jewish settlement in the Arab State to be? Who can guarantee today that a Jewish State will be established at all, and that we shall remain in the Arab State? When the time comes, if we find that we cannot maintain a Jewish settlement here, we shall demand a transfer to some other site, *en bloc*. Why should we split up now? I am convinced that if we decide to evacuate most of the family men our communal group will fall to pieces. In this way we shall destroy the work of years.

That is why I am strongly opposed to these proposals. We have not yet reached the stage for such a step. I wish instead to make a number of suggestions which can make our position here much easier:

a. Everything possible must be done to strengthen our defenses and to raise the siege.

b. We must transfer elsewhere a number of *haverim* who for reasons of health or age cannot help with the defense.

c. We must try to do as much work as we can on the farm. This is important not so much economically, but as a means of raising morale, and preventing the settlement from becoming a military garrison.

SHA'UL R.: Our position today is different from that of the settlements which were attacked during the troubles of 1936-39. Today we are fighting a war, and strategic considerations, as well as those of political and military prestige, are the factors that decide whether or not the settlement should be maintained; not pioneering.

However, this does not prevent the *kvutza* from considering the question of its own future. Some say that the Settlement Department proposal will bring about the liquidation of our collective, but in any case the *kvutza* will be liquidated if we do not begin to plan the evacuation here and now—either because of the reasons that have already been mentioned or because the Bloc will remain in the Arab State. I therefore favor the proposal.

YA'AKOV SH.: I am depressed when I hear veteran *haverim* ready to accept the proposal without acknowledging that it implies the disintegration of the *kvutza*. The Settlement Department has made this proposal partly because of the expense involved in supporting the families. I do not believe this is such an urgent problem. I am convinced that some solution can be found without our having to move. Maintenance will become a problem, not only at Kfar Etzion, but at many other settlements.

I see this place as our home and we are the ones who should protect it. The evacuation of Kfar Etzion, in the manner suggested, will lead to the disintegration of the Bloc. I am prepared to accept the proposal made by the Settlement Department only if it be resolved to evacuate the entire region.

AHARON Y.: The main point of our discussion is whether there is any future at all for our Bloc and whether we may not have to evacuate it eventually. The *haverim* who will join the women and children will not solve the problem of maintenance. The real reason for this proposal, as I see it, is not financial, but to keep the rest of us here until the time comes to evacuate the Bloc. We may have to remain here for a long time. The question facing us is whether we can undertake that task. Who can tell how long the Bloc, cut off from the rest of the country, will be able to hold out, and how long our families in Jerusalem will have to endure the separation from their husbands and fathers.

But there is another point to consider. The transitional period, once peace is restored, will be long and difficult. The Bloc will be beset by political, economic, and security problems. Some *haverim* will not be prepared to live in an Arab State, and a crisis will result. For that reason disintegration may threaten the *kvutza* even if we remain here, and perhaps even to a greater extent. Every inch of this place is dear to all of us, but sentiment alone will not help us to solve our problems. We must consider the proposal soberly and not reject it.

YA'AKOV A.: We have all invested years of our lives to make this place our home and now it is likely that we may have to start everything all over again. *Haverim* have said that it is our duty as pioneers to remain here in the Arab State. It seems to me, however, that to begin again and to reconstruct our lives and our settlement within the Jewish State demands far more from us as pioneers.

Speaking for myself, whatever happens, because of the security position I hold, I shall be the last to leave here. But we must all of us face the question: Have we the strength to begin again?

My main concern is the integrity of the *kvutza*. If it is correct that the *kvutza* will break up if we leave, because our people are attached to this place and cannot begin elsewhere, I am prepared to withdraw my support for the proposal. But those people who oppose the proposal are hiding their heads in the sand. The question is not a military one. Every place in the country has its military problems. The question is rather—whether we can remain in an Arab State. Our position is different from that of other Jewish settlements in Arab territory. They can hope for some rectification of the frontiers, while we must reckon with the distance between ourselves and the future borders of the Jewish State. We must ask ourselves whether we shall be able to live here, even if we want to. It may possibly, at the last moment, be necessary to evacuate us, whatever we ourselves want or think. Let a group of our own *haverim* prepare in good time and plan the future site of our *kvutza.*

SHALOM G.: I have been deeply moved by this discussion. I love this place, as all of us do. I planted the first seedlings here, I built my home here, and here our *haverim* fell. We have instilled the spirit of these hills and rocks in the hearts of our children.

And though our approaches differ, the political situation is clear. There is no doubt whatever that this area will not be included within the Jewish State, and the very grave question whether we shall be able to live in the Arab State must be faced. Reason compels us to face the prospect that we shall not be able to do so, though emotionally we cannot reconcile ourselves to such a possibility and all that it entails. The Settlement Department, it seems, is concerned about the future, and wishes to provide a solution to the problem in good time. What have the people who oppose the proposal to suggest?

It should be clear that this discussion is no more than an open exchange of views. We have been asked for our opinion of this proposal and we, as members of a kibbutz, are free to voice our thoughts. But once these deliberations are over, we are all soldiers with the duty to obey.

YITZHAK B.S.: None of us can leave this district so long as Jews continue to live here. There is no real difference between the Kaplan proposal and this proposal in its amended form. I do not think that it will be of any practical value to transfer part of the group elsewhere.

YA'AKOV K.: I envy the *haverim* who have been able to make up their minds. As for me, I still hesitate. The arguments in favor of the proposal are weak. We ourselves suggested the separation of families and when they were transferred we knew that we must prepare ourselves for a long period of separation. I must say that until today I have not heard anyone complain of it.

SHMUEL A.: We must carefully consider all factors before we reach a final decision. But once the majority reaches such a decision, every member should be prepared to abide by it. I, also, do not believe that the proposal has been made because of financial considerations; it reflects instead, the anxiety of the settlement authorities for the continued existence of our *kvutza* and its integrity as a settlement group.

DAVID B.D.: I am disappointed that so many *haverim* support the Settlement Department proposal. I would never have thought that responsible members of the *kvutza* could take up such an attitude. I appreciate that certain *haverim* cannot remain here, and of course there are also *haverim* ready to stay whatever happens. I do not understand the use of political arguments. Who can foresee the future? If we had made our decisions on the basis of political predictions on other occasions and reckoned with the hard facts of every situation, we would never have achieved what we have in this country.

YEHEZKEL A.: I was one of those who fought for the settlement at Kfar Etzion when the question came up in our work camp at Kfar Pines. But conditions have changed now that a competent institution has made this offer and is asking our opinion. We have had to abandon farming and other related work. This may increase the danger of our disintegration as a *kvutza*. The present proposal is therefore practicable and timely.

DAVID T.: The choice before us is whether to continue living in a communal framework or whether to live in a Jewish State. I can say for myself that I prefer to live in a Jewish State even if that means abandoning the collective way of life. I do not want to be a pioneer in a new *Golah*. We shall always be in danger while in "exile" in the Mufti's state. It is contrary to all that I have ever aspired to.

YITZHAK K.: In the first part of the debate my own attitude was clear. I was strongly opposed to the proposal, for I regarded the dispatch of a group as the beginning of the disintegration of the *kvutza*. It is impossible to break the cask and to preserve the wine.

As the discussion continued, however, I became perplexed; I assume that those who made us this proposal are also aware of what the future holds in store for the *kvutza*. If they propose and consent to the dispatch of a working party to establish a new settlement, there must be something in it. But have we reached a decisive stage when it is necessary for us to decide one way or the other? If it is, then we must decide now; but if we have not, then we had better adjourn this discussion until the situation clears up. Perhaps then we shall be able to decide unanimously, and the integrity of the *kvutza* will be preserved.

SHLOMO R.: Five years ago I was in the first group of members of the *kvutza* to come to Kfar Etzion. I came without thinking twice about what might await us here. I shall not be among the first to leave.

This discussion endangers every tree we have planted, every house we have built here. As it has been stated already, every stone here is dear to us and this soil, in whose defense some of the finest of our *haverim* fell, is sacred to all of us. But I regret to note that the undertone of love for our homes does not predominate in this debate. If someone should say that this is a matter of sentiment, then on this matter I am a sentimentalist.

Some of the *haverim* consider our situation as resembling that of Trumpeldor and his comrades at Tel Hai. People argued at the time that Tel Hai was not worth holding, but history proved them wrong. The defense of Tel Hai saved Galilee for our State to be.

AVRAHAM F.: In my opinion, this discussion serves no purpose since we are not in a position to reach any practical decision. The security authorities have decided that the Bloc will not be abandoned, and they will provide all means to ensure our successful stand. Should anyone have to leave the Bloc, *they* will be the ones to decide who it is to be.

Recommendations of the Committee Appointed to Draft a Resolution

On the basis of the discussions of the problems affecting the continued existence of our *kvutza* by the responsible bodies of the Yishuv, and taking into consideration the proposal made to transfer a number of members of the *kvutza* together with the women and children at present in Jerusalem to some other place in the country, we have arrived at the following conclusions:

1. In view of the lack of information regarding the plans of the national institutions for our future here and for the settlement of the problems which may arise in the period of transition;

2. And in view of the fact that because of current developments throughout the country the basic facts upon which we must make our decision are unsettled, we have resolved:

a. To bring to the knowledge of the institutions of the movement the opinions expressed at the General Meeting of *haverim* held on February 24, 25, and 26.

b. To urge the institutions of the movement to take an early decision on our future in view of present conditions and future prospects.

These conclusions are arrived at as a result of:

i. a wish to avoid taking a vote which might cause undesirable controversy among the *haverim;*

ii. insufficient knowledge of the plans proposed by the national authorities, preventing us from arriving at any final decision.

The above conclusions were unanimously endorsed by the General Meeting.

From a private diary—February 26

All members of the *kvutza* met for three days in the afternoon to discuss the Settlement Department's proposal. I sat hour after hour and listened to what each *haver* had to say. They are all the people who in everyday life seem to me so plain. Some of them, it is true, remind me of the youthful dreams we once shared; the stolidity of others reflects the rocky hills in whose midst we have come to build our homes. But I was conscious throughout of their concern for the fate of the entire Bloc, of the *kvutza,* of their own families. They were careful in their analysis of the situation and in the conclusions they drew. They obviously wanted to understand each other. They all felt that what they said would decide the fate of what they loved most in the world.

Sometimes the atmosphere became charged and the debate stormy, especially when the opponents of the proposal brought forward "patriotic" arguments. They honestly regarded themselves as representing the true aims of the *kvutza.* It seemed to me that they wounded the feelings of many *haverim.* Were the latter, who for so many years had borne the responsibilities of pioneering, in need of this sort of persuasion?

It was apparent that it was not easy for those who favored the proposal to give it their vocal support. They also do not want to evacuate the Bloc; perhaps they do not believe that it is possible to do so. Nevertheless, they did not wish to reject the offer out of hand.

I did not think that even those wholeheartedly in favor of the proposal were shirking their duty. I have known them for years as *haverim* who willingly perform all tasks with which they are charged. I appreciate the concern they voiced, and I know upon what it is based—the knowledge that there are dark days ahead of us, the fear of the unknown, and the feeling that even the authorities cannot decide the fate of the Bloc.

Of course, even the optimists, who are convinced that we shall emerge from the war unharmed, cannot foresee the shape of things to come. The majority of the *haverim* are afraid of life in an Arab State. Some of them regard it as the negation of all their work and their dream of a Jewish State.

Once one accustoms oneself to this way of thinking one is bound to conclude that the defense of the Bloc is a purely military objective. The *haverim* realize that they must share in the defense of the Bloc. But then their love for these hills, for the trees they have planted and all the work they have invested, becomes strangely irrelevant. They come gradually to the same conclusion: "In any case we cannot hold on to them any longer. This is our destiny!"

Some have no illusions about what lies ahead, but they do believe that in the end we shall win out. Those who hold that in any case the decision does not lie in our hands, and that the entire controversy is therefore superfluous, have adopted the most convenient attitude. They are prepared to let events take their course.

There is another consideration. It is not expressed openly but it causes real anxiety. What about our families? How can we forsake them at such a time? What will be the fate of the *kvutza* if we do?

Everyone is convinced of the correctness of his own attitude and motives, but the desire to safeguard what we have built up together decides the issue. The *haverim* appreciate that in such a crisis we must close our ranks. Otherwise the *kvutza* will break up and the entire Bloc will suffer.

Throughout these discussions an awareness of the bitterness of our dilemma oppresses me. No army in the world leaves its men to decide their own fate. The commander decides; the soldier must obey his orders and fight.

The enlisted men visited the hall to listen to the discussions of the *kibbutzniks,* half out of curiosity, half scornfully. They, after all, were not asked whether they want to leave or stay. They volunteered for service and someone else decided for them where they were to serve. *We* alone are offered the possibility to choose: whether to preserve the integrity of our group and to aid our families, or to remain in the settlement we have built up.—YISAKHAR

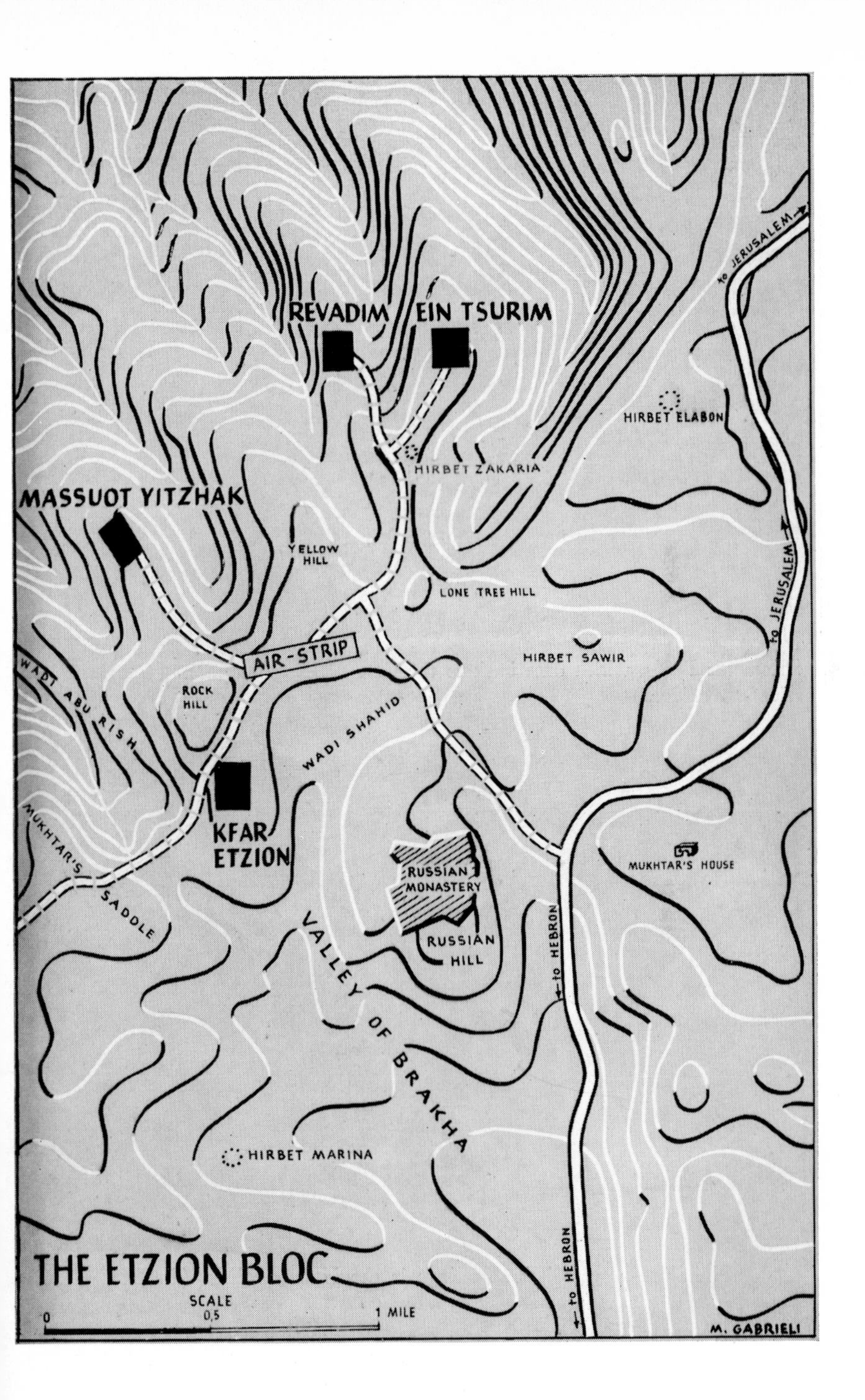

THE ETZION BLOC

Solomon's Pools, which date back to the time of King Solomon. (*Courtesy the Zionist Archives*)

Nahalin—a typical Arab village in the Hebron Hills. (*Barak*)

The German Monastery is occupied on the day of settlement. (*Keren Ha-Yesod*)

Overlooking the Valley of Brakha: the first ploughing on the "Holy Mount." (*Keren HaYesod*)

The western part of Kfar Etzion as seen from the foot of Rock Hill. (*Keren HaKayemet*)

Residential buildings in the southwest corner of the settlement. (The hill in the background is the Mukhtar's Saddle.) (*Keren HaKayemet*)

Massuot Yitzhak in 1947. (*Keren HaYesod*)

The bulldozer engaged in land clearance. (In the foreground an Arab herd passes through the settlement's land.) (*Keren HaYesod*)

Settlement day of the Bnei Akiva youth group. (*Keren HaYesod*)

Ein Tsurim at the end of 1947 as seen from the southeast. (*Keren HaYesod*)

Revadim as seen from the east. (In the rear-center is the Arab village of Jabba.) (*Keren HaYesod*)

The settlers of Revadim gathered in front of their houses. (*Keren HaKayemet*)

One of the trucks of the December 12 convoy. This convoy was escorted by British troops. (*Oron*)

The Hagana-escorted convoy of December 25 stops at the entrance to the Bloc near the Lone Tree. (*Ilani*)

Settlers recite the morning prayers after coming off guard. (*Ilani*)

Post No. 6 of Kfar Etzion in the southeast corner of the settlement. (Russian Hill is in the background.) (*Ilani*)

The funeral procession leaves Kfar Etzion on its way to the cemetery. (*Mendelsohn*)

The bodies are laid to rest in the mass grave in the Kfar Etzion cemetery. (*Mendelsohn*)

The airlift from Tel Aviv: supply planes (an Auster, left, and a Tiger Moth) stand near the airstrip. (*Courtesy N. Lerman*)

The February 21 "surprise" convoy: this convoy was escorted by the Hagana and brought reinforcements as well as supplies. (*Courtesy N. Lerman*)

The Monastery as seen from the west. (The entrance to the Monastery is through the arch on the left.) (*Raz*)

The entrance to the Monastery.

The Monastery detachment and their weapons. (*Courtesy N. Lerman*)

THE RUSSIAN MONASTERY UNDER SNOW

Looking westward from the Monastery. (The houses of Kfar Etzion are seen in the distance.) (*Courtesy N. Lerman*)

Diversion in the snow in the Monastery courtyard. (*Courtesy N. Lerman*)

The convoy on the Bloc feeder road, on its way back to Jerusalem. (*Courtesy N. Lerman*)

Arab irregulars preparing the ambush for the convoy. (*Archives of the Israel Defense Forces*)

While the surrender was being negotiated, the Arabs left their arms on the ridge and advanced toward the road. (The man on the left wears a Red Crescent armband; the soldier on the right is British.) (*Courtesy N. Lerman*)

A Jewish armored car, captured at Nebi Daniel, is paraded through Hebron. (*Archives of the Israel Defense Forces*)

THE GATHERING OF THE REMAINS OF THE ETZION BLOC DEFENDERS. (*Ba-Mahane*)

THE STATE FUNERAL OF THE ETZION BLOC DEFENDERS IN JERUSALEM. (*Jewish Agency Photographic Service*)

9 The Occupation of the Russian Monastery

The battle for the road from the coast to Jerusalem entered a critical stage as the food supplies of the city were depleted and the Arab attacks on motor transport grew in intensity. Almost every day a convoy would make the perilous run between Tel Aviv and Jerusalem, and hardly one arrived without sustaining casualties in drivers and escorts. A special Palmah force possessing armored vehicles provided the escort for these convoys.

Within the city the security situation deteriorated. Hit-and-run raids and ambushes continued unabated. The pressure on the beleaguered Jewish Quarter of the Old City was increasing. Other Jewish quarters that were also cut off from the main body of the Jewish populace in Jerusalem, such as the Hadassah Hospital and the Hebrew University on Mount Scopus, were also undergoing a siege within a siege.

The British Army was preparing to evacuate its camps in the vicinity of the Etzion Bloc. It had escorted four convoys to the Bloc over a period of a month and now refused to secure the passage of any more Jewish vehicles.

From the Journal of Kfar Etzion—February 26

Two representatives of the Regional Staff paid a visit to the Bloc to discuss some of the more urgent problems with the commanders and the leaders of the settlement.

February 27

One of the monks and the lessee of the Russian Monastery asked for a meeting with an official representative of the Bloc. They met with the Bloc Commander and the Mukhtar of Kfar Etzion and declared that they were threatened with starvation. They asked for our protection. They reported that an Arab band located in Beth Fajjar is planning to seize the Monastery. This band often breaks into the Monastery, threatens its occupants, and robs them of their food. The tenant informed us that the children of Jabba have been evacuated, while the villagers are planning to leave Nahalin for fear of an attack upon them.

We had to refuse their request for protection as we have neither the men nor the equipment to hold the Monastery. However, it was agreed that in the event of an attempt at robbery they will signal to us and we shall try to help them.

March 3-4

In the past few days planes have landed, bringing mail, newspapers and various other requirements. Our spirit has improved. M. Hazani, of the Agricultural Department of HaPoel HaMizrahi, arrived by plane today to observe at first hand some of the problems of the Bloc.

A large number of *haverim* are working on an extension of the air strip, now that the rains have stopped. The strongpoints of the Bloc are being reinforced. While we were fortifying Lone Tree Hill and laying mines in the vicinity, the Palmah unit occupied Hirbet Sawir to protect the workers. Everybody speaks highly of its advantages as a strongpoint and regrets that, through lack of manpower, we cannot hold it permanently.

March 5

The *haverim* are following the battle to keep open the road from Jerusalem to the coast very closely. We know that this struggle will determine our own contact with the rest of the country. . . .

Today, just before the Sabbath, we were in radio contact with the women and children in Jerusalem. Because of the atmospheric disturbances we could only catch the words: "Regards and *Shabbat Shalom* from the children!" It is planned to "converse" by means of radio from time to time.

March 7

We have pruned the apple trees and vineyards in the past few days, and have also plowed the orchards. These jobs help to keep up morale. It is good to feel like a farmer sometimes and not to have always to live like a soldier in barracks.

From private letters—March 7

M. Hazani spoke about the general situation in the country, and particularly on the prospects of Kfar Etzion. In his opinion the position will steadily improve. The steps being taken to establish a Provisional Jewish Government are of vital importance. People are hoping that Jerusalem will be the first city in the country to enjoy order and peace secured by the presence of an international force.

Hazani made it clear that all plans to transfer the fathers of families from the Bloc have been shelved. The national authorities are very anxious to settle Kfar Etzion's problems and have means to do so. He himself assured us that everything possible will be done to bring the necessary reinforcements and equipment, and to stockpile sufficient supplies for several months. A special appropriation will be allocated for the development of the farm. Even if only some of these promises are kept our people will be reassured and more capable of holding out.—SHALOM G.

The proposal regarding the transfer of some of the *haverim* came about as a result of lack of coordination between the financial and military authorities. Now it seems that the security authorities, who are interested in our remaining here, will bear the cost of maintaining our families.

We have not yet solved the problem of the future of the *kvutza,* and we have no doubt that many surprises are in store for us. Possibly all these troubles may soon pass and there will be nothing to hinder our future progress. We pray to God for health and peace.—YEHOSHUA L.

From the Journal of Kfar Etzion—March 10

The rain has stopped. Today was a beautiful spring day. So far sixteen inches of rain have fallen and all the cisterns, including the new one, are full. Kfar Etzion has three thousand cubic meters of water. This year we shall not have to bring water from Jerusalem. The cistern of Ein Tsurim and Revadim is also full. The flow of the spring at Massuot Yitzhak, which throughout the winter has never exceeded two or three cubic meters in twenty-four hours, now gives about eighty.

From a private diary—March 10

The sun is shining again and we are enjoying pleasant spring weather. The general depression has also lifted.

After work we went for a stroll to the strongpoints and the air strip. The rocks all around shone in the sunshine. The rain has washed them clean and little pools of water abound among the rocks. Between the rocks there are narcissi, cyclamen, and anemones. The young forest seedlings are now bright and green and seem to invite one to rest in their scanty shade and to breathe their fragrance. The trees in the orchards are blossoming and filling the air with their scent. The air is clean and pure. Far away in the west we can see the yellow strip of the coast, dotted with settlements. To the north, like a huge dark stain, lies the forest of Kiryat Anavim, and above it the Ma'aleh HaHamisha rest resort. Over there are our brethren and the rest of the Yishuv for whom we long so much.

God's world is beautiful, our home is beautiful on this spring day.

We usually finish work at four o'clock, and then every one changes into clean clothes. Just before *Minha* about twenty *haverim* gather to study their daily lesson in Tractate *Halla.* After *Ma'ariv* the Talmud circle, which has about fifteen members, meets. They are very keen on the first chapter of Tractate *Sanhedrin,* which they are studying now. Tsvi is an excellent lecturer, while Shimon, as usual, asks difficult questions. Ya'akov also remembers some of the learning that he absorbed at the Yeshiva; others too, take an active part in the lesson.

Another group has gathered in a neighboring room, and is enjoying Shmuel's lucid explanation of a chapter of the Prophets. *Haverim* and enlisted men gather in the reading room to listen to the radio or to read a book or a newspaper.

The shifts are changing in the dining room. Those who have come off guard duty are having their meal.

It is just another evening in Kfar Etzion.—YISAKHAR

From the Journal of Kfar Etzion—March 11

We were shocked to hear of the explosion in the compound of the Jewish Agency building in Jerusalem, when an Arab employee of the American Consulate drove the Consulate car laden with dynamite into the courtyard. The guards were deceived by the American flag flying on the car. Thirteen Agency employees were killed and seventy wounded. We were very worried, as the Agency building is near the Ratisbonne Monastery. Once again we must mourn our war casualties.

From a private diary—March 12

The discussions we have had with the representatives of the Regional Staff and with Hazani regarding the future of the Bloc have created a new spirit that is revealed in the fortification work.

It is clear that we cannot depend too much on outside aid, which in any case is slow in coming, so we must improvise with whatever materials we have. After a series of meetings and consultations we have worked out detailed plans to be put into effect as soon as the winter is over.

The proposal to regard the whole Bloc as one unit for work purposes has been accepted in principle. The settlements have been instructed to allocate more labor for the strengthening of the strongpoints and other key positions. The air strip, which is being extended and improved, is given priority. . . .

The various Settlement Commanders are hard at work on the construction of fortifications, trenches and communication ditches. In the absence of a pneumatic drill we must contrive all sorts of makeshifts.—YISAKHAR

March 14

A number of planes landed today, bringing arms and ammunition, including a light machine gun, two 2-inch mortars and ten Tommy-guns. . . .

The two Russian monks left the Monastery last week and went to Jerusalem. We opened negotiations with Ibrahim Hazboun, the lessee of the Monastery, about renting a number of rooms. Hazboun has always been friendly with his Jewish neighbors. He had been fearful for his life, because of a quarrel with the Arab extremists, and was glad that at last we decided to respond to his request to take the Monastery and its inhabitants under our protection. We signed a contract with him on the terms of occupation. The representative of the Bloc in Jerusalem has been instructed to contact the Russian Archimandrite in the Holy City and to obtain his confirmation of the contract.

During the past few days reports have reached us that Arab bands from outside Palestine, now stationed in our neighborhood, are planning to occupy the summer residence of the Mukhtar of Bethlehem on the Jerusalem-Hebron highway, and the Monastery, and to use them as a springboard for an attack upon us. Bloc HQ decided to forestall the attempt and to occupy the Monastery.

A detachment of thirty men was mustered from the various strongpoints and settlements. Dan of the Students Unit of the Field Force, formerly an officer with the French Maquis, was placed in command.

After occupying the Monastery the soldiers and the settlers set about putting up a barbed-wire fence, digging positions and communication trenches. The sappers mined the roads.

Posts were established in the upper story and on the balcony facing the road. Work continued at a brisk pace as we wanted to get the job done before the enemy got wind of it.

The occupation of the Monastery has been kept secret. We do not want the British authorities to hear of it as they might decide to intervene. We hope to surprise the enemy when the time comes.—YISAKHAR

From the diary of the Bloc's representative in Jerusalem—March 14

"Mosh" Silberschmidt has been appointed OC of the Bloc. I met him to discuss various matters. . . .

We have been informed that "B" Company of the Mikhmash Battalion of the Field Force in Jerusalem is to be assigned to the Bloc, relieving the students stationed there.

A radio message has been received from Tel Aviv Headquarters to the effect that a large convoy is being organized. It will leave on Friday, spend the night in Jerusalem, and continue on its way to the Bloc on the following day. It will bring fuel, foodstuffs, and building materials for the fortifications. The trucks at present in Jerusalem, loaded with supplies, galvanized iron sheets, and timber for the Bloc, will also leave with this convoy. An escort from Tel Aviv will accompany the convoy throughout its trip. We have been asked to let them know immediately how many armored cars we need and to dispatch as many men as we can for the escort. In addition we must get as many trucks with armor-plated cabins as possible and send them down to Tel Aviv on Thursday.—YOSEF P.

From private letters—March 19

In the last few days it has rained and snowed a good deal. It was the heaviest fall of snow we could remember in our district and one of the heaviest recorded in the country. Owing to the fuel shortage we suffered a lot from the cold. The air strip is a quagmire. We are cut off from the rest of the country. . . .

A plane that broke down on the air strip was completely covered with snow, and when the snow thawed we found that its wings were damaged. They were dismantled and we began to repair them, but we are not sure if we can carry out the repairs here. . . .

There is a shortage of food, especially of perishable foodstuffs. We have not had fresh meat, fish, or vegetables for some time now. There is little oil left, while the smokers complain of the small ration of cigarettes. There is a shortage even of medical supplies.

The Supply Committee has been very careful to conserve the supplies brought here by the convoy and has tried to put something by in reserve. Now we have to depend to an increasing extent on this reserve. One joke around the settlements is that as a result of the shortage food has improved. In the absence of staples we are compelled to serve canned meat, chocolate, candy, etc.

From a private diary—March 19

The *haverim* in charge of the Bloc's stores are making room for the supplies that we are expecting with the next convoy. . . .

Akiva of Kfar Etzion and "Jackie" of Revadim, together with their assistants, are busy extending and improving the telephone system to the settlements and the strongpoints.

The signalmen are also introducing improvements into their work and preparing their instruments for an emergency.—YISAKHAR

From the diary of the Bloc's representative in Jerusalem—March 19

We have been kept very busy organizing the large convoy. We asked the local Emergency Committee to arrange for a group of porters who are prepared to work on the Sabbath. We have supplies of gasoline sufficient for fueling fifty-five trucks. We have also the necessary wireless equipment together with a group of operators. We have got permission to park all the trucks coming from Tel Aviv and those already here in Jerusalem in the compound of the Schneller Camp. A store for our supplies has also been placed at our disposal for a short period. We have received all the supplies of foodstuffs approved for us from the Hagana stores.

We have discussed with the managers of the Egged Bus Company the supply of armored buses to transport the one hundred and fifty men of the Mikhmash Battalion "B" Company. We have also contacted the Hovala Company about heavy trucks to carry supplies from Jerusalem.

Twenty-five trucks have already come from Tel Aviv. We worked throughout Friday night until three in the morning to get all the supplies and material loaded.

Kfar Etzion has already been asked to make all arrangements for the arrival of the convoy.

March 20 (Saturday evening)

Everything was ready early this morning in the Schneller Camp. The trucks, the Egged buses, the drivers, and the men of "B" Company all waited for the word to go. Suddenly orders came from Tel Aviv that the convoy was not to leave and to unload the trucks. The Regional Commander explained that the order was to enable the trucks to return to Tel Aviv to bring essential supplies for Jerusalem. Groups of porters were mustered from all parts of the city and the goods were unloaded and stacked in the Schneller stores. In the afternoon another five trucks of materials for the Bloc arrived from Tel Aviv. These, too, were unloaded. Work continued throughout the day. Weary and hungry after working throughout the night and day on the Sabbath, depressed at the delay in the dispatch of the convoy, our *haverim* returned to the Ratisbonne Monastery.—YOSEF P.

From the Journal of Kfar Etzion—March 21

The weather is improving. Once again the planes are arriving, bringing supplies, letters, and papers. There was no mail from the *haverot* in Jerusalem, from whom we have not received any letters for the last fortnight. Apparently there has been some delay *en route*. The *haverim* are used to this sort of thing already and don't get excited about it as they had done in the past.

Replacements belonging to the "Orthodox Company" of the Tel Aviv Field Force are beginning to arrive by plane. We are dubbing them the "Airborne Platoon."

Dr. Windsberg, who has been appointed Director of the Field Hospital, has also arrived by plane.

From the diary of a member of Kfar Etzion in Jerusalem—March 21

Correspondence with the *haverim* in the Bloc is the pivot about which the life of the *haverot* centers. From time to time the *haverot* send their letters to the representatives of the Bloc in Tel Aviv for transmission by plane to the Bloc. Everybody is happy when the letters catch the Jerusalem-Tel Aviv convoy, and it arrives in Tel Aviv just as the plane is about to take off. But sometimes the letters remain in Jerusalem for a long time. Generally the convoys are attacked *en route* and the vehicles carrying the letters are held up or even forced to return to Jerusalem. Then again it is not always possible to send the letters on from Tel Aviv. And so delays in the dispatch of mail to and from the Bloc are frequent.

The situation has been eased since they began to broadcast regards from the Bloc every morning. The children are keenly interested in the special broadcast for them.—HA'IM Ts.

From a private letter—March 21

We listen eagerly to the radio. We read the newspapers closely, especially the reports of the debates in the United Nations. The declaration of the delegations of the United States, France, and China supporting an International Trusteeship for Palestine has depressed us. On the other hand, Ben-Gurion's statement that the Jews of this country will establish the State themselves if need be, expresses the feelings of all of us. We are of course worried about one question: What will the cost be in Jewish lives? This is a point on which we are too sensitive. We regard the killing of every Jew as a catastrophe. However, we appreciate that we have no alternative. This is life or death for us. We do not know what our personal fate may be, but we are convinced that our people will emerge the victors. . . .

Our *haverim* have reacted strongly to the courageous stand of the defenders of the Old City. There is a close parallel between the conditions under which the Bloc and the defenders of the Old City are fighting.—DAVID B.D.

From a report of the District Commander—March 21

According to reports reaching us over the past few days there is a lot of enemy movement in the vicinity. We have been informed of hundreds of local Arabs and strangers who apparently are preparing for an assault against the Bloc. Barriers have been set up on the roads. Abdul Kader el-Husseini and the members of his staff have taken up quarters in hotels in Beth Jalla. The British troops have evacuated the camp of Halhul, which is now being guarded by three hundred Arabs. . . .

Throughout yesterday there were exchanges of fire between our men and Arabs. One Arab approached quite close to our positions on Russian Hill and fired a number of shots. The pickets escorting the sappers who were laying mines near the Mukhtar's Saddle noticed an Arab coming from the direction of Saffa village. They fired a few warning shots and he made off. Another Arab approached us from the direction of the Valley of Brakha and fired at our positions. . . .

At 9:30 last night heavy rifle and automatic fire was opened on Kfar Etzion from the villages of Beth Umar and Saffa. About one hundred and fifty rounds, most of them tracers, were fired. The firing lasted for about a quarter of an hour, but no one was hurt.

Later a stand-to was declared and orders were given for everyone to sleep in his clothes.

Today we went out to work as usual. We pruned the trees on the Saddle. The picket guarding the men was strengthened.

We found many bloodstains on the Saddle. It seems that an enemy reconnaissance patrol came up close to our positions and picked up a pair of pliers—one of our booby traps. At least one of them was killed. The firing at the settlement was apparently in retaliation. Our scouts noticed a large crowd in Beth Umar, apparently for the funeral.

Jerusalem Radio reported today that a number of Arabs had been attacked near Hebron, and that one had been killed and two others wounded. Apparently the reference was to the incident at the Saddle.—YA'AKOV A.

From a private letter—March 25

The weather is beautiful and Purim is in the air. Yesterday and today we read the Scroll. They laid blazes into old Haman as usual. There was a terrific row in Nveh Ovadia. The guards probably thought that a battle was raging.

Everybody is happy. We are waiting for the show and then we'll drink *lehayim.*—DOV

From the Journal of Kfar Etzion—March 26

The Purim show staged by the dramatic troupe under the direction of Sha'ul was a great success. A large crowd came in from the settlements and from the strongpoints to take part. Yosef D., who was appointed "Purim Rabbi," put across a few good jokes. Then humorous articles from the "Vocal Newspaper" followed. A number of one-act playlets came next, including a parody based upon the partition of the country and the tactics of the Big Three in handling the Palestine question. Someone had got dressed up as the Wandering Jew, carried a pack of trouble on his back and sang "From the heights of Kfar Etzion, we greet you, Jerusalem!" The song poignantly expressed our loneliness.

The show ended with singing and dancing.

10 The Nebi Daniel Convoy

More than a month had gone by since the last convoy had arrived in the Etzion Bloc and the urgent need to transport the fortification equipment, fuel, and food supplies that had accumulated in Jerusalem for the Bloc, was appreciated by General Staff Headquarters. It organized for this purpose the largest convoy ever assembled until then in the period of hostilities.

From a private diary—March 26

We are all very glad to learn of the coming convoy. If it comes through, we should be able to hold out until the British leave the country and then the Hagana will have complete freedom of action.

Many of us are afraid that once again there will be some hitch, and the convoy will be delayed, as it was last week. Nevertheless, we are posting pickets to guard the road and have made arrangements to unload the trucks without delay. We all pray to God that it gets through and returns safely to Jerusalem. . . .

Tonight and tomorrow night the guards in the strongpoints are to be strengthened. Squads of settlers are to take over from the men of the Field Force and the Palmah. Patrols will be sent out along the main road and the Hebron-Jerusalem telephone line will be cut in order to interrupt communications between the enemy bases. The feeder road is to be closely guarded throughout the night. Traffic policemen have been appointed to direct the convoy from the moment it enters the Bloc to the time it leaves. Their duty will be to guide the trucks to the separate unloading points for men, food, and fuel. The air strip must be kept clear in case it should be necessary for a plane to land.

We are keeping our communication installations ready, in order to maintain contact with the exit base, with the trucks and reconnaissance planes, and with Staff HQ in Tel Aviv.—YISAKHAR

From the diary of the Bloc's representative in Jerusalem—March 26

The convoy is to leave on Saturday, which is the only day of the week when the armored cars are not busy escorting convoys on the Tel Aviv-Jerusalem road. It will comprise: thirty-three trucks loaded to capacity and carrying about one hundred and twenty tons of supplies and building materials, four Egged armored buses, and fourteen armored cars. The buses will carry one hundred and thirty-six men of "B" Company of the Mikhmash Battalion of the Jerusalem Field Force, and a small number of settlers of the Bloc who are returning.

It is to be escorted by one hundred and three soldiers from the Sixth Battalion of the Palmah, which has been stationed in Kiryat Anavim, and from the Field Force units in Jerusalem. An Auster plane is to fly overhead and reconnoiter the area.

The arms of the convoy will include: two Browning machine guns; one Spandau; two Bredas; thirteen light machine guns; two 2-inch mortars; fifteen Thompson sub-machine guns; forty-five rifles; thirty-two Sten-guns. The convoy will also carry explosives and will have four radio transmitters.—YOSEF P.

From the account of a Palmah soldier—March 27

We left Kiryat Anavim on Saturday, at five in the morning. Our convoy consisted of nineteen armored cars, headed by a big roadblock buster. Our car carried a squad of ten men and four sappers, whose job it was to blow up roadblocks, if necessary. Our equipment included two Bren-guns, eight rifles, and four Sten-guns. Our convoy impressed the residents of Jerusalem, who were on their way to the synagogue, and they shouted their blessings to us. We found thirty-three loaded trucks with armored cabins, waiting for us at the Schneller Camp. Here we were told that our destination was Kfar Etzion.

We set out for the Bloc at 8:00 A.M. The convoy was headed by a small armored car equipped with radio. Next came the big armored roadblock buster followed by a number of armored cars. The trucks came next, with armored cars in between. Five armored cars brought up the rear. Spirits were high, we sang and joked. Once the Jewish part of the city was behind us, however, faces became more serious and we were all tense. We reached Bethlehem without mishap. At the entrance to the town an Arab guard opened the roadblock and fled for his life. The sight amused our men and we began to feel something of the elation of victory. We could sense the panic among the Arabs of the town. The convoy rolled on proudly towards Kfar Etzion. On the road we passed a number of Arab cars, traveling from Hebron to Jerusalem. The green hills made us feel happy, and there was a magic about everything. Our good spirits were restored and once again we began to crack jokes. We passed Solomon's Pools, the danger spot for the convoys, without a shot being fired at us. The little Auster that was escorting us flew overhead. You cannot imagine how glad the people of the besieged Bloc were to see us. It was a real holiday.—YA'AKOV AI.

From a private diary—March 27

The convoy arrived at 9:30 A.M. We were very excited when we saw the trucks traveling along our feeder road. As the trucks pulled up at the roadblock near the Lone Tree they were directed to various unloading points. The trucks parked in a semi-circle to speed up the rate of unloading and to allow them to move as soon as they were empty.

At each unloading point a detail of men was waiting. We worked in chains, stacking the various kinds of supplies. Everybody did his best to finish the job as soon as possible. As the empty trucks moved off, new loaded ones came up.

Inside the Kfar Etzion compound everyone was busy. The fuel was unloaded and empty drums and boxes were thrown into the trucks. Within half-an-hour everything was completed. It took a little time to coax our bull, "Zimri," and two mules onto the trucks—for they were to be transported to the coastal plain where forage is more plentiful.

The men of the Palmah in the Bloc and the eighty-five students who were to leave got into the Egged buses which had parked by the Lone Tree. Their personal equipment was loaded onto the trucks.

The damaged plane on the air strip was loaded onto one of the trucks. This job took some time, and held the convoy up. We were worried at the delay.

An Auster plane with a radio operator and piloted by Daniel Buckstein, was parked on the flying field. It had been reconnoitering the Jerusalem-Kfar Etzion road all morning, keeping the commander of the convoy informed of the state of the road. . . .

While the convoy was unloading in the Bloc, news came in from Jerusalem that, according to a British Army report, Abdul Kader el-Husseini had been ordered by the Supreme Arab Committee to deal with the convoy on its way back. The pilot was ordered to carry out a reconnaissance along the road. He reported that the Arabs were putting up six roadblocks of rocks near Solomon's Pools, over a stretch of less than half-a-mile, and that he had been fired on while flying low. He noted a large number of Arabs descending from Beth Jalla in the direction of the main road.—YISAKHAR

[A British officer serving with the Arab bands, whose memoirs were later published in *Yediot Ahronot,* the Israel evening paper, described the preparations to waylay the returning convoy. According to him, as soon as the Arabs heard of the passing of the convoy fighters were mobilized throughout the entire area. British deserters were also brought to the scene. Among those directing operations in the subsequent fighting was a British officer who had deserted. Preparations to ambush the convoy were made with surprising speed. Reports of the impending battle spread like wildfire to Bethlehem and the surrounding villages. Hundreds of villagers carrying a large variety of weapons hurried to points along the road to take part in the fighting.]

From the accounts of members of the convoy—March 27

In view of the Arab preparations, the commanders of the convoy considered deferring their return but it was essential to bring the escort together with their armored cars and equipment back to Jerusalem, as they were needed on the Jerusalem-Tel Aviv road. In any case the commanders felt that with the force at their disposal they could deal with the Arab roadblocks. Zerubavel Horowitz, commander of the roadblock buster, was given orders to prepare for action. The second driver took up position by the crane.

The convoy left the Bloc at 11:30 A.M., with the scout car leading in the van, followed by the roadblock buster, the armored cars, the empty trucks and the buses. The command car traveled in the middle of the convoy. In the rear were the trucks that had been loaded in the Bloc. The armored cars were distributed along the long line of trucks, and brought up the rear. Not a single Arab car was seen on the road. Even the *fellahin* had disappeared from the fields.

Four miles from Kfar Etzion the "buster" encountered the first block and forced its way through easily. Two other blocks followed in quick succession. Then one of the trucks in the rear overturned and the Arabs suddenly opened fire. An armored car was ordered to extricate the driver and his mate. Neither suffered any harm, except for shock. Orders were given to all trucks to stand-to. Three other blocks were negotiated. The enemy was aiming at the tires of the armored cars and succeeded in puncturing one car's tires. The vehicle continued, however, to travel on its wheel rims.

Near Solomon's Pools enemy fire became stronger. At the point where the Al Hadar-Beth Natif road meets the main highway, the convoy was forced to pull up at the seventh roadblock.

Ya'akov Aiges, a survivor of the blockbuster, describes the attempts made to force a passage through this obstacle.

"This was the biggest block we had come up against, and it was made up of giant rocks. When we reached it we lowered the propulsor and Zerubavel and one of the men helped the crane-man. They began slowly to demolish the block. Then suddenly the car trembled under the impact of the rocks and slid into the ditch by the roadside. We were under murderous fire all the time. We tried to regain the road—but without success. The machine-gunner was wounded in the head and was bandaged by the orderly. Through the rear window we could see that the whole convoy had come to a stop two hundred yards or so behind us."—YA'AKOV AI. (Abridged from *LiDmutam,* published by HaKibbutz HaMe'uhad)

The trucks crowded in a long column on the road. Their tires were punctured by the flying bullets, and they were incapable of moving either forward or back. The drivers of some of the trucks that had overturned succeeded in reaching the armored cars. Now the Arabs began to descend the slopes, approaching to within three hundred yards of the convoy. Their cries could be heard clearly. We began to return their fire from the slits in the armored cars to prevent them coming closer. The convoy was in a serious position. Tsvika, the commander, decided to return to Kfar Etzion, and gave orders to the cars to turn round, but many of them had already been put out of action. There was no room on the road for them to maneuver and no more than five trucks and five armored cars, carrying thirty-five men in all, and the command car, succeeded in extricating themselves from the trap. One of these trucks carried the damaged plane.

From the account of a driver—March 27

We were at a standstill for about an hour at Nebi Daniel, before the command car turned about and drove from truck to truck, ordering the drivers to return to the Bloc. We succeeded in turning round on a side trail. On our way back to Kfar Etzion we encountered another roadblock which the Arabs had erected in the meantime. There was little we could do and so we drove straight onto the heaps of stone. We succeeded in getting through it, but barbed wire twisted round the transmission rod and ripped the brake tubes. The truck, however, kept on going to the rhythmic knocking of the wire below—like a heavy machine gun. But we paid no attention to it and went on, getting past all the blocks. Fortunately our tires were not hit, despite the incessant shooting, and we were able to reach Kfar Etzion.—SHLOMO

From the account of a Field Force officer in the convoy—March 27

Aryei T., the second in command, who was now in charge of the convoy, decided to take up position in an abandoned Arab building near the road, marked on the map as Nebi Daniel, and to concentrate the trucks about it. The gate was blown open. The trucks lined up two deep along the road, and, under the cover they gave, the men crawled up to the house. Throughout this operation the armored cars gave them covering fire. At four in the afternoon about half of the men of the convoy were already inside the building. A number of armored cars cruised along the road, picking up stranded drivers from the outlying vehicles. The wounded were carried into one of the rooms where they were bandaged as efficiently as possible under the circumstances. A transmitter was also moved into the house. Arms now remaining included three heavy and six light machine guns, one 2-inch mortar, rifles, and Sten-guns. The men took up positions on the roof and in the yard and began to reinforce them.

The building was an old Arab house with thick walls. It comprised two large rooms, a staircase and a small attic, from which it was possible to get to the roof. There was also a cellar, but we could not find the entrance to it at first.

Large numbers of Arabs took positions upon a ridge to the south and placed light machine guns and a two-inch mortar in a building one hundred and seventy yards away from us. They also fortified the buildings to the east and west, and the kilns to the north.

The commander of the convoy radioed the Regional Command asking for help to extricate his men and the vehicles. The prospects were extremely dubious of beating off the Arabs who were there in overwhelming numbers. We were informed by Jerusalem that the highest British authorities were being contacted.

But the British Army commanders refused to intervene on the grounds that "they had not been informed of the departure of the convoy and therefore could not accept responsibility for its fate." Orders were then given to burn the vehicles which could not be saved and to try to break through to Kfar Etzion in order to save the men and the arms. Staff HQ in Tel Aviv was asked to send planes to cover the withdrawal. The commander of the convoy radioed orders from Kfar Etzion to organize for defensive action during the night.

At 6:00 P.M. our defenses were deployed as follows: to the south of the building, in a ditch across the road, fifteen men armed with a machine gun had established a position. To the north, in the small orchard on the other side of the stone fence, another squad secured us from the direction of Beth Jalla. The main fire power was concentrated on the roof of the building: three light machine guns and one Spandau, each facing the four winds. Three armored cars blocked the entrance to the building, their crews covering the south and the west.

A number of armored cars continued to cruise among the trucks to gather up men and arms. After nightfall the commander of the Palmah detachment requested the men of the Field Force to relieve his men who were on guard in the posts.—YEHOYAKHIN K.

A number of attempts were made by the armored cars to dash to the rescue of the blockbuster two hundred yards in front of the leading truck of the convoy, and to remove its crew. The Arabs, however, concentrated their fire at the tires of these cars and not one of them reached the stranded vehicle. Several of them overturned and their men were extricated only with great difficulty.

From the account of a Palmah soldier in the blockbuster—March 27

Armor-piercing bullets were penetrating the walls of the blockbuster and there was hardly one of us who was not hit. However, those who could do so continued to stand at the embrasures and loop-holes and fired away at the Arabs whenever they approached. Zerubavel stood at the rear embrasure and from time to time would encourage the men, telling them that the armored cars were coming to rescue them. But after six hours had gone by and the stifling heat began to have its effects, he gave up these attempts and we all realized the severity of the situation.

The sun had set and most of the men were lying listless on the floor. The firing outside grew heavier and the Arab shouts louder. At 6:30 P.M. two Molotov cocktails struck the vehicle. One hit a rear wheel and the other struck the motor. The blockbuster slowly began to burn. It was then that Zerubavel called out that whoever wanted to make a dash for it should do so. But he himself refused to attempt to escape, as he did not want to abandon the wounded. I stared at him; he reminded me then of the captain of a sinking ship who refuses to desert the helpless passengers.

Ya'akov D., Y. Keren-Tsvi and I were the only ones to escape. As we raced away under cover of the darkness from the burning vehicle, it exploded and went up in flames, killing all the men inside.—YA'AKOV AI. (Abridged from *Li-Dmutam,* published by HaKibbutz HaMe'uhad)

From the account of a Field Force officer (Continued)—March 27

From time to time new reinforcements reached the Arabs. During the initial phase of the battle they kept up a desultory rifle fire, but towards evening they closed in to a distance of about two hundred and fifty yards and attempted an assault. We succeeded in dispersing them through heavy fire. Our men were in a very bad position. We had a large number of wounded, most of them only slightly hurt, but for the time being, at least, they were out of action. We could not contemplate any attempt to force our way through the enemy lines, both because of the large number of wounded, and the shortage of arms and ammunition. More than half of our men were unarmed. In addition, only the men of the Palmah and the Field Force were organized in military units. The non-combatants included the drivers, their assistants and a small number of settlers who were traveling with us to Jerusalem—about sixty to seventy men in all. When we started fortifying the building at dusk, it was already clear that the only chance of withdrawal was with the aid of British troops. Our forces outside could help only by dropping food and arms, but they could not save us.

The morale of the men in the positions facing the enemy remained high throughout the battle and they did not lose their nerve. Inside the building, however, the situation was difficult. The men sat crowded together on the ground. They were dazed, tired, hungry, and thirsty. It was only after considerable persuasion that they were induced to carry stones to the roof or to relieve men in the forward positions. We sent out appeals for arms and ammunition, and asked that the Arabs be bombed and that British troops be dispatched to put an end to the battle.

We got the following reply from Jerusalem HQ:

> If you are unable to withdraw in the direction of Kfar Etzion you must fortify your positions, save your ammunition, and hold out until morning. We shall send you air support at dawn. Because of the mines on the road a large force cannot leave before morning.

The men within the building were gradually organized. The civilians also began to do their share. The girls took care of the wounded, loaded the magazines, and helped the men carry stones to reinforce the positions.

The men in the forward positions were given blankets and sacks. They were relieved for a short while to allow them some rest before the attack, which we were sure would be launched at daybreak. Arms and ammunition left in the trucks were collected and we took out the batteries in order to work the transmitter.

Just before midnight firing grew more intense. The Arabs began to burn the vehicles closer to the building and we could hear their cries clearly. After midnight they approached to within seventy to eighty yards of the building. They called out to us in Arabic, Hebrew, English, and even German to lay down our arms and surrender. Later they advanced under the cover of rifle and Bren-gun fire. A two-inch mortar also went into action but did not succeed in hitting our defenses. When the Arabs tried to stage an assault our men drove them off with grenades. Apparently their losses were heavy as they did not try again. During the Arab attack we once again radioed HQ asking for air support.

Headquarters informed us that two Austers had already taken off and were bringing us ammunition and food. They were flying without lights and we should identify ourselves by radio.

Soon it was reported from the building that the planes had dropped their load nearby, but the Arabs were raking the whole area with fire and it was very difficult to pick up the supplies. The planes were asked to bomb the enemy in a wood about three hundred yards to the east so that we could pick up the parcels. The planes surprised the Arabs, who aimed very heavy fire at them, so that they had some difficulty in getting away. Nevertheless they continued to drop supplies and to bomb the enemy until daybreak.—YEHOYAKHIN K.

From the diary of a member of Kfar Etzion in Jerusalem—March 27

When it became clear that there was no hope for the convoy to extricate itself by its own efforts, the Jewish authorities in Jerusalem decided to ask for help. Chief Rabbi Herzog exhorted the International Red Cross to intervene and arrange for the evacuation of the women and the wounded men. Dr. Katzenelson of the Va'ad Leumi also contacted Dr. de Reynier, the Red Cross representative. De Reynier got in touch with the British forces but was told that the troops could not advance owing to the roadblocks. He was also informed that the Government forces could accept no responsibility for the convoy, as they had not been informed of its departure. Despite the sanctity of the Sabbath, Rabbi Herzog phoned the High Commissioner's Office and called upon him to intervene.

The Jewish institutions had to decide whether to order the men to fight to the very end, with only a slim prospect of victory, or to try every possible means of saving the lives of one hundred and eighty men who could still play an important part in the war. Once the decision was taken they had to swallow a bitter pill and submit to the humiliating attitude of the British Army. The British finally agreed to extricate the men at Nebi Daniel, but insisted that the Hagana forces hand over their arms to them and they would transfer these arms to Jerusalem.—YOSEF P.

From the account of a Field Force officer—March 28

At half-past six in the morning Jerusalem reported that a detachment of British troops had left in the direction of Nebi Daniel. It was being held up by many roadblocks but was making steady progress. The news encouraged our men who had made good use of the lull in the fighting to rest by turns, for their fatigue was growing.

At seven we radioed that the batteries of the transmitter were fading and we should have to use it less. The enemy now renewed their attacks with increased ferocity, and once again Headquarters was asked to send planes to bomb them.

By nine the number of wounded was thirty, two of them seriously hurt.

By ten the situation was grave. An attack was launched from the north, the Arabs advancing in military formation under a smoke screen until they were about four hundred yards from our positions before falling back again.

There was continued heavy sniping. One of the boys of the Students Company was killed. Despite the cover provided by the armored vehicles parked outside, Arab fire penetrated into the building. Within a few seconds two men had been hit, one being killed, and the other severely wounded in the lungs. The building was closely secured on all sides, but the windows and doors were of wood. We had not paid much attention to a wooden door facing north and a solitary bullet which came through it wounded another man severely. The men were tired and hungry. The heat was intense and a number of them fainted. About forty wounded men lay in the next room, including four who were badly hurt. Reports reached us that the troops were being held up on the way and despair grew.—YEHOYAKHIN K.

From the diary of a member of Kfar Etzion in Jerusalem—March 28

Major Allen, commanding the British relieving force, contacted the Arab commanders, who warned him that any attempt to remove Jewish trucks or to aid the Jews would be strongly resisted by the Arabs. The negotiations lasted for hours. Major Allen reported to Jerusalem that Jewish planes were bombing the Arabs and that bombs had fallen near his men. He was ordered to make no move in the direction of the building as long as the Jews did not withdraw their aircraft. The British in Jerusalem also threatened to open fire on the planes. After some haggling it was agreed in Jerusalem that only one plane would remain in the air for reconnaissance.

Major Allen radioed to his superiors in Jerusalem: "The Jews seem to be running short of ammunition. The Arabs are continuing to attack and the Jews will not be able to hold out much longer. Why can't we get them out of here?" The reply was: "These are the Brigadier's orders. He does not want the troops to clash with the Arabs."

At 2:20 P.M., after lengthy negotiations, it was reported that the Arab commander had consented to the British troops evacuating the Jews on condition that three of his men accompany the British to make sure that the Jews did not take any weapons with them.

Fourteen half-tracks and five trucks were sent out to the British force from the El Alamein Camp in Jerusalem to transport the Jewish force to Jerusalem. A delegation consisting of representatives of the International Red Cross and the Red Crescent, including Arab medical officers, to assist in the evacuation of the wounded, accompanied this force.—YOSEF P.

From the accounts of members of the convoy—March 28

At 4:45 P.M. a British officer of the rank of Lieutenant of the Corps of Engineers drove up in an armored car. He stated that he had been ordered to transmit the terms of the cease-fire: We must leave all arms and military material behind on the spot. When I asked about the personal equipment of the men and the weapons of the Settlement Police who were authorized to bear arms he declared that he could give me no answer, but was willing to take Aryei T. and me to his superior officer in the rear.

As we were traveling in the officer's car we were subjected to heavy fire and forced to take cover in a ditch by the roadside. A few minutes later two police armored cars came up with a Lieutenant-Colonel of the Army and a police officer of the rank of Inspector.

Together with Aryei I went up to the Army officer who stated shortly: "You must leave everything you have on the spot, in return for which we shall take you to Jerusalem." When Aryei asked him for an undertaking in writing he asked angrily: "Isn't the word of a British officer sufficient for you?" Just then orders were received from our base to the effect that we must not surrender our arms to the troops before reaching a Jewish area. I repeated these orders to the officers who replied simply: "Either you do as you are told or we shall leave you behind here." . . .

The end came suddenly. All at once firing stopped. The Arabs got out of their positions and advanced in the direction of the building. Resistance was out of the question. The Army convoy appeared on the scene. Our men succeeded in destroying only some of their weapons. The heavy and light machine guns were dismantled and parts were thrown into a well. The transmitter was destroyed. Our men began to emerge from the building and from their positions. They handed over to the soldiers the arms they had not had time to destroy. About three thousand Arabs surrounded the building; they stormed the cars and tried, despite the orders of their commanders, to enter the building, where the wounded were still lying. The British soldiers were very nervous, for any chance shot might cause a massacre of both the British and the Jewish convoys. . . .

At first the Arabs tried to search our men, but after we had protested strongly orders were given for them to keep their distance. The search was conducted by British officers and men. I wanted to insure the transfer of the wounded but the officer in command gave orders that those who were unhurt should leave first.

I turned to the representative of the International Red Cross and asked him to come with me to supervise the removal of the wounded, but he refused and returned to his car without so much as a look into the house to see how they were faring. I returned to the building and saw that only the seriously wounded remained behind. It turned out that there were no spare stretchers and we were compelled to take the dead off the stretchers so that we could move the wounded. I wanted to transfer the dead but the orders were first to remove the wounded. At about that time the Arabs entered the building, roaming about among the wounded. There was an Arab doctor there. When he was about to leave I stopped him and asked him to remain behind until the last wounded man was removed. He agreed and drove the Arabs out. The English doctor, too, remained behind—at my insistence—until the transfer of the wounded was completed.

The military convoy carrying the one hundred and eighty

defenders left the battlefield. When the trucks reached the Jewish suburbs of Jerusalem the defenders burst into song. The wounded were transferred to the Hadassah Clinic, where doctors and nurses had been waiting throughout the night. Near the Jewish Agency building we were given a very warm welcome by the people of Jerusalem.—EHUD

The thirteen members of the convoy who were killed in the course of the battle of Nebi Daniel were buried in the Sanhedria Cemetery in Jerusalem. The funeral left the Bikkur Holim Hospital to which the bodies had been brought by the British troops. Dr. A. Z. Eshkoli spoke on behalf of the Hagana. Two companies of Hagana soldiers marched behind the cortege.—A.

From the Journal of Kfar Etzion—March 29

The capture by the Arabs of the armored vehicles and the arms of the Convoy Escort Company of the Sixth Palmah Battalion has resulted in the break up of the unit. Convoy traffic from Jerusalem to the coast has been interrupted and the siege of the city has tightened.

The battle of Nebi Daniel indicates that the method of maintaining communications with isolated settlements must be changed.

II

JERUSALEM'S SOUTHERN OUTPOST

"For I will defend this city to save it."
Isaiah 37:35

11 A New Bloc Commander

The fate of the Nebi Daniel convoy signified that for all practical purposes the Etzion Bloc was totally cut off from Jerusalem. From now on the only line of supply open was the airlift from Tel Aviv.

Moshe Silberschmidt ("Mosh") assumed command of the Etzion Bloc. His arrival in the Bloc coincided with the emergence of a new factor in the battle for Jerusalem—the Trans-Jordan Arab Legion. Units of this modern force, which was trained, equipped, and led by British officers, had been in Palestine during the entire period of hostilities, but hardly took part in the fighting. Now, however, it was taking up positions in the area, following the withdrawal of the British troops, preparing for the showdown to come after the total British evacuation of the country in another six weeks.

From a private diary—March 29

During the fighting at Nebi Daniel our outposts on Russian Hill and in the Monastery compound harassed Arab traffic on the road and no enemy vehicles could pass by. The Arabs complained to the British authorities that we had seized the Monastery, and today Mr. Williams, accompanied by several police constables of the Bethlehem Police Station, arrived to investigate the matter. Ibrahim Hazboun told them that he had sub-leased to us several rooms in the Monastery of his own free will. There was little the police officer could say to that. He warned us, however, against firing on any vehicles traveling on the road.—YISAKHAR

From a private letter—March 29

Everything is quiet here in Kfar Etzion. Not a single Arab shows himself throughout the entire neighborhood. They do not dare travel, not even on the main road.

Our people are tense. The prospects of a convoy getting through to us have diminished and of course this has had its effect on everybody here.—YA'AKOV A.

From a private diary—March 30

This afternoon, Yig'al Allon, Commander of the Palmah, who came here by plane during the battle at Nebi Daniel, spoke to us. He discussed our methods of fighting and the part we are expected to play in the war.

In spite of the defeat at Nebi Daniel, he said, there is reason to hope that other convoys will get through to the Bloc and that reinforcements will continue to arrive. The Etzion Bloc constitutes a forward position in the defense of Jerusalem, and if we did not control this area it would be necessary to occupy it. The fact that the Bloc commands such an exposed section of the enemy's communications constitutes a very important factor in the strategy of the entire struggle. What a difference it would make if we had a similar Bloc in the Tulkarm-Jenin-Nablus triangle! The Etzion Bloc is destined to serve as a springboard for Jewish penetration into the Hebron district and the Negev. Yig'al added that he appreciated the difficulties caused by our isolation from the main body of the Jewish forces. Our position, he said, was similar to that of Tobruk during the Second World War. The evacuation of the Bloc was not to be thought of. We must close our ranks to form a single disciplined force. "You must strengthen your positions as much as you can and then you will be able to hold out," he concluded.—YISAKHAR

From the Journal of Kfar Etzion—April 4

For the past few days we have had heavy rain and stormy weather. We are completely cut off. The airstrip is a quagmire and until it dries out no papers, mail, or supplies will arrive. The dismal situation is reflected in the features of the *haverim.* Our only comfort is that in such dreary weather we need have no fear of an attack.

From the diary of a member of Kfar Etzion in Jerusalem—April 4

The road to Jerusalem has been cut and there is no contact whatever with the coastal plain. The siege of the city is beginning to leave its mark. There are no newspapers or mail. Food stores are shrinking, and rations are decreasing from day to day. Vegetables, eggs, and milk are unobtainable. The water pipeline has been cut and water is being rationed to a few pints daily. The shortage of fuel and electricity has aggravated the situation.

The monks of the Ratisbonne Monastery are kindly and courteous. They have placed the cisterns at the disposal of the refugees living in the Monastery, so we do not have to wait for hours in the water queues. When the shelling of the city began the monks vacated a number of rooms in the cellars to be used as shelters by the residents.

The general mood in Jerusalem is very subdued and in

the Monastery the situation is often more depressing than elsewhere. When we are lucky and letters arrive the spirits of the womenfolk rise. The letters written by the *haverim* are a source of encouragement, inspiring us with the hope that they will succeed in holding out.—HA'IM TS.

From a private letter—April 4

The mood of depression which was so noticeable after the battle of the convoy has lifted. Tension has slackened. Nevertheless from time to time misgivings regarding the outcome of our struggle and what the future holds in store for our "Tobruk" come to the surface.

Despite all this the days are passing quietly and even cheerfully. We crack jokes, stage parties, vocal newspapers, play the piano, and kick a ball about. Often, it is true, our gaiety is forced, but we laugh nevertheless. Often one thinks uncomfortably about the strange caprices of fate. We wanted to improve the position of our wives and children, so we sent them to Jerusalem. Now they are living in congested conditions, worried about us and exposed to bullets, bombs, and a food shortage.—BEN ZION G.

From the letter of a member of Massuot Yitzhak—April 4

The good spirits prevailing here are not born of ignorance or self-deception. The people here are fully aware of the situation, but I believe that it is precisely because of a consciousness of the onerous nature of their duty that they have called up their spiritual reserves in order to preserve the normal tenor of their lives. We are aware of events both in this country and abroad and follow the fluctuations in the military and political situation with keen interest.

Normally a soldier has leave now and again to visit his

relatives and friends; we, here, however, are tied down but we do not complain. Each of us does his job as well as he can; indeed as if he were not used to anything better, as if this is just how it should be.—AHARON M.

From a private letter—April 4

In time of trouble one tends naturally to turn to the Supreme Power. It is good to derive encouragement from the consciousness of the existence of that Supreme Power above us. I am not a great chanter of Psalms but it is interesting, nevertheless, that at a time when the barometer of our moods is so unsteady, I can always find some chapter in the book of Psalms suited to the occasion.

At the memorial service for the ten victims of the first convoy on the Thirtieth Day we read Psalm 83: "Keep not thou silence, O God; hold not thy peace and be still, O God," which applies so well to our own political and psychological situation.

On Friday night on January 16, after we had driven off the Arab attack, we read Psalm 18 during the Sabbath evening service: "To the Chief Musician, a Psalm of David, the servant of the Lord, who spake unto the Lord the words of this song in the day that the Lord delivered him from the hand of all of his enemies."

At the funeral of the thirty-five we read Psalm 94 at the open graveside: "O Lord to whom vengeance belongeth . . . show thyself." And on the Thirtieth Day we read that wonderful Psalm 144: "Blessed be the Lord, my strength, who teacheth my hands to war, my fingers to fight."

The Psalms is a wonderful book. It is David's Lyre with a hundred strings, each giving expression to one particular mood, and in its entirety it is the book of feeling and of faith of all our people throughout the generations.—YOSEF D.

From the diary of a member of Kfar Etzion—April 4

The victory at the battle of Nebi Daniel has raised the morale of the Arabs throughout the district and has encouraged them to tighten the blockade. The booty they captured includes, besides the guns and equipment, a considerable number of armored cars, which they did not have previously. Both the vehicles and the weapons will probably be used in operations against the Bloc and in safeguarding Arab traffic along the roads.

One result of the battle is that we are compelled to relinquish our strategy of passive defense; we must now try to harry enemy traffic. The result of our new tactics may be a direct clash with the Arab Legion encamped close by, which provides escort for the Arab convoys. This change has come about before the Bloc has had time to prepare for it. The convoy did not bring all the reinforcements we require; only a small number of soldiers has been added to the Bloc's manpower. Moreover, we have not yet got all the materials we need to reinforce the Bloc, not even the necessary arms.—YOSEF P.

From private letters—April 7

We have been having a heat wave for the past three days, and the hot *sharav* wind threatens to scorch every flower and shrub. The trees in the orchard are in blossom. Weeds are high, however, even though the orchardmen are doing their best to plow and hoe as much as they can. But in spite of everything the trees will bear bumper crops of fruit, and help to relieve the supply problem of the Bloc. . . .

We are getting ready for the wedding of Yehezkel and Rahel. At first they wanted to fly to Tel Aviv to celebrate their wedding together with their relatives, but seeing that that is impossible at the present time they have decided to get married here. . . .

The bulldozer is working overtime, extending the air strip. The convoy escort and the drivers are helping. They hope that they will be able to return home when the strip is widened and two-engined planes can land. The strip has already been improved and small planes land easily. . . .

An aircraft engineer has arrived in an Auster to repair the damaged plane stranded here. . . .

The mines workshop is very busy. The workers have been released from guard duty and they work night and day. In all the settlements the work of strengthening the defenses is being carried on energetically. We are trying to dig in, as far as this is possible, with the simple implements we have here. We are working hard improving the defenses of the Monastery, the Mukhtar's Saddle, and Hirbet Sawir.

From a private diary—April 7

The *haverim* are following with the keenest interest the news of the battle for control of the heights dominating the road to Jerusalem. We were overjoyed when we heard of the capture of Kastel, after it had been taken and lost again several times in the course of a few days. We were also pleased at the news of the death of Abdul Kader el-Husseini, who upon several occasions had operated against our Bloc. . . .

We are following the battle of Mishmar HaEmek with special anxiety, and are shocked by the news of the heavy damage caused by the enemy artillery. The *haverim* have begun to ask, "How can *we* hope to withstand such an attack, when we can't even dig proper bunkers in our terrain?"—YISAKHAR

Memorandum dispatched by the Bloc Commander to the General Staff, Tel Aviv—April 9

The following is a list of the arms and ammunition required by the Bloc:

Arms: thirty sub-machine guns; one thousand hand grenades; one thousand mines; one light machine gun; one 3-inch mortar. (Our establishment includes three 3-inch mortars and we have only one.)

Ammunition: five thousand rounds of .303; five thousand rounds of .300; one hundred 3-inch mortar shells (we have only twenty-nine); five thousand rounds of Italian ammunition (these must be examined carefully; a large part of what we have here can't be used!); five thousand rounds Schwartzlause ammunition (the ammunition we have is old and cannot be relied upon).

Two members of Kfar Etzion who served with the Engineers of the Jewish Brigade are proficient at making mines. So far we have produced fifteen different varieties of mines. We began with scare mines and now can manufacture lethal ones. But the workshop is operating under very difficult conditions and to continue production we urgently need the following materials: two hundred and twenty-five pounds of explosives, ammonal, fifteen hundred detonators #6 and #8, three hundred yards of 1 mm. steel wire for springs, twenty-five yards of 1.5 mm. copper wire.—MOSH

From a private diary—April 9

We were at the close of a comparatively quiet period.

For several weeks we had got used to the thought that of all the isolated outposts in the country, the Etzion Bloc was the quietest. We had made considerable progress in our defense plans and the air strip had begun to serve as a link with the rest of the Yishuv. Indeed, conditions in the Bloc were not too rigorous. The settlers began to believe that they could develop their own way of life and preserve their social and economic framework. Our *haverim* looked forward to the big convoy which was to bring reinforcements, arms and supplies, and to embark upon the execution of the many plans which had been discussed at the meetings. Then Mosh arrived.

At first we did not know anything about his responsibilities or his past career. We saw a tall, neatly-dressed young man, with calm, sad eyes, stepping off the plane. We could not fathom the look he gave. Was it no more than a reflection of his character or did it express an evaluation of the perils of our situation?

His quiet, modest demeanor, his good manners, his courtesy towards everybody—officer, enlisted man or civilian—soon captivated everyone in the Bloc. Serious, resolute, and courageous in the fulfillment of his military duties, there was no swagger or arrogance at all about him. We had appreciated these qualities in Danny Mass, the Palmah man; we were glad to see that Mosh, the Field Force soldier, also represented the best type of Jewish officer. Neatness and a love of order were his outstanding characteristics. He was meticulous about the small things, which might so easily be forgotten. There was hardly anything bearing upon the defense of the Bloc to which Mosh did not devote his personal attention. His working hours were from early morning to about midnight. Often we wondered at his staying power and capacity for work.

He saw that his first task would be to weld the entire Bloc into a single, disciplined fighting force. It was no easy undertaking. There were misunderstandings between the various settlements and between them and the commanders of the military units. There were also difficulties caused by the different organizational traditions of the Field Force and the Palmah. Mosh straightened all these out, always seeking a compromise but when necessary imposing his authority as commander of the Bloc. Throughout he has had to reconcile the interests of the soldiers and the settlers, of the religious section and the non-religious, always in a spirit of moderation and understanding. A farmer himself, he is able to understand what we have achieved here; he understands the farmer's desire to safeguard his farm, but at the same time he has been successful in inducing the farmers to integrate themselves into the military regime. He speaks their language and that is why he can convince them. They respond willingly to the many demands he makes upon them.

He shows an understanding for our religious problems and in this field he is very chary about imposing his authority. He prefers to confer with our Halakha Committee and to try and convince us of the vital necessity, for the defense of the Bloc, of any demand he has to make which conflicts with religious observance. He is always given a good hearing and in the end usually he gets his way.

After some time we learned something of what lies behind his conduct. "Mosh" (Moshe) Silberschmidt is a former member of the Bachad in Germany who was later active on the *hakhshara* farms in England, and so he is not unfamiliar with the way of life of religious settlements.

He has introduced a new spirit. The period of passive defense has passed. If the Bloc is to carry out the function for which, in the main, it is being held, namely to serve as an outpost in the defense of Jerusalem, it must accept the risks involved and pit its meager forces against the enemy. Possibly this increases the danger threatening it, but in war fortune favors the brave. Mosh's conduct and actions give us confidence, and though we are aware of the perils of this new policy, we support him wholeheartedly.

He has insisted upon the extension of the network of fortified strongpoints, especially in the Russian Monastery and on the Mukhtar's Saddle, and is planning occupation of additional positions. Together with the commanders and the sappers he works out the plans and supervises their execution. He has urged the Settlement Commanders to extend the network of defense posts and trenches in every exposed sector. He is not satisfied with positions above ground, but insists that we dig in deep and build bunkers as shelters in keeping with the latest developments in the war. For the time being, until our defenses are stronger, we must lay in arms and wait for the necessary reinforcements and do no more than harry Arab transport.—YISAKHAR

From the diary of the Bloc's representative in Jerusalem—April 9

The following is the composition of the manpower in the Bloc:

Settlers:			
Kfar Etzion	65 men	25 women	90
Massuot Yitzhak	59 "	32 "	91
Revadim	57 "	23 "	80
Ein Tsurim	33 "	21 "	54
			315

Enlisted personnel and others

"B" Company, Mikhmash Battalion, Jerusalem Field Force	135
Other details attached to the Company (medical orderlies, etc.)	19
Orthodox Detachment, Tel Aviv Field Force	20
Nebi Daniel convoy detachment (Palmah, drivers, etc.)	48
Other members of the convoy	8
	230
Total	545

YOSEF P.

From a private diary—April 11

A few days ago the newspapers published a statement made by Salah Jaber, Mayor of Hebron, that the Arab Legion had taken the Hebron area under its protection. He called upon the Jewish settlements in the district to come to peaceful terms with the Arabs. His conditions were:

a. an undertaking not to attack the Arabs;

b. the surrender of our arms.

On behalf of the Arab leaders he gave an assurance that we should suffer no harm, provided we conducted ourselves as loyal citizens of the Arab administration.

Our immediate reaction was one of derision. We asked each other: Are we the aggressors in this district? Do the Arabs really think that there is a single Jewish settlement ready to give up its arms and to rely upon Arab promises? Has the Mayor of Hebron forgotten the fate of the Jewish community in his town, during the bloody riots of 1929? Of course this is not the purpose of the statement. There is something behind it.

The Arabs, and not the Mandatory Government, now control the district. The Arab Legion, a regular military force, well-equipped and armed, has taken the field against us even before the Mandate has expired. It will control the roads; it will train and protect the Arab villagers. Now we must reckon with a disciplined force. But the British Army which, ostensibly, has concluded its duties after the Nebi Daniel affair, has not withdrawn completely. British officers continue to command the Legion and, there is no doubt, the Army will extend whatever aid it considers necessary when the occasion arises.

Our situation is fairly clear. There is not much chance of our receiving reinforcements for the approaching battle. Large forces cannot be diverted to our district.

The main struggle hinges upon Jerusalem proper and the Negev. The settlements around Jerusalem, "the islands in the Arab sea," can serve only as auxiliary outposts in the Jerusalem campaign.—YISAKHAR

From the account of a Field Force soldier—April 11

In his talks with the commanders of the settlements and the various units, Mosh reviewed the military situation in the Jerusalem district and the role the Bloc must play. In addition to their own defense, the settlements must help to insure control of the capital and of the roads linking it up with the rest of the country. We must endeavor to tie down the large enemy concentrations in the Hebron area and hinder the incursion of regular or irregular troops from Trans-Jordan.

For that reason we cannot confine ourselves to local defense. We must integrate our operations within the overall strategy.

a. We must strengthen our defenses to enable us to resist an enemy far superior to ourselves in numbers, training and equipment.

b. We must concentrate particularly on communications. The lesson to be learned from the Nebi Daniel convoy is not encouraging but we cannot resign ourselves to complete isolation. We must prepare some more imaginative plan to get a convoy through, whether from Jerusalem or from Tel Aviv, by way of Hartuv-Al Hadar or Beit Jubrin, to flank the larger concentrations of the enemy. Our fate depends upon our ability to keep our lines of communication open. For all these tasks we need three more companies of drafted men, besides more arms and equipment. We particularly need anti-tank weapons.

c. One of the major tasks of the Bloc is, by laying mines and also by mounting direct attacks, to harry Arab traffic using the main road and the internal roads linking up the various concentrations. By depriving them of their freedom of movement we can relieve enemy pressure on our own communications.

d. We must carry out sabotage and harrying attacks upon military and economic objectives. An increase in the forces at our disposal, better equipment, and improvement of our combat capacity will enable us to operate over a wider area in this district.

We hope that as soon as the British leave the country our forces in the Jerusalem area will be able to move more freely and establish contact with us. It would be excellent if we could create and secure such contact by capturing strongpoints along the main Jerusalem-Hebron road and link up with our forces in the Negev and other sections of the southern district.

Following the defeat and capture of the convoy at Nebi Daniel it has been decided that the Bloc will remain in contact mainly with General Staff Headquarters in Tel Aviv. Operational and administrative problems will be dealt with through representatives attached to this Headquarters.

This setup constitutes an improvement, as it allows for greater co-ordination with our source of supplies. It suffers, however, from the absence of close-range familiarity with the situation and requirements.

Relations with the Jerusalem Regional Command will be confined to problems of regional planning.

Mosh has set up his command in Kfar Etzion. It is divided into two branches: General and Operations. The staff of the first is headed by Mosh, his deputy is Ya'akov A., and its other members are the people in charge of the various services: signals, fortifications, supplies, transportation, work coordination, and medical service.

The staff of Operations, also headed by Mosh, consists of Avraham T. ("Abrasha," the commander of the Field Force company), Ya'akov A., and the settlement and outpost commanders.—H. A.

12 Blocking Enemy Traffic

With little more than a month remaining until the end of the Mandate, large scale warfare broke out in all parts of Palestine. Many volunteer para-military bands from the neighboring Arab States took part in these hostilities. A joint Iraqi-Syrian "Yarmuk Army" heavily attacked Mishmar HaEmek, in the Jezreel Valley. This force employed artillery for the first time in the Palestine warfare, but was nonetheless repulsed after having suffered heavy casualties. An Egyptian volunteer force assaulted Kfar Darom in the southwest corner of the country but did not succeed in penetrating the defenses of the settlement.

But the Jewish forces were also taking the offensive. Their most important campaign, "Operation Nahshon," was launched to secure the heights dominating the coastal road to Jerusalem, in order to send through several giant convoys to the beleaguered city. In this operation Kastel, five miles northwest of the Holy City, was captured after a seven-day battle. This was the first time an Arab village had been assaulted and captured by the Jews.

Within Jerusalem the fighting also grew in fury and the Etzion Bloc was charged by the Regional Command with preventing the transfer of Arab reinforcements from the south.

From a private diary—April 12

Fierce battles are raging in Jerusalem and the immediate vicinity. The enemy is shelling the city with artillery.

We have laid mines and have begun to attack enemy traffic on the highway. The roadsides have also been mined.—YISAKHAR

The Bloc Commander transmitted the following message to Staff H.Q. in Tel Aviv:

> I have been ordered to cut communications. I need one hundred 3-inch shells, two thousand hand grenades, ten thousand rounds of .303 ammunition.

From combat accounts—April 12

Two squads set out at dawn to lay an ambush, and occupied a position near the cisterns, on the main road, near the entrance to the Bloc. The men kept well out of sight and were well camouflaged.

The force garrisoning the Monastery, which was equipped with one heavy and two light machine guns, was ordered to cover the attacking unit and to block traffic along the road if it should prove necessary. So far we had not attacked the enemy from the Monastery building, as we wished to maintain its neutrality and did not want to reveal in what strength we were holding it.

A motor vehicle carrying a large number of armed Arabs came in sight on the road, just opposite the spot where our picket had taken up position. The car was attacked from the rear. According to the men the number of casualties they inflicted was high. The driver, however, kept going and disappeared over the ridge. Meantime two trucks and one automobile of the Arab Legion appeared on the scene from the direction of Hebron. They were joined by an armored vehicle equipped with a two-pounder. They halted several hundred yards from where the squads had taken up position. The Legionaries alighted and advanced along the road, keeping up heavy fire all the time, and covering their vehicles. A fierce battle ensued.

The men lying in ambush were ordered to withdraw. One squad managed to get down the hill and reached the wadi while the other covered it. The Legion's armored car drove into the Bloc's feeder road and cut off the line of retreat. In order to save the men, the officer in command of the operation was compelled to order the Browning crew in the Monastery to open fire on the armored vehicle, whereupon the latter withdrew to the main road. The commander of the ambushing picket, who was wounded in the hand, ordered a retreat. The garrison of the Monastery kept up their fire at the armored vehicle, the tires of which were already punctured. Its crew suffered a number of casualties and those who were uninjured left the car in a panic and fled to the hills. We discovered an enemy machine gun detachment which had taken up position in a building located on the road leading to Beth Fajjar. We forced them also to take to their heels.

A number of men of the Legion and the Arab bands were hit. The vehicles and arms were abandoned on the road. Despite the fact that our men knew that reinforcements would arrive soon, they decided to pick up whatever booty they could. A platoon of the Palmah, which had been held in reserve, and a squad of sappers were dispatched in an armored car for this purpose—and also to destroy whatever they could. But just when they reached the road a large enemy convoy came in sight and opened fire. The convoy included trucks and armored buses which had been captured at Nebi Daniel, and was escorted by five armored cars. They began to extricate the vehicles that were stuck, all the time keeping up heavy fire on our armored car which was forced to withdraw towards the Bloc.

In the Monastery a state of alert was declared. The machine-gunners took up position in the wood and on the slope facing the main road in order to hold up the enemy convoy. The enemy opened up with intensive fire on the Monastery. One volley hit the balcony where the machine gun was posted, and two of our men were wounded. Meantime all the Arab positions on the surrounding ridges opened up heavy fire on the Monastery, Kfar Etzion, and our strongpoints. As the convoy came up the incline heavy fire was opened up on it from the Monastery. One armored vehicle traveling in the van was hit and put out of action. A number of cars stopped and others barely managed to get out of the mêlée. Many of the Arabs who jumped out of the cars and trucks on to the roadside were wounded by the anti-personnel mines our men had laid the night before.

Heavy fire at the Monastery and the other positions in the area was kept up. It included artillery, mortars, and light and heavy machine guns. Fortunately no one was hurt. This was the first battle in the Bloc in which the enemy used artillery.

At first the shelling dazed our men, but Mosh and the other commanders encouraged them, warning them to take care that none of the enemy approached under cover of the artillery barrage. The Monastery's upper story was evacuated and the men distributed in well-camouflaged defense positions in the wood. Despite the murderous enemy fire our machine gun was also transferred to the wood. Two more men of the crew were hit and we had to call up another squad from one of the strongpoints. As soon as our men got used to the screech of the shells and saw that not every one had its billet, they began to look more cheerful.

As the fighting grew heavier, the pickets in the various strongpoints were reinforced. One squad was dispatched to hold Hirbet Sawir. The shoulder of the Russian Hill, commanding the Valley of Brakha and Hirbet Marina, was also occupied.

About midday a British military convoy passed in the direction of Hebron. Our men did not interfere with it as they had been ordered not to attack military convoys. The troops dismantled and blew up a land mine. Arab sniping continued without respite.

At about quarter-past two in the afternoon a large Arab convoy, escorted by about ten armored vehicles equipped with artillery, passed by. Our men fired at the trucks and the troops replied with artillery, mortars, and machine guns. About forty shells fell in the Monastery area, and five, at least, hit the walls.

Just before evening the enemy began to shell the Monastery and the area again. Shells fell in the vicinity of Kfar Etzion, Wadi Abu Rish, and the Mukhtar's Saddle.

The three-inch mortar posted on the Yellow Hill was ordered to shell enemy concentrations and transport. The fire was directed from a forward observation post in the Monastery. Four of the six shells fired scored direct hits, damaging trucks and causing casualties among the enemy. However, owing to the shortage of shells, we used the mortar very sparingly.

Meanwhile, under cover of a heavy artillery and machine gun barrage, hundreds of Arabs mustered from the surrounding villages got ready for an assault on the Monastery. When the shelling stopped we discovered large groups of Arabs, who tried to rush the Monastery from the eastern section of the stone fence. As they came closer the machine gun got its sight on them. The defense positions opened up with rifles and grenades. The mortar, too, started shelling a concentration of the enemy in a dead area, hidden from the Monastery's garrison. Within a quarter of an hour, after a short brisk battle, the Arabs were in flight, dragging their casualties after them.

Another group of about one hundred Arabs had come up from the Valley of Brakha and had reached a southwestern spur of Russian Hill. The men in the Kfar Etzion positions saw them advancing but let them come within close range before opening up with heavy and light machine guns. The Arabs suffered a number of casualties. Others tried to creep up the other side of Russian Hill, but the area was mined and they fled in alarm.

The garrison in the Monastery had been under fire all day and the "Airborne Platoon" was sent to reinforce them. *En route* they were attacked and a soldier was wounded in the leg. One of the men was ordered to stay behind with him while the rest of the men got through the dangerous sector. They reached the Monastery safely. A few more shells came over, but as darkness fell, quiet reigned.

From reports of the Bloc Commander to Regional Headquarters—April 13

Throughout the night Arabs concentrated in various spots in the neighborhood. We estimate that in yesterday's battle the Arabs suffered at least forty casualties. Seven of our men were wounded. I am awaiting orders regarding future operations. . . .

We cannot avoid clashes with the Arab Legion, who provide an escort for traffic on the road. We cannot refrain from retaliating when troops open fire on our units. During the recent battle we were compelled to attack the Legion as we could not extricate our men in any other way.—MOSH

From a private diary—April 13

During yesterday's fighting the old Arab woman who lives in the Monastery was slightly wounded. Ibrahim Hazbun, his sister, and his nephews have gone to live in Kfar Etzion. They have been given two rooms and will get their supplies from our stores. They were given a friendly reception.

For several nights we have been busy strengthening the defenses of Hirbet Sawir. From the beginning of the fighting the Command has recognized the importance of this strongpoint, but owing to the shortage of men we could not occupy it and had to rest content with the construction of provisional but properly camouflaged defense positions. The area has been mined in breadth and depth. In view of the plans to harry enemy transport, Mosh has now decided to occupy Hirbet Sawir.

Work at the Hirbeh is continuing under cover of darkness. Defense positions and communication trenches are being dug, barbed-wire entanglements are being constructed and other security measures have been taken. The men return home before dawn.—YISAKHAR

From a report of the District Commander—April 15

Since last Monday's fighting everything has been quiet

here. We have learned that in Hebron preparations are being made for a new attack, to be supported by the Arab Legion.

We need reinforcements. Once again there is a delay in bringing up our men from Tel Aviv. There are two damaged planes here. One of them could not take off properly because of a defect in the engine, and made a forced landing. The other was damaged during the attack. We do not know whether flights to the Bloc have been held up because of lack of aircraft or because of the apprehensions of the pilots regarding our air strip. We are hoping that tomorrow one of the planes will be able to take off. If we get the spare parts we can repair the other plane also.

We are lengthening the air strip and within a month it will be five hundred yards long. . . .

We are suffering from a shortage of men. The settlers of the *kvutzot* are bearing a heavy burden. For a week in every two they are on guard duty at night. In addition they have a few hours of guard every second day, various chores in the dining hall, the dairy and the chicken run, and other special duties. About fifteen members of Kfar Etzion are permanently occupied in work on behalf of the Bloc, including outside representatives, signal men, sappers, and commanders. The daily duties have therefore to be carried out by a comparatively restricted number of *haverim*. The work co-ordinators have difficulty in completing their daily rosters because they know how fatigued the men are. A number of people should be flown out of the Bloc for health reasons, but we can't let them go. We are short of girls for the essential domestic services. Work on the fortifications of the settlement is being held up, because priority must be given to the strongpoints in the Monastery, the Mukhtar's Saddle and the occupation of Hirbet Sawir.—YA'AKOV A.

From the Journal of Kfar Etzion—April 17

The choir rehearsed the *Seder* songs in Nveh Ovadiah today. Everybody is sorry that the children are not here to sing with us. We haven't decided yet who is to ask the "Four Questions."

We tuned in to the Kol Hagana broadcast from Tel Aviv. This was the Hagana's first broadcast to include both local and foreign news. We heard that the Arabs had evacuated Tiberias and that a Jewish local administration has been set up.

From private letters—April 18

Spring is here, and the days are warm and bright. The men who are not essential for work on the fortifications are busy plowing and hoeing in the orchards. There is such a lot of work to do and so few people to do it! The trees are covered with fresh, green leaves, presaging a good season.

Jerusalem Radio has reported that a large convoy of two hundred and forty-seven trucks containing supplies for Passover has reached Jerusalem safely.—DOV

April 19

Supplies for the dairy barn are satisfactory. We have sufficient fodder until May. At present we are mowing green fodder in the Arab fields. There is a chance that we shall be able to sow some barley and insure a further supply for the cows.—ME'IR F.

From a report of the Chief Medical Officer—April 19

There are at present nine wounded and two other patients in the hospital. All beds are occupied and, indeed, the place is already crowded. We have asked Headquarters to evacuate a number of the wounded by plane.

We have decided to transfer the hospital to the so-called "new" children's house. We have ten beds provided by Kfar Etzion, with bed clothes supplied by the Medical Service. Our equipment is barely adequate for emergency operations. We still need twenty beds and the necessary equipment, a small X-ray apparatus, a microscope and equipment for a small laboratory; a field operating table, and metal sterilization containers. We also need a qualified surgery nurse and an X-ray technician.—DR. WINDSBERG

From the private letters of a member of Kfar Etzion—April 20

Following our victories at Kastel and Mishmar HaEmek, our people here are confident that our superior fighting spirit will enable us to beat the Arabs off. We have no alternative but to fight. In war only those who are strong, who have fortified themselves by devotion to an ideal can hope to triumph.

A month ago, if any one had said that the Hagana would capture Kastel, he would have been laughed at. And now we see how peace-loving workers, who might have been considered no match for people who are thought to be warriors from birth, can also fight and win battles.

Even the heavy weapons of the British, which are at the disposal of the Arabs, cannot destroy the fighting spirit of our men. Our victories in the last few weeks have done much to encourage us. . . . Those who thought that we could not defend ourselves, now see their mistake. Perhaps the enemy will be compelled to make more desperate attacks; they may even get help from the Arab armies. But all this cannot undermine our morale. We must maintain the fighting qualities which already distinguish the thousands of soldiers manning the strongpoints and convoys.

When we consider our own future position we believe that the weak, if they have the necessary courage, can defeat the strong. Our numbers are small and the prospects of obtaining aid from outside are not very bright; for that reason we must be ready to take risks and to strike at the enemy bases. We can hope in this way to upset all their plans. Our stand here can help besieged Jerusalem.

We cannot do anything else but fight. Otherwise the Arabs will defeat us and force us into a Ghetto. How happy the youth of the European Ghettoes would have been had they the chance to do what we are doing now, standing up to our enemies with arms in our hands. Our readiness for self-sacrifice will preserve the six hundred thousand Jews of this country. Knowledge of this must encourage our families, who, even if they are not in the front line, do their share in the war we are waging.

The Russian Monastery outpost is commanded by Tsvi Ben-Yosef, a composer whose songs are being sung throughout the country. He is also a musician, and when he plays a wave of emotion surges up within me, a storm of disquiet. "What will the future bring?" But then the measure becomes more lively and gay. "Never mind! Don't worry! Let us have faith in our own strength and in our future. Let us march towards the light that is breaking over the horizon."
—Ben Zion G.

13 Passover

While the British were systematically withdrawing from Palestine, the Hagana forces stood poised to capture the cities with a predominantly Jewish population. Meantime, the plans to establish the Jewish Provisional Government were being completed.

The Etzion Bloc was no longer an unrelated sector of the front, but had become a key strategic point in the battle for Jerusalem. The settlers and soldiers were gratified to know that their nearly five months of resistance had served its purpose, and that they were playing a major part in the military struggle.

From private letters—April 21

Passover, the Festival of Freedom, is near. This year we shall not celebrate it together. But our hearts are united by a single will and a single hope: May God grant that in the future we observe the *Seder* in peace and that our children once again repeat the "Four Questions."

I pray that it should be granted us to celebrate the Festival of Shavuot here, together.—Ben Zion G.

April 22

We are getting ready for the Passover. Speaking for myself I don't feel the usual holiday spirit. When the guard duty roster for the *Seder* night was drawn up I said that it made no difference to me if my spell was from six or eight or even from ten o'clock. If you and the children are not here the festivity means nothing to me. I suppose that in spite of everything we must keep our spirits up and not allow despair and bitterness to get the better of us.—SHALOM G.

April 22

I have just finished the *bedikat hametz*. Our Ya'ir wasn't here with me and so I did not have any one to hold the candle. At a time like this I feel your absence very much. However, the reports of our victory in Haifa make the isolation more bearable. Perhaps we are closer to victory. We have no illusions about an early end to the war. But the feeling that we are strong enough, with God's help, to achieve statehood, strengthens us in this gloomy period.—SHMUEL A.

April 23

A few nights ago we heard the sound of the firing and the explosions preceding the campaign to clear the road from the coast to Jerusalem for the convoys. We could even see the tracer bullets fired from Ma'aleh HaHamisha. We knew something big was happening. Next day we heard of the results over the radio. I did not believe that our forces would be able to do the job. The fact that they did strengthens me in my faith that we have a Father in Heaven who has not forsaken us though for some time He has hidden His Face. As Rabbi Akiva once said to the Emperor of Rome: "The Shepherd who keeps the sheep from the seventy wolves is mighty indeed!"

The Hagana Radio reported yesterday at noon on the street-fighting in Haifa. We sat by the radio until eleven o'clock. When we heard the good news during the last broadcast that the entire city had been captured by our forces, we were tremendously elated. This may help to create something of a holiday atmosphere here.

This morning we celebrated the traditional conclusion of a tractate of the Talmud in which the firstborn sons participated. I, too, took part, on behalf of our firstborn son, who is still too young to partake himself in such a ceremony. Cake and drinks were served. The good news has encouraged us a lot; indeed we started dancing when we heard it.

At present we are in a hurry to finish our last meal of *hametz.*—AKIVA G.

April 25

The Cultural Committee decided that the *Seder* be held in the dining hall. The room was tastefully decorated and depicted the highland countryside in spring. On the walls verses from the Bible describing the spring in this part of our country were inscribed. In the corners of the room there were boxes of flowers and fruits, adorned with suitable verses from the Song of Songs: "The fig tree putteth forth her green figs"; "The vines with the tender grapes give a good smell," etc. The intention was to link the idea of spring in nature with the new springtime of our people. We all wished to stress the connection between the Festival of Freedom and the impending liberation of the Jewish people.

After the festival service in Nveh Ovadia we sat down at the table. Participants at the Seder included the members of the *kvutza,* some of the enlisted men, and some of the drivers and escort of the Nebi Daniel convoy who have been stranded in the Bloc.

The Seder opened with the traditional ceremony of the

washing of hands, eating of herbs, and breaking of the *matza.* We chanted *Ha lahma anya* and *Ma nishtana* in the traditional melody and then recited the Haggada with Yosef D., who acted as the "King" and expounded the meaning of the various passages, stressing the significance of the service for all generations, and especially for our own. After we had sung *Vehi she'amda,* a passage from Lamdan's poem *Outlook-Point in Judea,* was recited. When we came to the verse from Ezekiel, "And I passed by thee and saw thee polluted in thine own blood," we read a paragraph from the late Shalom Karniel's last article, *In Thine Own Blood Live.*

During the meal the choir sang, "Behold the Days Come and They Shall Beat Their Swords into Plowshares," and "He Who Leads His Sons Over the Red Sea," and other songs. The singing grew livelier as the meal progressed. After the meal Yehoshua L. read the verses from the Song of Songs: "The voice of my loved one cometh, leaping upon the mountains, skipping on the hills." We all felt as if the verses spoke for us and our own time.

The guards who had meantime been relieved read the first part of the *Haggada* in the library and then joined us in the dining hall. They put their rifles against the walls and sat down to eat. When we sang the verse from Psalms, "Place guards for Thy city, all day and all night," once again we were conscious of the actuality of the prayer.

After we had recited "Next year in the rebuilt Jerusalem" we began to dance gaily, though many *haverim* refused to join in, saying that they could not forget those members who had fallen—to whom it had not been granted to join us in this *Seder.*—Dov

In the Russian Monastery

From the diary of a Field Force soldier stationed in the Russian Monastery—April 25

Despite the tense situation and all our hardships, the holiday spirit prevails. On the day before Passover a large caldron was placed in the spacious courtyard of the Monastery, a fire was kindled beneath it, and when the water was on the boil the work of seething the utensils for the Passover began. They went into the boiling water *hametz* and emerged *kasher* for Pessah. . . .

The kitchen is sporting an entirely new look. On the window sills sheets of white paper have been spread. The quartermaster was very generous and issued a tin of boot polish for every ten men. We all sat around polishing our shoes and rifles. . . .

Spick and span, in full equipment, the guards of the strongpoints went down in threes to the Lone Tree. The Bloc OC took the parade. Mosh said things sublime in their simplicity. He stressed the tasks with which the Bloc has been intrusted and the part it must play in the days to come. He called for an honorable stand, and brought out the analogy between the Passover observed by our forefathers in Egypt and the events of our own day. The company returned to the Monastery and got ready for the *Seder*. Shorter spells of guard duty were arranged so as to allow everybody to partake in the festivities. . . .

The Monastery was ready to welcome its many guests for the *Seder* night: the soldiers manning the various strongpoints, headed by Dr. Windsberg, our medical officer, Mosh, and Abrasha, the Company Commander. After the recitation of the Haggada had been concluded, the officers put on their aprons and served the chicken. The fellows burst into song and began to drink. . . .

The men in the posts were attracted by the singing in the building. It was dreary, dark and cold outside. I remembered my own family and asked myself, what are they feeling now? Mother, I suppose, looked at the empty chair and her eyes filled with tears.

An approaching rustle disturbed me, but it was only one of the guards. He slipped down into the trench and asked: "Well, what's new"? He waited a moment and then continued on his round, in the direction of the southern post. I remained alone again in the gloom of the night. It would be a good while before I was relieved and I longed to be with the people in the lighted hall.

At last my turn came to join the gaiety in the hall. By the time we had emptied our third and fourth glasses we were happy and slightly drunk. The guards changed every hour, so spirits remained high, and as soon as a new group entered there was general rejoicing. At midnight our visitors left us and we, too, went back to our quarters or to our post.—AHARON K.

From the letter of a member of Kfar Etzion in Jerusalem—April 25

Pessah has come again. We sat down to the *Seder* in the Ratisbonne Monastery in a very depressed mood, our thoughts concentrated upon what was happening in Kfar Etzion. We wondered how they would organize the *Seder* without the women and children. We recalled other Pessahs that had passed, the preparations to welcome the festival, and the late Shalom busy, tireless in his efforts to give it a proper form. The question welled up within us: "Can we hope to spend next Pessah at home?" A deafening rattle of rifle fire comes to our ears, heralding the Hagana attack on the enemy bases of Beth Iksa and Nebi Samuel, commanding the approach to the city.

During *Hol HaMo'ed* the siege of the Holy City was raised and a convoy comprising three hundred trucks reached Jerusalem. There is a feeling abroad that things have changed for the better. Apparently our own situation has improved.—HA'IM TS.

From the Journal of Kfar Etzion—April 26-27

Despite the shortage of men the Bloc Command has decided to station two squads at Hirbet Sawir night and day. . . .

The Commander of the Field Force unit is going to move his headquarters, which up to the present has been stationed in Kfar Etzion, to the Yellow Hill strongpoint. On the slope of the hill facing Massuot Yitzhak tents have been pitched, trenches dugs, and suitable security measures taken. Bloc Headquarters will remain in Kfar Etzion.

April 28

Over the radio we have heard the declaration of Abdullah, King of Trans-Jordan, that he will aid the Arabs of Palestine. It was also reported that the Arab Legion has crossed the Jordan to occupy Jericho and that the Arab States have promised the help of their forces to fight the Jews.

From a private letter—April 28

We heard over the radio of King Abdullah's declaration. A few months ago such a statement would have caused anxiety but today we are much better prepared throughout the country. But can Kfar Etzion, isolated as it is, hope to hold out against regular troops? . . .

We are fully conscious of the inevitability of this struggle. Our spirits are stronger, and for that reason, perhaps, we shall be able to hold our ground when the time comes. We hope that we shall know how to fight back.

We are very anxious about the battle raging in Jerusalem. A desperate struggle with the enemy is in progress there. Every victory in the Holy City strengthens us in our hope that the siege of the Etzion Bloc will be lifted.—BEN ZION G.

From the Journal of Kfar Etzion—April 29

According to reports coming in our forces in the Jerusalem Region have been very active. The fighting on the roads has been intensified and our men are operating against enemy transport. The object is to hold up all movements of reinforcements coming from Trans-Jordan headed for southern Jerusalem. . . .

An Arab informer reports that five hundred Legionaries from Jericho have arrived in Hebron. They have brought with them four Bren-carriers, and a light gun drawn behind a truck. They are under the command of Captain Abdul Jawad.

The unit held a parade in the streets of Hebron where the men were addressed by their Commanding Officer. The latter told them that the Legion must defeat the Jews and that they would be intrusted with the task of capturing Kfar Etzion. If they failed, the officer told them, the courage of the rest of the Legion would fail. He called upon the men of Hebron to help the Legion in its task and to place all their vehicles at its disposal and to be ready to go out to battle. . . .

The state of vigilance among our men is being strengthened. Two squads composed of members of Ein Tsurim have been ordered to occupy the Hirbet Sawir positions permanently. A squad of ten men is being sent every night from Kfar Etzion to guard the Mukhtar's Saddle strongpoint. The pickets guarding the strongpoints are being reinforced by members of the other settlements of the Bloc. The burden on the settlers, who are already overwhelmed by work and guard duty, has now been considerably increased. The settlements have been ordered to place rifles, machine guns and mortars at the disposal of the strongpoints.

April 30

Acting upon orders received from the Regional Command, today we attacked a convoy of Arab irregulars on the main road. Over fifteen vehicles were damaged and held up. The Arabs panicked and rushed out of the cars. However, they called up reinforcements, and armored cars of the Legion and of the British Army once again launched an attack upon the Monastery, and other positions, using artillery and heavy machine guns. Bullets even landed in the area of Kfar Etzion. Fortunately we suffered no losses. There are large enemy forces in the hills around Beth Fajjar.

From a report of the District Commander—May 1

We have been busy since the early hours this morning blocking the road. We attacked a large convoy traveling from Jerusalem to Hebron. A number of the cars were hit and abandoned by their passengers. Some struck mines. In the course of the day other cars were damaged. One car which could not be removed was set on fire by the Arabs. The Monastery and Hirbet Sawir were attacked by two-pounders. The Monastery sustained some damage but no one was hurt. Arabs have been seen gathering in the neighborhood. Other concentrations were reported from Beth Surif. Some shots were fired from Beth Umar and Saffa.—YA'AKOV A.

Radiogram from the Bloc Commander to Staff Headquarters—May 1

During our attack on the enemy's transport we succeeded in putting six vehicles out of action. It is difficult to estimate the number of casualties. With the exception of a number of armored cars, not a single vehicle succeeded in getting through the section of the road under our control.

We have spent: one thousand rounds of .303; two hundred rounds of Italian ammunition and two hundred of .300. If we do not get supplies of ammunition we shall not be able to continue our operations.

Send five hundred anti-personnel mines.

From the diary of a member of Kfar Etzion in Jerusalem—May 1

The Jews of Jerusalem anxiously followed the battle being fought out in the Katamon Quarter yesterday. After forty hours of fighting, the quarter, which was an enemy stronghold reinforced by Iraqi volunteers, was taken. A threat to the southern Jewish quarters of the city has been removed.

At Headquarters it was stated that the fighting on the Jerusalem-Hebron road pinned down enemy forces and prevented the dispatch of reinforcements to the Iraqis in Jerusalem. We were very pleased to hear that the defenders of the Bloc shared in the victory.—YOSEF P.

14 Facing the Legion's Guns

With only several weeks remaining until the total evacuation of the country by the British, the Hagana forces were sweeping ahead to capture vast stretches and key communication points in the proposed Jewish State. After the fall of Haifa and Tiberias, the Arabs began to evacuate Safad in Upper Galilee and the port city of Jaffa. Strategic points in the Jordan Valley and in Western Galilee were also captured.

Local Arab resistance was slowly disintegrating before the Jewish onslaught, but in the neighboring Arab countries the plans to invade Palestine were being completed. And though Mr. Bevin, the British Foreign Secretary, made an announcement in the House of Commons that the forces of the Arab Legion would be removed from Palestine before the termination of the Mandate, the Legion continued to strengthen its strategic position in the country.

The Security Council of the United Nations, seeking to create an authoritative neutral body in Palestine, established a Truce Commission whose members were the consuls of the United States, France, and Belgium in Jerusalem.

From a private diary—May 2

Mosh has coined a motto for the operations in which we are now engaged: *Netsah Yerushalayim*—the eternity of Jerusalem. It captures the mood prevailing among us.

A major part of the fortification work has been suspended and our efforts are now concentrated on the road. We have learned from Mosh that our blocking of the road has disrupted enemy traffic and contributed to the victory in Katamon. That is truly gratifying. We are aware of the fact that the Arab Legion is far superior to us in arms and manpower and that we cannot rely on aid being rushed to us, if necessary, against this formidable foe. Only the airways are open to us, and the meager reinforcements that the Austers and other planes can transport to us in time of need can hardly be of any consequence. And yet, in spite of these overwhelmingly adverse conditions, we must carry out the missions with which we are charged.—YISAKHAR

From the account of a sapper—May 2

We have been ordered to destroy enemy communications with Jerusalem. Mosh's orders were: "Blow up the bridge crossing the culvert on the main road and cut the telephone lines between Hebron and Jerusalem." The Palmah unit, which serves as the Bloc's reserve force, was ordered to provide cover.

We were woken last night. The sappers met near the store house. The officer in charge of the operation gave us a briefing on our objective. We prepared the explosives and completed the preparations. One of us kneaded the gelignite, someone else wound electric wire on a reel, others got the ignition apparatus and the anti-personnel mines. Within an hour we were ready and waiting for the armored car which was to take us to the main road. We loaded the stuff onto it and set out.

We stopped a short distance from the last roadblock. We stored our materials in a trench in the ground, which would also serve as our meeting place. The men repeated their various tasks. Mordekhai would blow up the telephone pole near the Mukhtar's house, "Gingi" the pole near the entrance to Beth Fajjar and David the bridge on the main road. As soon as the road bridge was blown up the others would carry out their missions and withdraw towards the rendezvous, near the feeder road.

We reached our immediate objective. The Palmah men took up positions along a stone fence, running parallel to the road, and we moved up to the bridge. We examined the area carefully and set to work. First we laid anti-personnel mines all round the bridge, then we mined the ditches by the roadside and the fields nearby, as the enemy soldiers would use the earth of the fields to fill the mine hole. Finally we laid the charge under the bridge, led the wire over the fence, and blocked the hole with sandbags.

When everything was ready a detail of men advanced towards the Mukhtar's house, making a wide detour around the mined ditches. We laid a charge under a telephone pole and a few mines nearby. It was darker than we had thought it would be, so we changed our plans and instead of leaving a sapper behind to set off the charge when the time came, we decided to blow up the pole immediately. We wanted to avoid the risk of one of our men treading on one of our own mines in the pitch darkness.

The sappers took up their positions at some distance from the pole, only one of them remaining behind to set off the charge. The order was given: "Ready? Go!" There was a slight buzz, then a flash, followed immediately by a deafening blast. The pole flew skywards. The hills round about us resounded with the echo of the explosion, punctuated by the sound of rending wires. The twisted wires lay contorted on the ground, and somehow reminded one of a carcass. One look, however, was enough for us. We did not know what surprises the night might hold for us and we made off.

"Who goes there?" we heard the deep voice of a sentry. "What happened to you? Have you set off the charge already?"

We explained that we had changed our plans and why.

The men got ready for action. A long column of Palmah men and sappers formed up in single file along the fence and we waited expectantly.

"Connect the detonator!" we heard a hoarse order.

"Heads down! Ready! Go!"

The sapper gave the handle a half-turn. Another flash and a mighty blast. A cloud of dust covered us. The acrid smell of gunpowder filled our nostrils. We could hear a series of dull thuds as stones hit the ground. Two other explosions followed, apparently of mines set off by the falling stones.

The boys jumped up to have a look at their handiwork. The job was well done. "One hundred percent!" someone exclaimed. A deep ditch had been plowed across the road. Even a tank couldn't get over it now.

"Come on boys! We've another job to do—the two telephone poles near Beth Fajjar."

We marched ahead confidently. The enemy at Beth Fajjar had not ventured even to fire a single shot. We had no doubt whatever that they had heard and probably even seen the explosion. The Palmah men took up positions along a fence at the entrance. The sappers quickly and expertly laid their charges and exploded them.

We made our way back to the rendezvous. As we passed the Monastery, its garrison fired a few rounds to mark their appreciation of our good work. We got into the armored car and ten minutes later were back in Kfar Etzion.—DAVID B.D.

From a report of the District Commander—May 2

This morning a British military convoy passed along the road from the direction of Hebron. It was forced to make a wide detour. After midday another military convoy came in the opposite direction, from Jerusalem. It tried to get round the trench and landed in the mine field. One car was put out of action and two soldiers were wounded. Later on troops arrived to repair the road. They dismantled a number of mines, but we do not know if they found all of them. Not a single Arab vehicle tried to get through. At any rate no traffic will travel on the road for a number of days. The neighborhood is very quiet.—YA'AKOV A.

From the diary of a member of Massuot Yitzhak—May 3

On Saturday Shmuel L., who is in charge of all fortification work, and I were called up by Mosh. We were informed of the plan to block the road again. The plans had been worked out in great detail and Mosh told us of the assignments of the various jobs and the timetable. Four eight-ton trucks loaded with heavy rocks would go out onto the road. A Field Force platoon would give them cover, while a detail of sappers under command of David B.D. would dismantle the mines we had laid on the road previously. This would allow our trucks to pass; afterwards we were to lay the mines again elsewhere on the road.

We were to take charge of the loading of the trucks and the setting up of the block. A group of *haverim* from Revadim would give us a hand. The job, we were warned, must be done quietly, quickly and efficiently. Otherwise the enemy might get wind of us.

Zero hour was eight last night. The men were assigned to their trucks, final orders were given, and the convoy moved off slowly from Kfar Etzion. At the crossroads by the Lone Tree the trucks pulled up and in a few minutes an opening was made in the roadblock there. We continued on our way slowly in order to deaden the noise of the motors. The sappers dismantled the mines laid by the side of the blocks on the internal road. We lay quietly on the ground and listened intently.

We reached the main road. Abrasha, commander of the Field Force unit, came up to give final instructions. The leading truck turned left, in the direction of Jerusalem, and parked crossways on the road to prevent the approach of hostile traffic. The second turned right towards Hebron and did likewise.

The word was given and the work of unloading the rocks began. The enemy positions were not far off and we had no doubt that they had heard the sound of the trucks. In spite of that we felt reasonably secure. Then came the turn of the second truck but the ignition would not work. We were wasting valuable time but there was nothing we could do. We tied her up and gave her a tow. The sappers warned us not to slip into mined ditches. We finished unloading and made the block as high as possible. We had done well. Dimly we could make out the platoon that was giving us cover, under the command of Tsvi Ben-Yosef, emerging from concealment and moving confidently over enemy ground.

Just as we were getting onto the feeder road shots and rockets pierced the air. The sappers were announcing that they had done their job and that everything was in perfect order. It was midnight when we got back.—ELIEZER S.

From a report of the District Commander—May 3

At half-past three in the afternoon, an Arab convoy from Jerusalem, comprising four trucks, escorted by British troops and Legionaries, approached. When they came near the turn to our feeder road they opened fire with machine guns and light artillery at the Monastery. They were held up by the roadblock and could not get ahead. We took all precautions not to hit the military vehicles and directed our fire against the trucks. Soon they were put out of action.

Shortly afterwards another convoy, comprising seven heavy armored vehicles armed with two-pounders, and a number of ordinary troop carriers and other cars came up. They took up positions along the road and opened fire at the Monastery and Hirbet Sawir. The Monastery was hit by hundreds of shells and thousands of bullets. The building still stands, however, and can be lived in. We have suffered no casualties in the last few days, mainly because the enemy fire was directed against the building, while our men were in the defense positions outside. During the attack the truss ring of the three-inch mortar broke. Please send a spare. Also try to send us another mortar. There is plenty of work for it to do here.

The British troops forced a way through our block and the Arab Legion extricated the cars that had got stuck on the road. They struck some of the mines on the roadside and Medical Corps cars removed the wounded. After dark they withdrew, making a wide detour by way of Beth Fajjar, to avoid the dangerous sector. At night we could hear the sound of much movement along the road and in the hills surrounding us.

We are waiting for the transport plane to bring us a big consignment. These supplies have a good effect on morale. —YA'AKOV A.

From a radiogram and report of the Bloc Commander—May 3

> . . . We were glad to get the anti-tank rifle. For a rifle of this type forty rounds of ammunition you sent us are next to nothing.

. . . The air strip is about five hundred yards long now. We need instructions how to continue it. Please send an engineer. We have neither the qualified men nor the instruments to draw up the necessary plans. The engineer will be given top priority to return by plane, even if he stays only for a single day. What are the prospects of sending a large plane? You know how much we depend upon it. The hour of decision is very near.—MOSH

15 The Attack of May 4

From the diary of a Field Force soldier stationed at the Russian Monastery—May 3

I was posted at the observation post behind the Monastery fence. From time to time I would survey the area with my binoculars. Several weeks ago this highway carried a heavy volume of traffic; now it was silent as a desert trail. Bullet-ridden vehicles lay in the ditches, on both sides of the road; we had put them "to rest." On the face of it, it appeared that we had succeeded in stopping all enemy traffic to Jerusalem. But what counter measures were the enemy planning? . . .

With the exception of some desultory sniping it was quiet now. Meantime the enemy was being reinforced from all the villages in the neighborhood. Mosh was with us and swept the area with his field glasses, watching every enemy movement. He exclaimed: "We must expect a full-dress attack! A state of alert tonight and reinforced guards in all positions!"

We ate a hurried meal and then returned to the positions. More men were added to each watch. The atmosphere was tense and the features of our officers grave. Ben-Yosef made the rounds of the positions, giving last instructions.

I was in the square position, commanding the rear from the direction of the Valley of Brakha. We could hear heavy movements of enemy transport and saw lights lighting up the horizon. It was a wearisome night. The hours crept by and every few minutes I peered at my watch. We tried to sleep but could not. Thoughts crowded into my mind; the sum total of them was no more than fear of the unknown. I tried to cast them out of my mind and my lips muttered a prayer: "God, strengthen me to stand the test this once!"

Somehow the night went by. The sun's rays lit up the countryside. At dawn sniping grew more and more intense. It became difficult to get from one position to the next. One by one the fighters gathered in the kitchen to have their breakfast. A number of sharp shooters were posted in the various positions to silence the enemy snipers.—SHMUEL S.

From the report of the District Commander—May 4

In the early morning a convoy of Legion armored cars and British tanks deployed on the road, facing the Monastery and Hirbet Sawir.

The attack began at eight with a heavy bombardment by artillery and the spraying of the area by machine guns, mounted on the tanks and vehicles. The bombardment was methodical and very accurate. Shells fell over the entire Monastery area: in the building, in the trenches, and on the surrounding fences. Simultaneously hundreds of Arabs who had come on foot and in trucks launched an assault on the Monastery under cover of their artillery. . . .—YA'AKOV A.

In the Monastery

From the diary of a Field Force soldier (Continued)— May 4

When the bombardment began, the alarm was sounded and the men filed quickly into their positions. A fierce battle developed. Shells rained down over the whole area, the terrible screech of their flight having a bad effect on us. I continued to dig in my slit trench and I was only sorry that I had not done so previously. Above the noise of the bombardment and the rattle of the Vickers I heard cries of "First-aid! First-aid!"

I had fired about fifty rounds when I noticed that my ammunition had almost run out and decided to hold my fire until I got further supplies. Suddenly I became conscious of the fact that our fire was weakening. I looked around to discover the reason. The first-aid man came rushing by and shouted: "The Browning position has been hit by a three-inch shell. The crew has been killed. A medical orderly who rushed up to help them was also hit." The thought flashed through my mind, "Our chief weapon has been destroyed! . . ."

A squad came up from Yellow Hill and took up positions behind the fences in the hope of stemming the Arab advance, but they were unsuccessful. The word was passed round that the wounded would be removed in the armored car and on stretchers. The car arrived on the scene but could not take all the wounded. Meantime the bombardment was becoming weaker, and this we regarded as a bad sign. We literally prayed for a continuation of the shelling, as we knew that when it stopped the assault would begin. Ben-Yosef went out to reconnoiter. He soon came back, breathing hard, and ordered a hurried retreat, before the enemy, who were only a hundred yards away, trapped us. Our front line positions had already been occupied. Rafi N. gathered whatever weapons he could still carry and tried to destroy the rest. He managed to save two mortars, seven rifles and two Sten-guns.

Our casualties were three dead and ten wounded. Abrasha T., commander of the Field Force company, was one of the wounded.—SHMUEL S.

At Hirbet Sawir

From the diary of a settler of Ein Tsurim—May 4

As the attack on the Monastery mounted in intensity, our position, too, came under very heavy fire. We lay in the trenches waiting for the enemy assault. At ten o'clock Headquarters ordered Ein Tsurim to dispatch a crew with a machine gun to Hirbet Sawir, as three machine guns had already been put out of action. Soon the squad put in an appearance and joined the defenders of the position. The shelling was very heavy and before long a number of men had been wounded, fortunately only slightly. Our spirits were not very high as it was reported that the Monastery had been taken. Our own situation was not good as we had very few men and the number of wounded was constantly increasing. The enemy bombardment continued unabated. In the orchard near the house facing our position a three-inch mortar had been posted and was making things very uncomfortable. Suddenly we saw a number of Arabs who had advanced unobserved over the dead area and were very close. They surprised us. Apparently the mines had been dismantled previously, for we did not hear a single explosion. We succeeded in driving them back. . . .

At about four in the afternoon another attempt was made to rush our position. Six to eight armored cars took up position on the sector of the road facing the Hirbeh and opened up with heavy artillery and machine gun fire. Under the cover they gave several hundred Arabs succeeded in advancing to within fifty yards of our positions. They advanced methodically, led by men equipped with mine detectors. When they had come close enough we opened up with everything we had, throwing grenades as well. The assault was broken. Meantime the armored cars, who had held their fire while the Arabs were trying to charge our positions, had withdrawn to Beth Fajjar. Another squad of men from Ein Tsurim, who had been stationed at Hirbet Zakaria, arrived to reinforce us.

We suffered seven casualties: one dead and six wounded.
—Tsvi S.

The Battle on the Mukhtar's Saddle

From the diary of a member of the "Airborne Platoon"—May 4

I advanced with a squad of men to reinforce the southern end of the Saddle. With us was a heavy machine gun and its crew from Kfar Etzion. Our orders were to halt the advance of enemy forces who were threatening the Monastery from the direction of the Valley of Brakha.

At the kiln we met a squad of rifle men who had been sniped at constantly. They looked a little tired and harassed. They were depressed by their isolation and were glad to see us. We posted the machine gun at some distance from the south kiln, facing the valley, but the Arabs did not show up from there. They were advancing upon the Monastery from the east. However, we could not change our position, as the whole area was mined and enemy sniping made movement difficult.

In the afternoon the enemy suddenly began to shell us with artillery and mortars, keeping up heavy machine gun fire all the time. The attack was meant to soften us up before an assault, but we did not budge. Then, without warning, four tanks appeared, advancing rapidly upon our position. Their fire was so heavy that we could not raise our heads. We stuck to the ground. The tanks, followed by infantry, came closer and closer. We opened up with light machine guns and rifles—the heavy machine gun had been put out of action—aiming at the infantry, but the tank crews soon discovered our positions. They were already on top of our forward positions, and their infantry was charging the west flank of the strongpoint. Orders were given to beat a retreat, before the enemy occupied the whole ridge. The men on the west flank managed to effect their retreat at the very last moment. But we seven who occupied the southern sector of the Saddle did not receive the order to retreat, as the telephone wires had been cut in the meantime by shell fire.

I lay by the mortar and Avraham L. served as my observer. Suddenly he cried out and I saw that he had been hit in the neck. I took out my personal bandage and began to dress the wound. He kept on repeating *Shema Yisra'el*. Just then Aryei H.Z. came running up and ordered us to retreat. Four of us picked up Avraham and made haste to leave the strongpoint. Two members of Kfar Etzion carried the machine gun and ammunition. But as soon as the tanks took up positions on the ridge of the Saddle, they opened machine gun fire on us and hit two of us. We placed Avraham behind a rock, intending to come back later to take him.

By the time we had reached Kfar Etzion, several hours later, thanks to the covering fire from the settlement, only two of our men were unhurt. Late at night Avraham was removed from the area under the cover of darkness. Towards morning he died in the hospital.—MORDEKHAI M.

The Attack on Kfar Etzion

From a private diary—May 4

Some time after two in the afternoon our Observation Post noticed suspicious movements on the Mukhtar's Saddle and the men were ordered into their positions. Soon we could make out tanks moving along the ridge of the Saddle and advancing upon our strongpoints. We were very anxious about the fate of our *haverim,* whom we could see retreating at a run. We could also make out groups of Arabs entering the tents of the strongpoint. We were ordered to open heavy fire to cover the retreat and to harry the enemy who now occupied the strongpoint. At the other end of the western sector a machine gun that had been placed on the roof of the strawshed was working very effectively. It was placed high up and commanded a wide field of fire. We also noted a number of hits scored by the three-inch mortar, from its emplacement on Yellow Hill.

The enemy replied by covering the entire western area with murderous fire. Shells hit Nveh Ovadia and the row of buildings on the western side of the settlement. Direct hits were also registered on the dining hall, the kitchen, and other buildings in the middle of the farmyard. The explosions of the mortar shells were deafening and the whole area was swept by machine gun fire.

Fire was concentrated upon the dairy barn, the stable, and Post Eight, compelling the men stationed there to abandon their positions and to take shelter in slit trenches nearby. But the fire of the enemy followed them. Direct hits were scored on the positions, and after a number of men had been wounded by splinters it was decided to withdraw to a reserve position. Alexander N. and Moshe W. who had suffered only scratches, retreated with the rest of the men, but a ricochet broke the right arm of Dov K. He was treated for his wound and sent to the hospital.

Throughout the battle, Ya'akov A. and Avraham F. conducted the defense of the village from the western positions and directed the covering fire.—YISAKHAR

On Russian Hill

From the accounts of a settler and a Field Force soldier—May 4

In the afternoon we saw the tanks that had occupied the Saddle shelling Kfar Etzion. At the same time a large crowd of Arabs concentrated on the road, south of the Bloc. In regular military formation the Arab Legion began to advance from the direction of the Valley of Brakha towards the strongpoint.

The exchange of fire between ourselves and the Arabs who had occupied the Russian Monastery positions continued without interruption. We asked for the three-inch mortar to concentrate its fire upon the Monastery. Some of the shells fell quite close to us and caused alarm among our men. At 3:30 P.M. a fire broke out in the Monastery. After another bout of firing quiet reigned.

Aharon L. was ordered to prepare his squad in the tent of the strongpoint for the counterattack. The whole area was exposed to enemy fire and it was only with the utmost difficulty that the men could get out of the ditch. They were tired and hungry and were waiting for the rations that had been promised. They lay around on the beds and the floor, and some of them in the posts nearby, which could not be seen from the Monastery.

Then one of the tanks on the Saddle opened fire on us. After the first shell had exploded near the tent the men were ordered to scatter, but they did not have a chance to do so. We saw the flash of one of the tank's guns and a shell hit the tent. Mosh had left the tent a few moments earlier and so was unhurt. . . .—TSVI S. and AHARON L.

From the report of the Bloc Commander—May 4

The tanks opened up with a heavy bombardment of mortars and artillery upon Kfar Etzion. Then they turned their fire upon Russian Hill. As a result of one direct hit on a tent, in which the reserve force was concentrating for the counterattack to recapture the Monastery, seven men were killed outright and a large number wounded. Meantime the advancing Arabs had entered the minefield on the Mukhtar's Saddle where they suffered heavy casualties. A large number were also hit by our rifle and machine gun fire from Kfar Etzion and by the three-inch mortar.

The tanks began to withdraw in the direction of the road. The Arabs continued to snipe with rifles and machine guns, and opened up once again with a heavy artillery bombardment from the main road on Hirbet Sawir, followed by repeated attempts to mount an assault. We were successful in beating them back, inflicting heavy losses. At dusk the armored vehicles left the battlefield in the direction of Jerusalem. Their withdrawal gave the signal to the enemy infantry also to retreat.

After dark we sent out scouts to the Monastery and the

Saddle. They encountered no opposition and we reoccupied both outposts. Our men took up positions for defense.

The enemy was constantly reinforced by men from the neighboring Arab villages, who came from both directions. It is difficult to form any estimate of the enemy's forces, but there is no doubt whatever that there were many hundreds of men, perhaps even more than a thousand. It is certain that we inflicted a good many casualties, dozens of killed and wounded, mainly in the vicinity of Hirbet Sawir and the Mukhtar's Saddle.

The enemy's success was mainly the result of his use of artillery and armor. The accuracy of their fire and the deployment of their vehicles by far exceeded that achieved in previous attacks. We had no effective anti-tank weapons and they could operate quite freely. In addition our men were psychologically unprepared to resist these weapons. The enemy had unlimited supplies of ammunition and every attempt they made to charge our positions was preceded by a hail of automatic fire. They tried to cover the road with heavy fire and to cut communications between our various positions. However, thanks to the outstanding courage of our men contact was maintained throughout.

The main force used in the attack was the Arab Legion. In one sector alone we counted eleven platoons of the Legion, deployed for attack and dispersed over the area. It is reasonable to assume that the tanks and the heavy armored vehicles belonged to the British army. A number of half-tracks armed with Bren-guns also took part. This is the first time in our engagement with the Legion that these weapons have been used.

Our defenses are not strong enough to withstand artillery. If the enemy had continued their pressure and advanced our plight would have been very grave and we might not have been able to hold our ground.

We need more effective weapons and also reinforcements. In the earlier phases of the operation I was compelled to throw all our forces into the engagement and not a single unit remained in reserve. If the fighting had continued for a number of days our men would have dropped from fatigue. I must also remind you of the shortage of ammunition. Another day of fighting and we shouldn't have had a round left.

The three-inch mortar—the only "heavy" weapon we could use against the enemy—proved very effective. However, the balance of firepower was one mortar against dozens of cannon, mortars, and heavy machine guns. For that reason I must stress again the need to send at least another two 3-inch mortars and larger supplies of shells and ammunition. We had only eight shells left by evening.

In the light of the above, the Bloc's defenses cannot be regarded as adequate. It is essential that you send us a qualified officer, with experience in artillery and tank warfare. We stand in need of reinforcements in arms, experts and implements, and I do not wish to take a decision solely upon my own responsibility.—MOSH

The Re-occupation of the Monastery

From the account of a settler of Ein Tsurim—May 4

Flames could be seen coming from the Monastery and the sniping ceased. Mosh decided to send out a reconnaissance patrol. The patrol, led by Nahum F., made its way along the ditch to the breach in the Monastery fence. Meeting with no resistance Nahum decided to advance. They made their way cautiously through the yard and the orchard, until they were quite close to the building. Dead silence reigned. The enemy, it soon became clear, had evacuated the building and Mosh was informed accordingly. The withdrawal of the Arabs was a surprise to us. We could not understand why they had withdrawn. Had they been afraid of mines or of a counterattack? Or perhaps the evacuation was a trap?

At 10:00 P.M. a detail of men re-occupied the building. Some of the walls had been destroyed, but the shell of the building was still intact. On every hand there were signs of an Arab attempt to set the building on fire. Everything that could be removed—furniture, clothing, personal equipment of our men—had been plundered. The enemy had left behind them sufficient evidence of the heavy losses they had suffered in the battle and from mines.

During the night the Monastery was held by two squads of the Field Force and two from Revadim and Ein Tsurim, under the command of Mosh. Those who were not manning the defense posts were hard at work, digging new positions nearer the dead area in front of the Monastery, in order to forestall any surprise attack.

Beds, mattresses, furniture, and utensils, all of them collected from the various settlements of the Bloc, were brought over on the next day and life in the Monastery reverted to normal. Patrols were sent out to the battlefield to study the enemy's methods during the attack. Everywhere they found signs of the losses the Arabs had suffered. Red Crescent ambulances carrying wounded to the hospitals could be seen on the road.—TSVI S.

In the Hospital

From the account of a medical orderly—May 4

The first wounded men began to arrive at the hospital before noon. Dr. Windsberg laid down a detailed program for operating on the wounded. A reception room was set aside where two nurses took care of the men as they were brought in, and gave them food and drink. Then they injected them against blood poisoning. The men were very patient and some of them gave up their turn in the operating room for a friend who was suffering greater pains or whose condition seemed more serious.

That day about thirty men were operated on. We worked from nine in the morning to about eleven at night, practically without a break. Dr. Windsberg was untiring in his work. Throughout he retained his self-command and directed the work in the hospital firmly and efficiently.

Soon the hospital was completely crowded and the empty children's house next door had to be cleared for the wounded. The latter were tended devotedly by the girls of the settlements, and of the Palmah and the Field Force.—NAFTALI G.

From the account of an Arab officer, a member of the Trans-Jordan Delegation at the Rhodes Armistice talks, who had taken part in operations against the Etzion Bloc.

[The Hebron Area Command of the Arab Legion, operating as part of the British Forces and guarding lines of communication and Government property, planned taking over control of the entire Hebron District immediately after the evacuation of the remaining British troops and officials.

From the middle of April the inhabitants of Hebron, and especially the mayor and notables of the town, urged the Legion to destroy the settlements of the Etzion Bloc, as their proximity constituted an affront to the Arabs. A number of well-armed Arab bands in whose ranks British and German volunteers were serving, were operating in the area at the time. In addition, hundreds of villagers of the district possessed arms and roamed around in Hebron and the vicinity in the hope of taking part in an attack on the Jews. The Arabs of Hebron, and particularly one Arab band which had a number of European instructors, had in their possession some twenty armored cars, plundered from the Jews and from the British police. However, the experiences of the Arabs of Hebron and the villages in their attacks on the Etzion Bloc had not been happy. They were lightly armed and could not hope to penetrate the Jewish defenses.

The Legion did not submit to the pressure of the notables.

From April on we sent out patrols to reconnoiter the Jewish positions. The information at our disposal was obtained mainly from Arabs familiar with the settlers of Kfar Etzion and from the commanders of the bands who had launched attacks on the Bloc. On the basis of these reports we placed the number of defenders far higher than the true figure. We also overestimated their firepower and arms. After the battles were over we were astonished to see how much we had been mistaken and misled by the information given by the leaders of the bands.

In the middle of the first week of May the Jews began to attack the transport of the Arab Legion traveling along the road skirting the Jewish positions. We suffered casualties and as a result of one attack six men of the Legion were killed and their car set on fire. On other occasions military vehicles of the British troops were also attacked. The road was closed to civilian traffic, while military transport continued to be exposed to ambush. After a series of these attacks, it was decided to take punitive action against the Jews and to destroy the positions dominating the road. British tanks and transport and Arab Legion armored cars accompanied by infantry attacked the Jewish positions, the object being to destroy them and to compel the Jews to withdraw to their own villages. No capture of the Etzion Bloc was contemplated at the time.

These reprisal operations lasted several hours, the Jews defending themselves with great courage. Despite the superiority of our arms they fought obstinately and inflicted many casualties, mainly among the Arab bands who, because of their inexperience, advanced into machine gun fire and were mercilessly mown down. For the men of the Arab Legion too, this was their baptism of fire, but they conducted themselves cooly and intelligently. Some of them were caught in the minefields and were blown up; others were trapped and hit by Jewish fire. Generally speaking, however, the Legion's losses were small. A number of Legionaries were hit as they were trying to help men of the Arab bands, who had been wounded by the Jews, or were caught in the crossfire between the tanks and armored cars and the Jewish positions. The British fired only from their tanks and took care not to come too close. It was obvious that they were more interested in overawing the Jews than in hurting them. All they wanted was to safeguard their transport along the road.

This operation failed because it did not result in the destruction of Jewish positions commanding the road and forcing the Jews to withdraw. Undoubtedly one of the factors operating in favor of the Jews was the participation of irregular Arab troops who mustered from the neighboring villages in order to share the victory. The Jews derived much moral encouragement from the slaughter they inflicted upon these Arabs.

When we felt that the Jews had been adequately punished and it was necessary to look after the dozens of wounded, the battle was brought to an end and the Legion's troops returned to Hebron. The British also left the scene after they had given the Jews a dose of fire. Patrols of the Legion remained behind to observe the movements of the Jews and to make sure that no planes brought them supplies. Transport of all kinds was kept busy for hours collecting the wounded of the Arab mob, whose groans and screams had a bad effect on the inhabitants of Hebron and Bethlehem, who in any case were downcast at the "victory" of the Jews and the large number of casualties sustained in the battle. Those Legionaries who had been severely wounded conducted themselves well and bore their sufferings with fortitude.

During a session of the High Command of the Arab Legion, it was resolved that the military power of the Etzion Bloc must be liquidated. For some time afterwards the officers were kept busy on their plans for the capture of the Bloc.]—(From an interview printed in *HaTsofe,* April 8, 1949)

From the diary of a Palmah soldier—May 5

The bodies of the twelve men who had been killed in the battle were brought to Nveh Ovadia, where they lay in state. The hall, the walls of which were perforated with seven shell holes, and the fine Holy Ark, which had also been hit by a shell, provided a somber background for the occasion.

Work was suspended and the *haverim* gathered to pay their last respects to the fallen.

Meanwhile a burial party was digging another common grave among the rocks of Abu Rish, under the shade of the young wood. It was hard work and it was only after an exhausting effort that the grave was completed just before evening.

The funeral procession made its way silently to the slope of Abu Rish, headed by a guard of honor and the commanders of the Bloc. The bodies were borne on stretchers, followed by the men serving in the various units and the settlers.

The fallen men were given a military burial. Psalms were recited and then the *Kaddish*. Mosh delivered a short address by the open grave:

"What are we, and what are our lives? Nothing at all. The main thing is the work we are doing, by which we live. We will strike the enemy wherever we can get at him; we shall not permit him to carry out his designs. Our reply is: *Netsah Yerushalayim*—the eternity of Jerusalem!"

URIEL O.

16 The Strokes of the Pendulum

A little more than a week remained until the end of the Mandate, and in Tel Aviv the Jewish Provisional Government to be was assembling for the first time. The Hagana forces successfully continued their occupation of strategic points in the country. In Jerusalem the High Commissioner was pressing for a cease-fire in the city before the British withdrawal.

From a private diary—May 6

Yesterday morning a number of Austers landed to evacuate the wounded. They also brought arms: two light machine guns, rifles, and ammunition to replace what we had lost the day before yesterday, as well as two rarely seen anti-tank Piats. In addition a two-engined plane flew several times over the Bloc and parachuted medical and other supplies, ammunition, clothing, and kitchen utensils—all of which our Command had asked for. Everybody is interested in the planes and what they are bringing. The feeling that we are not isolated and abandoned to our fate is very encouraging. But everybody is asking, "When are we going to get reinforcements?" . . .

We are making every effort to extend the flying strip. Many men are working on the extension though they are needed elsewhere. We hope that two-engined planes will be able to land on the strip within another four days. Then there are prospects that reinforcements will be flown in.

We live with the feeling that we are running a race with the enemy and with time. Can we hope to anticipate May 15 and strengthen the Bloc with men and arms, or shall we have to fight it out with the enemy while we are still weak?

All other work has been suspended and everybody has been mobilized for the fortifications. Positions must be changed and strengthened to withstand artillery. We must repair the breaches made during the last attack. Above all we must get as deep as we can underground. The soldiers and the settlers work day and night. . . .

They are manufacturing land mines in the metal workshop. The sappers go out at night to lay the mines. After the battle we found that the Arabs had cleared some of the fields, but in spite of that there is no doubt that mines are our most effective defensive weapon. It is a pity that we have no more mines for use against heavy armor. The few we have have been laid in vital spots, where we must expect an enemy armor attack.

In the settlement, also, we are being kept busy. Headquarters and the radio station have been transferred to the German Monastery, which seems stronger and better protected than Nveh Ovadia. The cellar has been equipped to serve as a shelter for the wounded and non-combatants. In addition it has been decided to empty the small cisterns within the farmyard and to convert them into shelters. We are also working hard extending and deepening the trenches around the defense posts and the communication trenches.

All these defense works are being executed under the direction of Ya'akov A., the District Commander, and Avraham F., the Settlement Commander of Kfar Etzion.

Avraham is an experienced Palmah veteran. He is resolute and energetic, and rushes from one post to the next, inspecting the excavation work and discussing each job with the men on the spot. Everyone who comes into contact with him is infected by his tireless industry.

Ya'akov has a quieter temperament. Many people believe that he is devoid of all emotion and that he is incapable of losing his temper. He has been familiar with the defense problems of the Bloc from the very first days of Kfar Etzion, and has recognized the gravity of our situation from the beginning of the siege. The leading members of the *kvutza* have been aware for many weeks of his pessimistic view of the position. At the same time he knows that we must carry out our duties like soldiers and that we cannot retreat. He also appreciates that he himself, holding the most responsible position among the settlers in the Bloc, must practice the highest degree of self-restraint. Mosh has found in him a loyal aide; quiet, moderate, responsible, always ready to compromise on minor points in order to insure attainment of the main objective.

Ya'akov is kept busy inspecting our military potential, our establishment, our arms and ammunition, and the preparation of plans for the distribution of arms in an emergency. He drafts memoranda and messages to the various institutions, in which he insists on the reinforcement of the Bloc.

He and Avraham provide examples worthy of emulation.—YISAKHAR

From the diary of a wounded member of Kfar Etzion—May 6

I have had time to rest after last week's battle, and to

recover from the pain of the operation and innumerable penicillin injections. Now I feel a little stronger.

On the day following the battle my turn came for evacuation by plane. Together with my ward mate, Yitzhak K. —who was also wounded in the hand during the battle—I was taken to the air strip, where we were to await the arrival of the plane. Meanwhile I observed much activity on the strip and in the strongpoints nearby. After a long wait the Auster landed and the two of us were put into the narrow seat. The pilot, a tall, pleasant youngster from South Africa, who had already seen service in the Second World War and had only arrived in Palestine the day before, did his best to make us comfortable. The belts were strapped about us and we got ready for the flight. The plane taxied along the runway eastwards, then turned and taxied again along the entire length of the strip. But just as it was about to rise, one of the wheels struck a rock. The tire burst and the plane overturned. The people on the air strip rushed up, raised the plane and lifted the three of us out. None of us was seriously hurt, though the jolt had been painful. The pilot was very sorry about the whole affair. We assured him that we were not hurt and invited him to have something to eat in the village. Meanwhile he could rest until the next plane came. . . .

Soon *haverim* had come to see how we were—in the hospital again. They told us of the receipt of a cable from Regional Headquarters reading: "Tomorrow morning at ten a Jewish doctor and a representative of the Red Cross will proceed to the Bloc in three Red Crescent ambulances. Take care that they don't strike any mines." It seems that we still have a chance of reaching a hospital and getting proper treatment.

Our commanding officers are pleased at the message. They hope to be able to send all the wounded to Jerusalem, and so ease the situation here. The people tending them can be transferred to other work and we shall be able to save precious rations. It is essential to empty the hospital in case of another emergency in the near future.—Dov K.

From the account of a member of Ein Tsurim—May 6

Our Observation Post, which was expecting the arrival of the Red Cross ambulances, observed British Bren-carriers traveling up the road opposite Hirbet Sawir. Officers in British uniforms emerged and climbed up towards the Hirbeh. For a long time they lay on a rock, surveying the area through their field glasses, making notes on the maps they held in their hands. We thought that this had something to do with safeguarding the Red Cross ambulances and, in keeping with our orders, did not open fire.

Afterwards we noticed a large Arab herd being driven onto the Hirbet Sawir lands, but for the reason already mentioned held our fire.

We reported these movements to Headquarters.—Tsvi S.

Radiogram from the Bloc Commander to Staff Headquarters—May 6

Yesterday and today officers of enemy armored units patrolled the areas close to our positions, plotting and mapping terrain. We assume that this is in preparation for a renewed attack to be launched by enemy armor. We have observed many flocks are being pastured in the vicinity, apparently with the intention of discovering mine fields.

Anti-tank weapons must be sent to the Bloc without delay. No planes have arrived. Our supplies of ammunition are very low.

From the diary of a wounded member of Kfar Etzion—May 7

I got up in the morning anticipating the arrival of the ambulances. One of the *haverim* helped me to pack my things. Then I went for a walk round the village, to see the damage suffered during the attack and to say goodbye to the *haverim.* I was worried all the time by the question: "Is this goodbye to Kfar Etzion? How long will the *haverim* here be able to hold out?"

Memories returned of various periods in my life, connected with the settlement of Kfar Etzion. That is why the shattered walls of Nveh Ovadia were very dear to me, that is why the eyes of the portraits on the walls—of Rabbi Kook, after whom our *kvutza* had been named, of Dr. Avraham Ovadia, whose name the building bore, of our member Avraham Katz, killed in the defense of Hanita, and whose name had been given to the main hall—looked down so sadly at me. I asked myself, "Can the hopes and aspirations that pervade this mountain village withstand the avalanche?"

Then I went to the positions surrounding the village. Everything I saw testified to the battle that had been fought. The damage accentuated my fears for the future. Everywhere I found *haverim* busy at their duties. In the dairy barn, Avraham Sh., together with some of the girls, was helping the engineer Tsvi M. to repair the plane that had been damaged a few days before. In the metal workshop they were busy turning out mines. On the vacant lot nearby other *haverim* were twisting pieces of barbed wire. In the kitchen, the sewing room, and the laundry the *haverot* were all busy at their tasks.

In a trench near the stable some veteran settlers, experienced at rock-hewing, were deepening the communication trench connecting two important positions. I came up to them. Shalom, an old Hagana man, greeted me with the question: "What do you think of last week's rehearsal? When you get to town don't wait. Explain our situation to them." Yisrael, who is always so reticent, chimed in. "We can't hope to hold out like this, with empty hands, against so powerful a force. You must be our representative and arouse them." Shmuel said: "You know that I have always been an optimist. But now . . ." Immediately he stopped short and added: "Never mind! Within a few days the State will be proclaimed. Happy is he who lives to see that day. Everything is worth it, for its sake."

I took my leave with a heavy heart. I thought of Shmuel's words and recalled another conversation we had once had, under other circumstances. It was in 1930, when we were together in the Youth Movement in Poland and the Passfield White Paper of the British Government had just been published. The prospect was gloomy. We were discussing the situation of the Zionist movement, and Shmuel had remarked: "If only we had half a million Jews in Eretz Israel things would be different." I thought: Now we have more than half a million Jews. We are the precursors of Israel's independence. Why are our hearts so sad as we stand on the threshold of the realization of our ideal?

On my way I met Tsipora, the only mother in the village, who had chosen to remain behind with us, sending her child to Jerusalem. She gave me a message for the *havera* who is looking after her son Yosef. "I have asked Ya'akov to let me go to Jerusalem with the wounded," she added. "Ya'akov did not refuse. He only explained to me how short we are of men and women. We have agreed to decide when the ambulance arrives. I don't know what to do. I have to choose between my duty as a mother and my obligations as a *havera* under conditions of siege."

May 8

The ambulance did not arrive on Friday. In the evening I went to the service, and afterwards ate the Sabbath meal in the dining hall. Despite the events of the week there was a gay atmosphere in the hall, and we sang the regular *zemirot*. On Saturday morning, after services, the *haverim* went out to work as usual.—Dov K.

From letters of members of Kfar Etzion—May 8

It was Saturday today and we were all assigned to work on fortifications. The last attack has had a bad effect on morale. The shell holes in the western wall of Nveh Ovadia and in other buildings are not a pleasant sight. The funeral and the crowded hospital did not encourage us either.

According to a report received here the Red Cross were to come to evacuate the wounded. We waited for them all day yesterday. No plane has landed for the past three days. All this is depressing, though the reports of the cease-fire in Jerusalem have raised our spirits. But according to the radio, it seems that it is very doubtful whether this cease-fire is worth anything.—YITZHAK K.

Saturday night. I have just come back from the Secretariat, where the loudspeaker has been installed. We heard of the proposed cease-fire in the Holy City, and though it is not clear whether this is "good for Jews," we rejoice at the prospect of peace being restored where you are.

Pessah has passed and it is already the Fifteenth Day of

the Omer. It is interesting that this period of awaiting the State should coincide with the Counting of the Omer. We have sufficient reason to count each day that passes, and brings us nearer to the date of decision. The Counting of the Omer links Pessah and Shavuot; Pessah, the festival commemorating the liberation of the people and Shavuot, the day when Israel became a nation, by accepting the Torah. Today we are again in the period between the declaration in favor of a Jewish State and the implementation of the declaration. When our forefathers went forth from Egypt they had to surmount many obstacles. Our situation today resembles theirs. We have to avoid many pitfalls and hope that, with God's help we shall achieve our ultimate goal, and our Counting will be complete.

You pray for a miracle, like the miracles of the Exodus. I believe that we have already witnessed many miracles. Whoever thought that we should make such progress before May 15, under such difficult conditions, despite the interference and intervention of the British. Not a single settlement has been abandoned and we already control most of the territory of the proposed Jewish State. Is this not a miracle? I know that our main objective lies still ahead. Let us hope our success will continue.—YOSEF D.

Life is back to normal and the tragedy of last week has almost been forgotten. . . . We are waiting for May 15, which is just a week away, with growing apprehension. Then the invasion of the country by the Arab armies will probably be launched. There are big battles ahead and we cannot foresee the outcome. One thing is certain—losses will be heavy.—SHIMON H.

Our *haverim* behaved very well during the battle. It was an acid test. It was a hard-fought battle, but we can already see signs of our just victory on the horizon. True, the price is high but those who will live to see the day can hope to live in liberty, in their independent homeland. I do not know if we shall see it but our children will be free citizens of a free country, and for that we are ready to fight.

The people here are not conscious of any self-sacrifice but they do not regard their job as an adventure. We are soldiers who have been ordered to hold this position at all costs. We are doing our duty. This is a forward position of Jerusalem and we are defending the ramparts of the Holy City.—SHALOM G.

The arms we received have cheered us up. It is a pity that so many rounds were damaged when they were dropped without parachutes. Only one package dropped by parachute was intact. Two other packages were damaged.

We are still strengthening our defenses but we are short of men and the work is proceeding very slowly. We have reached rock in most places and have no drills to get deeper. The extension of the air strip is also being held up. The bulldozer is not working properly.

We have been informed that Regional Headquarters will soon send a representative to the Bloc for consultations. We are very short of men. It is difficult to decide whether we should continue to occupy the strongpoints around the Bloc. We need all the men we have to hold them, but this means that the base will be weakened. We have no reserves. The alternative is to dig in in the settlements, but then we shall leave the approaches to the settlements exposed. We are doing all we can to hold the strongpoints in the hope that reinforcements will come. If we are not reinforced we shall soon reach the point of exhaustion, particularly if there should be further attacks.

We are waiting further orders. We should prefer to defer our harrying operations for a few days, until we have time to reorganize and strengthen our positions. However, if in the meantime our help should be required, or if we have to repulse another attack, we shall do our duty.—YA'AKOV A.

From a private diary—May 9

This morning a plane landed and took away the pilot who had been stranded here. We were told that the number of planes at our disposal has been diminished by various mishaps and that all the planes that can fly are essential for operations elsewhere. For that reason it is difficult to comply with our requests. The delay is giving rise to much concern. The wounded must be evacuated to Tel Aviv, we need more arms, and above all the sense of isolation is very irksome. Meanwhile a mist has covered the entire area and planes can't land in any case. It is very worrying. . . .

From the papers we have received and from the radio bulletins we can form some picture of the progress of the war. The BBC has reported that British troops took punitive action against Kfar Etzion because of the attacks on military transport. Apparently they are referring to the transport of the Arab Legion, which, so both the High Commissioner and Bevin promised, would be sent out of the country. . . .

King Abdullah, in an order-of-the-day to his troops, has declared: "I call upon you to save Palestine. Upon this war depends the honor and the glory of the Arab States!"

. . . The High Commissioner has gone to Jericho, now occupied by the Arab Legion, for talks with Azzam Pasha, Secretary General of the Arab League. Agreement was reached between them. The High Commissioner announced that a cease-fire would be imposed in Jerusalem. The city would be placed under the supervision of the International Red Cross. The Hagana favors the proposal in the hope that it will give Jerusalem, which is already exhausted, a respite, and will enable the Yishuv also to concentrate on the strengthening of other fronts. . . .

Meanwhile the situation in Jerusalem is becoming more and more serious. Enemy artillery emplaced at Nebi Samuel and elsewhere, is continuing to batter the city's Jewish quarters. Food and water supplies are very low. . . .

Jewish forces have launched a number of attacks. One of them, "Operation Maccabi," is intended to free the road from Jerusalem to the coast. We have heard reports of the attacks around Beth Mahsir, Dir Ayoub, and Latrun. Apparently our forces in this area are being strengthened considerably.

We listen in to these reports with rejoicing and also with envy. When will our turn come? Do not these operations reduce the aid that should be extended to the Bloc? Or perhaps one result will be to relieve the pressure on us.—YISAKHAR

From the diary of the Bloc's representative in Jerusalem—May 9

Reports have been received of the fighting in the Etzion Bloc area, according to which we have suffered more than forty casualties and lost important weapons. They express doubt whether the Bloc with its present forces can withstand an attack of Arab Legion armor. Mosh has called for a high-ranking officer to visit the Bloc in order to encourage the men and to plan operations. Regional staff officers have discussed the prospects of the Bloc.

The consensus of opinion is that if it is not possible to strengthen the Bloc very substantially within the next few days it must be evacuated with the aid of the British troops. This can still be arranged. It must be borne in mind that with the fierce fighting in progress on the Tel Aviv-Jerusalem road and in other parts of the country our small air force is being kept fully occupied, and it is not likely that it will be able to extend aid to the Bloc in case of a major attack.

These conclusions have been transmitted to the General Staff.

I have heard that a number of members of the General Staff support this view. Others, however, argue that there are many weak and isolated areas in the country and that we cannot agree to voluntary evacuation of any one of them as the Yishuv's morale and fighting strength might be affected. Thus far not one Jewish settlement has been evacuated. We must hold on to every settlement as long as we can.

The discussion has affected me very much. I am very worried about the future. Who knows better than we do how short the Etzion Bloc is of men and heavy arms to meet a major attack. Even a month ago, at the time of the Nebi Daniel convoy battle, the Bloc had no reserves or even a necessary minimum of arms. Forty men have now been put out of action; the Palmah platoon has practically been destroyed, and the Field Force company now comprises no more than three platoons. The enemy have exposed the weak links in our defensive system and can now improve their tactics. Can the Bloc hope to hold its forward positions in this situation? And if these strongpoints should fall there is no second line of defense.

Must we rely on miracles and bank on the Arabs not attacking the Bloc before May 15? The Arabs of the district are getting ready to take their revenge for the attacks on their transport, which have upset their plans. According to reports which have reached us, the Arab Legion will play an active role in this attack.—YOSEF P.

From the account of a Field Force soldier—May 9

In view of the concern that has been expressed in the Bloc, Mosh called a meeting of all unit commanders and all leading members of the Bloc and explained the situation to them. He did not conceal his own anxiety regarding the ability of the Bloc to withstand an attack after the fighting of last Tuesday. He voiced his doubts whether we could hope to complete the airfield before May 15, or whether reinforcements could reach us before the decisive battle. Under these circumstances the next battle might well be the last. He expressed his view that it must be a "Massada," comparable to the last stand of the Zealots against the Romans after the destruction of the Temple. This time, however, we are imbued with the consciousness that by fighting to the last we shall help to save Jerusalem.

In reply to someone who asked why the General Staff had not dispatched reinforcements, he declared that he was convinced that we had received whatever could be allocated for us. Possibly there were other areas in the country whose needs were even more urgent. The decision must rest with the General Staff. We must accept the situation and do our duty as best we could.—H.A.

From the account of Palmah soldiers—May 9

Our platoon suffered heavily in the last battle. Five of our best men were killed while a number of others were wounded. Our unit can no longer serve as an effective reserve force.

When we asked Mosh to urge the General Staff to dispatch reinforcements to the Bloc, he replied: "I make it my business always to outline the situation as it is, without diminishing the importance of anything and without exaggerating it. I do not complain if they send us two Piats and inform me that that is all they can spare. Perhaps that is a bad policy, but I cannot do anything else."

We felt that a storm was brewing. Nevertheless we tried to raise our own spirits, though we had a premonition of the evil that was to come. One evening we had a party, complete with a concert of recorded music, community singing and the usual yarning.

We maintained the Palmah spirit.—NAOMI T. and URIEL O.

From a private diary—May 11

This morning a brief notice (after the style of the Counting of the Omer) appeared on the bulletin board:

"Today it is eleven days in May; there are four days to the proclamation of the State."

We have learned indirectly from a reliable non-Jewish source that the Arabs have decided to destroy the Jewish settlements south of Jerusalem at all costs. Large fighting forces are concentrating in the neighborhood of the Bloc and are constructing strongpoints in the hills facing the Jewish villages, in order to prevent the arrival of reinforcements. Mine fields have been laid at a distance of more than half a mile from the Bloc. An all-out attack will be launched at any hour and its objective will be the surrender of the Jewish forces.

According to this informant, armored units of the Arab Legion under the personal command of the Deputy OC of the Legion will participate in the attack.—YISAKHAR

III

THE SACRIFICE

"Thy beauty O Israel, upon thy high places is slain."
II Samuel 1:19

17 The Outposts Fall

The Arab Legion laid its plans carefully and well, drawing upon its experience in the attack of May 4. They left the Bloc alone for a whole week, but in the meanwhile they were gathering themselves for the assault. Flocks of sheep were driven over the fields to reveal mines. Aerial photographs taken previously were now supplemented by patrols who, from positions close to the Bloc, carefully mapped the whole area.

In Jerusalem a cease-fire was in force, enabling the Arabs to transfer men and armor to support the main body of their troops, mustered in Hebron and Bethlehem. The Legion's armored force was of substantial proportions and included tanks, half-tracks, and other armored vehicles. Indeed, in some phases of the attack no less than forty armored vehicles, equipped with two-pounders and heavy machine guns, took part simultaneously. According to the defenders, three-inch mortars and heavier guns were also used. Other components of the Arab force that took part in the attack were units of the "Arab Liberation Army" and the local Arab bands, who were reinforced by thousands of armed Arab villagers.

The forces defending the Bloc, numbering less than five hundred men and women, were weakened by the ardors of their long stand. Their equipment consisted of rifles, Stenguns, a few light machine guns, one heavy machine gun, a number of two-inch mortars and one three-inch mortar, two anti-tank Piats, and one anti-tank rifle. These arms were supplemented by hundreds of anti-personnel mines which had been scattered around the various approaches to the outposts and settlements, and by about a dozen anti-vehicle mines which had been placed at strategic spots. Ammunition stores were meager, and any attempt to reply adequately to the heavy volume of enemy fire was out of the question.

A small quantity of arms and ammunition which had been prepared at the Tel Aviv Airport for transport to the Bloc did not arrive in time.

Decisive battles were being fought throughout the country during this period, requiring all the support that the modest Jewish Air Force with its tiny, fragile planes could give. Bitter fighting was raging on the coastal road to Jerusalem, with detachments of the Legion joining the fray. Egyptian units had already crossed the southern border and were assaulting Kfar Darom; the main body of Egyptian troops was preparing to follow in their wake. Iraqi forces were in Trans-Jordan, ready to cross the Jordan River. And in the north, the Syrian and Lebanese armies were poised to invade Galilee.

It was under these conditions that the last battle of the Etzion Bloc began in the dawn of May 12, 1948.

The Attack on the Mukhtar's Saddle

From the account of a member of Ein Tsurim—May 12

In the early hours of Wednesday morning we made our way to the Saddle, as was our practice every day, to strengthen its fortifications. We were guarded by a detachment of the "Airborne Platoon," who were armed with a machine gun, rifles, and sub-machine guns. The patrol took up position and we began work.

At about five o'clock we suddenly heard an order in Arabic, *"Udrub! Wahad al wahad,"* (Strike! One after the other) and immediately afterwards machine gun and rifle fire was opened up on us from the lone house near Beth Umar. At the same time three armored cars appeared on the scene, which began to shell us as they advanced, followed by infantry. We took cover in the dead area but, as the telephone communications became disrupted and the armored cars continued their advance, the commander ordered a retreat from the forward positions. The men without arms were ordered back to Kfar Etzion. Just then a shell exploded nearby and wounded David C. He was immediately taken to the hospital.—Aryei A.

From "A Report on the Final Battle of Kfar Etzion"—May 12

A heavy shelling was opened up on Kfar Etzion from the direction of the Mukhtar's Saddle, and the settlement's Striking Squad, under the command of Avraham S., left for the Saddle on the double. The men were armed with a Lewis gun, two sub-machine guns, seven rifles, and about two thousand rounds of ammunition. Every man had hand grenades. At the gate, Avraham F. caught up with them and took over the command of the squad. Just outside the settlement they met the men who had been working there and at the turn in the road they met the Field Force detachment retreating from the Saddle.

The squad was ordered to disperse and took up positions on the rocks, about one hundred and fifty yards from the road leading from Kfar Etzion to the Saddle. Enemy fire was aimed mainly at the farmyard and Russian Hill. The three armored vehicles advanced slowly. Orders were issued: If the armored cars advanced in the direction of the settlement, the men were not to fire or reveal the ambush; when the cars had passed, the men were to attack the infantry with hand grenades. The ambush party, however, was pinned down by heavy fire, and was unable to follow the enemy's movements. Shells began to explode in the area around them. The three-inch mortar placed on Yellow Hill fired some shells which landed in between the advancing armored cars. Fire was now opened up on the cars from Kfar Etzion. They lurched off the road and were unable to advance. About one hundred and twenty yards separated the ambush party from the armored cars, but the squad was unable to fulfill its mission.

Tsvi Glazer was wounded, and Dov L. was dispatched to Kfar Etzion for further orders but, owing to the heavy fire, was unable to return. Before noon Aryei Kl. was wounded by a mortar shell which exploded only about two feet from him. He was knocked down by the concussion, and sprayed with splinters. He was in severe pain and covered with blood. Nahum Z. and Aryei H.Z. dressed his wounds and the latter went to Kfar Etzion to bring a stretcher but was also unable to get back. Nahum took Aryei on his back and carried him to Kfar Etzion. The journey took two hours.

The ambush party remained in the field. It did not suffer any other casualties.

The Battle in the Monastery and on Russian Hill

From the accounts of Field Force soldiers—May 12

Twenty-eight men under the command of Tsvi B.Y. were stationed in the Russian Monastery, and twelve men on

Russian Hill, under the command of Rafi N. They were armed with one Spandau machine gun, three Bren-guns, one two-inch mortar, an anti-tank rifle, rifles, sub-machine guns, and grenades.

On the night of May 11, Tsvi B.Y. sat with us and played a number of tunes he had composed on an accordion. He repeated one of his latest melodies several times. I went out for my regular spell of guard duty. A thick mist covered the entire neighborhood. It was very quiet but I had a premonition of evil. At five that afternoon, a number of enemy armored vehicles had concentrated on a hill on the other side of the main road. The three-inch mortar opened fire on them and scored several direct hits. The enemy, however, had not replied.

When my watch was over I lay down to sleep. At about one in the morning we were ordered to get dressed and go out to the defense positions. The Observation Post had reported suspicious movements around the Monastery and cries in Arabic. Within two minutes the entire force had taken up positions. After half-an-hour of tension, our nerves already frayed waiting for the shooting to begin, we were told to go back to our rooms.

The Monastery was surrounded by a ring of defense posts. The mortar was placed south of the building. To the east, facing the road, there was a defense post equipped with a Bren-gun. On the north there were two trenches commanding the woods that cover the area down to the cisterns near the main road and the feeder road of the Bloc. Both of these positions were equipped with Bren-guns and rifles. The western post, facing Russian Hill, was also manned. There was a wide ditch in a northwesterly direction that connected the Monastery with the outpost on Russian Hill. Near the southern section of the Monastery fence, facing the main road, there was a dugout where a Spandau was placed. Two breaches had been made in the stone wall for snipers to operate against enemy infantry.

At five in the morning heavy firing began. We rushed to our positions. I and four others ran to the post overlooking the road. A few days before we had dug a bunker and hoped that it would be able to withstand a bombardment. We had a Bren-gun, two rifles, and two Sten-guns.

The shelling was very heavy. Every time I heard the whine of a shell overhead I thought, "This one is going to get me!" But the shells exploded several yards behind us. The sound of firing and the explosion of shells were punctuated by bugle calls from the road, where the enemy transport was parked. We appreciated that this time we had to deal with regular troops of the Arab Legion. We decided to hold our fire until the assault began.

Above the noise of the battle we heard orders being given in Hebrew: "Forward! Leave the wounded by the roadside!" For a moment we thought that our men were coming up, but straightaway saw through the enemy's trick.

Then the first assault began. Our Bren-gun opened up. I stood up to observe from where the enemy was firing when two ear-splitting explosions followed one another in quick succession. I saw that the bunker had collapsed. Two shells had come in through the embrasures and had destroyed it. Miraculously no one had been killed, but two of us were wounded. The Bren-gunner had been wounded in the head by splinters. Apparently he was shell shocked because he began to run for the Monastery. His "Number

Two" was hit in the hand, and had his wound bandaged on the spot. The Bren-gun was knocked out. The attackers came quite close to our position, and we began to throw hand grenades. Our situation was desperate. We waited for orders from Tsvi B.Y., but the telephone lines were cut and the entire intervening area between our position and the Monastery was being peppered with shells and fire. It is difficult to describe the fateful moments when our lives hung by a hair and we had only a few grenades left. My Sten-gun was jammed and I had no time to fix it.

The fellow with me went out to the Command Post to find out what we should do. A few minutes later he returned, breathless, and shouted: "Let's get out of here, the Arabs are already in our positions!" We retreated without delay. Apparently the Arabs thought that there was no one left alive in our post. As we were leaving we saw the Arabs under the terrace of the bunker. They were Legionaries wearing steel helmets and armed with sub-machine guns and knives. They were caught by surprise at our appearance but recovered immediately to give us a heavy dose of fire from the rear. The path, however, was lined with poles which gave us protection and so we managed to get by the building and to reach our men who were waiting by one of the terraces in front of the Monastery. As we passed the mortar position we called to Yehuda Feist, who was in charge of it, to retreat, but he did not budge. Apparently he did not believe that we were retreating and wanted to get the order from our commander. He was killed by the Arabs, as was Shimon G. the first-aid man, who remained behind in the Monastery.

Tsvi B.Y. gave orders to withdraw slowly and to fight from terrace to terrace. But the men were no longer in a state to understand his orders. We were behind the last terrace, in front of the entrance to the Monastery, when Mosh appeared. He had already been wounded in the head, but he paid no attention to the wound and ordered us to carry on the fight. He hurried away in the direction from which Tsvi and the Spandau crew were to come, intending to return with them to the Monastery. . . .—ELIMELEKH B.

From the account of a Squad Commander—May 12

Yitzhak W., a Squad Commander, who was in the Spandau post on the south fence of the Monastery recalls:

"We were a squad of five men, stationed at the southern fence about one hundred and fifty yards from the Monastery. We covered the Valley of Brakha and the main road, with effective fire. For weapons we had the Spandau with twenty-four hundred rounds, sub-machine guns and rifles.

"At about half-past-five we heard bugle calls from the direction of the main road. Immediately afterwards I observed eight platoons of infantry advancing towards us in military order, and accompanied by bugle calls. About two hundred and fifty yards from our position they entered a dead area and we lost sight of them. When we saw them again they were only one hundred and fifty yards away. We could see three platoons of the Legion, and five of the Arab Liberation Army quite clearly. Their rear was brought up by an armed Arab rabble. Then someone in an officer's uniform emerged from their ranks and began to address them. When he finished we heard the bugle sound the attack. The platoons deployed in squads. As they charged I ordered my men to open fire with the machine gun. When we had finished three belts (one hundred and fifty rounds) we stopped firing, and then emptied another belt into that human mass.

It was a terrible sight. Most of the men in the front rank lay on the ground dead or wounded. The rest fled in disorder towards the road. A few tried to find cover in a gully at the foot of the hill, and ran into a mine field. The assault had been broken. Nahum F. lay on the ground near a breach in the fence and began to snipe at the retreating Arabs. He was joined by David Sh. who took up position beside him.

"After an interval of about half-an-hour the enemy began a heavy bombardment of our position, using three-inch mortars, two-pound and twenty-five pound guns. Shells and bullets covered the earth around us. We decided to withdraw to our secondary position, about thirty yards in the rear, giving each other cover. This position was concealed among the trees, and we waited for a renewal of the enemy's assault. A runner brought us ammunition and told us that on both sides of the Monastery a hand-to-hand fight was in progress. The enemy had learned a lesson from the previous attempt to rush our position and now advanced in squads formation from different directions. All the time we could hear bugle calls. The Arab heavy machine guns worked without a pause. When the enemy entered the dead area the artillery began to fire smoke shells, to conceal their advance. The sound of firing mingled with cries of *'Aleihum!'* The Spandau and our rifles again opened up and mowed them down without mercy. The second assault was also beaten back. We had suffered no casualties.

"After a lull in the firing a runner came with orders from Tsvi B.Y. to retreat. I did not understand the reason, for up to then we had had the upper hand. I called out to Nahum F., who was lying near the breach in the fence, to retreat but received no reply. I figured that he had been wounded or killed. Giving each other cover we got back to the barbed-wire fence. On our way we came across five Legionaries with a Bren-gun, opened fire upon them, and hit some of them. We heard a number of shots from the two-inch mortar position. I saw Legionaries fire at the position and kill Yehuda Feist who did not want to leave his post and retreat with us. We joined our men who had taken up position along the stone fence and were sniping at the enemy trying to get into the Monastery. I mounted the machine gun on the fence but it was out of order and only fired single rounds. We saw Mosh's tall figure. He ran in and out among the men, encouraging them. After a few minutes he was hit in the head, but it was not a serious wound and the first-aid man dressed it for him. Then once again he went from man to man urging, 'No retreat!' "—YITZHAK W. (As recorded in the diary of Uriel O.)

From the account of a Field Force soldier (Continued)—May 12

Suddenly Mosh ordered us to fall back on the ditch in the rear. He had observed tanks advancing upon our position and was afraid that our last line of retreat would be cut off. We took our arms and began to crawl along the ditch. Large rocks impeded our progress. Just then heavy machine gun fire was opened up on us. The Arabs had placed a heavy machine gun on the balcony of the Monastery. Our losses were heavy and from all along the ditch we could hear cries for help. One soldier whose knee had been shattered kept crying out: "Don't leave me! I want to live!" Nahum F. dragged him along as far as he could and then was forced to leave him where he lay, promising, "Soon the stretcher bearers will come along." Tsvi B.Y. came up, carrying a Tommy gun in one hand and a two-inch mortar in the other. He tried to get past the exposed stretch but a boulder blocked the ditch. He lifted his leg and immediately was wounded in the hip and the blood gushed out. Moshe K., the medical orderly, tried to stanch the flow but it was useless. The men near Tsvi said his last words were two lines from the song, "Immortal Soldier," which he had composed: "If I should fall in battle, comrade, take my rifle and avenge me."

Time was pressing and we continued to fall back. Mosh was at the other end of the ditch, covering our retreat. He wanted to get the men together in the strongpoint on the other side, but he was hit again by a bullet and fell in the ditch. This time the wound was fatal. He did manage, however, to move to one side so as not to hinder the passage of the others.

Shmuel M., a squad leader not yet seventeen years old, covered our retreat until he was hit in the hand. "Itzik" W. mounted his Bren-gun and prevented the Arabs from entering the ditch. A number of them were killed. Me'ir S. ran with his Bren to a forward position. Yosef G., the mortar man, kept sniping with a Canadian rifle, until he fell wounded in the stomach. Ovadia H. was wounded in the head as he was trying to get Yosef out of the position. The fight in the ditch lasted about half-an-hour.

Only I and two other men succeeded in crawling to the end of the ditch. From time to time the Arabs fired smoke bombs which blinded us. During the retreat something happened that shocked me to the core. I was lying at the bottom of the ditch when I felt someone crawling behind me. It was David Sh., who throughout had fought like a hero, encouraging the others all the time. He was groping his way blindly. "What's the matter, David?" I asked him. "I can't see a thing," he answered. He caught up with me and lay on top of me.

When we got to the end of the ditch we joined a number of other men who were retreating and helped some of the wounded along. We also succeeded in taking some of our weapons. We were unable to do anything for those who were seriously wounded.

We intended getting to Kfar Etzion down the slope of the hill, but we noticed a number of Arabs trying unsuccessfully to advance through the fig orchard, towards the eastern fence of the village. Kfar Etzion was being blasted without respite. Heavy fire was opened up on us once again and we made our way across the dead area to the air strip. We rapidly crossed the strip, from which armored vehicles were shelling the village, and slid down into the valley which lies between Yellow Hill and Massuot Yitzhak. We were completely exhausted when we got to Massuot.—ELIMELEKH B.

At Hirbet Sawir

From the account of a settler of Ein Tsurim—May 12

There were eighteen of us at Hirbet Sawir on the night of May 11. In addition to personal arms—rifles, Sten-guns, and grenades—we had one Spandau machine gun, one Bren and a two-inch mortar. At 4:50 in the morning we observed a long armored column traveling northward on the Jerusalem-Hebron road. We immediately took up positions. Within a few minutes the column had split up, the larger section turning in toward the Monastery and the Mukhtar's Saddle, while three tanks came straight at us, then halted in the dead area, about four hundred to six hundred yards away.

When the assault on the Monastery was launched we opened fire with the machine guns in the direction of the cisterns and the internal road—the only area leading to the Monastery which had not been cut by the enemy—so as to give flank cover to the garrison and to pin down the attacking force. The tanks then began shelling our strongpoint systematically and very precisely.

Contact was maintained with the Bloc by field telephone. As soon as we went into action we informed Lone Tree Hill and Yellow Hill of the situation and tried to find out if there were any prospects of our being reinforced. The telephone lines, however, were cut by the very first shells, and the operator who went out to examine the damage was slightly wounded. Sometime afterward we were reinforced by a squad that was sent from Lone Tree Hill.

The shelling became heavier. Meanwhile we could see the enemy infantry, consisting of several companies of Legionaries and a large number of irregulars, deploying for the attack. The enemy advanced in waves, under cover of heavy mortar, artillery, and machine gun fire. The attackers were repulsed by heavy counter fire from our machine guns, rifles, and Sten-guns. After these unsuccessful attempts the Arabs called up their tanks for support. We had no anti-tank weapons, not even Molotov cocktails. The tanks advanced to about one hundred yards away and covered us with heavy fire. Thanks to the communication trenches the number of men hit during the shelling was small. Adi A., commanding the strongpoint, was killed outright by a bullet in the head. Then Moshe S. was hit in the chest by a two-pound shell. The tanks made a sudden flanking movement and took up positions between ourselves and Lone Tree Hill, to cut off our line of retreat. The pin of the mortar broke and the

Spandau ceased to operate. The infantry renewed their advance. At half-past nine, in keeping with our orders, we decided to fall back.

We withdrew under cover of the Bren placed upon one of the stone fences. The men crawled successfully to Lone Tree Hill with all their arms, by way of the wadi to the north. We could not remove the two bodies because every moment was vital. Then we saw Hirbet Sawir blacken with the advancing hordes.—TSVI S.

On Lone Tree Hill

From the account of a Field Force officer—May 12

Lone Tree Hill was held by a Field Force squad armed with a Piat, a Breda machine gun, a two-inch mortar, and rifles. Early in the morning Mordekhai D., the Deputy Company Commander, inspected the position and weapons and told the men to stand to. He went on to Hirbet Sawir. By the time he returned the battle for Lone Tree Hill was raging. This is how he described the decisive hours of the strongpoints afterward:

"Tsarfati came up and asked for more ammunition for Sawir. We could see an armored car making its way up between Sawir and Lone Tree Hill, with the intention of cutting the strongpoints off from each other. I told Tsarfati to run back to Sawir and to order them to fall back immediately. Soon the squad that had been holding Sawir reached us. I sent some of the men on to Hirbet Zakaria, others to Yellow Hill, and ordered the latter to take up defensive positions along the perimeter of that hill. The last men to reach us took up positions on our hill. I was planning to fight a delaying action for as long as possible, in order to delay the cutting of the Bloc in two; we were aware that the battle was over in the Monastery.

"While I was still making my plans, I observed wave upon wave of the Arab bands coming down the slope from Sawir in our direction. Our position was being heavily shelled throughout and subjected to heavy machine gun and rifle fire. The hut was burning and, if we moved at all, it was in a crawling position. But all along we returned the fire and sniped at the Arabs coming down from Sawir. Meanwhile armored vehicles were coming straight at us. We opened fire with the two-inch mortar but it was not in good working order. The Breda machine gun was also out of action for some time. The dugout was the only position which continued to operate effectively throughout the action.

"Suddenly I was told that armored cars and a tank were coming up from the feeder road. As soon as I observed the swaying radio antenna emerging from the dead area I ordered a retreat to the dugout and to a rear position. I sent a number of men to take the Breda and the Piat to the other side. The Piat's first shell landed about five yards in front of the armored car; the second also missed, and with the third it broke down. After a short spell of confusion the retreat began. Shmuel B. was the last to leave. Suddenly I noticed a long column of men following him. 'Who are they?' I wondered. Then I saw their white *keffiyehs*. They were Arabs following us at a distance of no more than thirty yards.

"When we were together again I ordered the men to fall back on Yellow Hill. Ezra S., the machine gunner, remained behind to cover our retreat and was killed. Tsvi S. reached Yellow Hill and shouted to me, 'Motke, there is no one here!' I cursed the whole world in my heart and replied:

'Impossible! Have another look!' But when I reached the hill with the rest of the men I saw that he was right. The men gathered around me, discouraged. 'Fellows,' I muttered, 'things are in a bad way! Let's take whatever we can with us and retreat to Revadim!'

"As we were going down into the wadi we saw the Legion's armor already on Lone Tree Hill. After an hour or so we reached Revadim, broken and exhausted."—MORDEKHAI D. (As recorded in the diary of Uriel O.)

On Yellow Hill

From the account of the Yellow Hill Commander—May 12

Yellow Hill was regarded as the central point of the Bloc and dominated the nearby air strip. The telephone exchange of the Bloc and the Command Post of the Field Force were located there. Because of its commanding position overlooking a section of the main road and the nearby hills, the three-inch mortar had been placed on it. The strongpoint comprised a complex of defense posts and deep communication trenches.

During the morning of May 12, when the attack began, the reserve force stationed on the hill was dispatched to the outlying strongpoints. One Piat was transferred to Kfar Etzion, the other to Lone Tree Hill, and the anti-tank rifle to the Monastery. In the strongpoint there were the three men of the mortar crew, about twelve girls engaged in communication and administrative work, and a number of injured men who were on their way to recovery and had returned to limited duty. Arms included one Browning with a small quantity of ammunition, three rifles, and two submachine guns.

At first regular telephone communication was maintained with the Bloc Command in Kfar Etzion and with the various sectors. At 6:00 A.M. the line with Kfar Etzion was cut and we kept in contact by runners. Mosh, before leaving Kfar Etzion for the Monastery, sent his instructions to the picket on the strongpoint and to the mortar crew.

In all we had no more than sixty shells for the three-inch mortar. During the morning it operated very effectively against the enemy vehicles on the Mukhtar's Saddle, against transport on the road, and later against the Arabs occupying the Monastery. Our supply of shells, however, dwindled rapidly and soon we had no more than ten left.

When we saw enemy armor advancing on Lone Tree Hill and a group of men falling back from the hill upon Hirbet Zakaria, we decided that in view of our small numbers there was nothing we could do but to follow suit. We destroyed the telephone exchange and hid whatever arms and ammunition we could not take with us in a ditch. The first to leave were the girls, with the mortar, the remaining shells, and the ammunition. They were followed by the wounded, with the mortar crew taking up the rear. As we were making our way to Hirbet Zakaria, Avraham B. was hit in the head by a bullet and was killed instantaneously.

Weary and discouraged we reached Hirbet Zakaria.—MOSHE B.

18 The Battle of Kfar Etzion —May 12

The capture of the eastern outposts by the enemy between 10:00 and 11:00 A.M. *cut the Bloc into three: Kfar Etzion and Massuot Yitzhak, with virtually no link between the two settlements, and the northern sector—Ein Tsurim, Revadim and Hirbet Zakaria. The air strip was dominated by the Arabs and there was no longer any prospect of landing reinforcements or supplies.*

The brunt of the attack was now directed against Kfar Etzion and, this time, unlike previous attacks, the village's defense posts, constructed in a wide circle round the crest of the hill, were attacked simultaneously. The difficulty of defending the settlement, whose rocky soil had not allowed for the digging of communication trenches of proper depth, was soon apparent.

The other three settlements and Hirbet Zakaria were not directly assaulted by the enemy. They were, however, attacked by harassing fire and were unable to join in the fighting raging about Kfar Etzion. Only a small picket which had been stationed in the early morning on Rock Hill, consisting of settlers from Massuot Yitzhak, was in a position to block the enemy's advance.

Now it became obvious what the death of Mosh meant. The battle had taken a fateful turn, and there was no longer a central command—an eventuality which, apparently, had not been foreseen. The cutting off of the strongpoints and settlements and the shock of the enemy armor, artillery and mortar fire undermined the Bloc's powers of resistance.

From the accounts of members of Kfar Etzion—May 12

At five in the morning, when the assault on the Mukhtar's Saddle, the Monastery, and Hirbet Sawir was launched, the alert was sounded and the men hurried to their positions. Soon a heavy shelling of the village had begun, and the Striking Force proceeded to the Saddle. Shortly afterwards the wounded and the men who had been fortifying the Saddle returned to the village. Reports were dispatched to Headquarters in Tel Aviv and Jerusalem on the attack and the strength of enemy armor. Sometime afterwards telephone communication with the strongpoints, the other settlements, and between the village's positions was cut, and a system of runners was established.

The Palmah detachment arrived from Massuot Yitzhak and remained in reserve near the hospital. When it was learned that the various strongpoints had fallen, they were distributed among the village's defense posts. The first men to retreat from the Monastery succeeded in reaching the village by way of Wadi Shahid and the fig orchard. The wounded were accommodated in the shelter and the hospital and those who were unhurt went to the defense posts.

Posts Seven and Eight operated against the enemy forces that had taken up positions on the Saddle and they were reinforced by a machine gun that was placed on the straw shed and the Schwartzlause that had been mounted near Nveh Ovadia. During the morning, while the armored cars were advancing from the Saddle towards the village, a Piat squad was sent out to these positions to halt them. But its men were caught in enemy fire before they reached their objective. Azriel S. was killed here.

At 9:30 A.M. David B.D., in charge of sappers, was called to the Command Post and ordered to distribute Molotov cocktails to the northern defense positions which were threatened by enemy armor. Me'ir F., who was in command of the northern section, transferred the Piat which had been stranded on the southern section to the positions facing the gate. David D. was charged with exploding the electric anti-tank mine when the enemy armor approached.

After we had learned of Mosh's death, Ya'akov A., his deputy, directed the battle operations in Kfar Etzion and in those parts of the Bloc with which there was still contact. He was assisted by Aryei H.Z., in command of the "Airborne Platoon."

Notwithstanding the intensive fire, the men in the defense posts conducted themselves well, holding their fire until ordered to open up. They were worn out by their constant guard duty, hungry, and thirsty. During the day it was impossible to get food to the positions. The pump house had been hit and there was no water in the pipes. But all doubts about the ability of the Bloc to hold its own were cast aside. They were determined to fight as long as they could, and, if possible, to keep the enemy at bay until the State was proclaimed. Then they hoped to be reinforced.

After the strongpoints to the east and north had been occupied, the enemy tried to come down from Russian Hill into the village through the fig orchard. This sector was the weak link in the defenses of the village, because most of its gentle gradient was a dead area for the men in the positions. The avenue of approach for the armor was the air strip. Time and again the armored vehicles succeeded in coming up close to the farmyard from this leveled-off stretch of ground. The Arabs also made good use of the concealed wadi on the southwest, for the redeployment of their men, and tried to assault the settlement from this direction.

When the bombardment became heavier the men took shelter in the trenches near their positions, but later they were compelled to remain at their posts. They had to use their ammunition sparingly and opened fire only when the Arabs were within close range. The Arabs were being constantly reinforced and replacements for the attacking force and the armor came up repeatedly.

After ten o'clock, two runners were dispatched to Massuot Yitzhak to ask the commander of the settlement to send reinforcements to Rock Hill. Akiva L., one of the runners, returned to Rock Hill, bringing with him arms and ammunition for the picket stationed there.

Meanwhile the attack was mounting in intensity. The enemy had stationed men in each of the occupied strongpoints and continued to pound the village. Between 11:00 A.M. and 2:00 P.M. a series of messages were dispatched describing the situation.

> We are being severely shelled. Our situation is very bad. Every moment is vital. Send planes without delay.

> We are in a ring which is becoming tighter. All Arab villages of the neighborhood are participating in the attack. Send planes.

> The enemy has occupied the Monastery and all other strongpoints. About two thousand Arabs are taking part in the attack. Twenty heavy armored vehicles are advancing upon us. We have no weapons to use against them. We have many killed, including Mosh. Our situation is desperate. No planes have come so far.

The number of wounded is growing. Could you get in touch with the Red Cross? Send help. The shelling is very heavy.

At 2:30 P.M. a signal was received from Jerusalem:

To: Massuot, Ein Tsurim, and Revadim.

Massuot, Revadim, and Ein Tsurim must organize a force for a flanking attack. Try to break the ring of encirclement and re-establish contact with Kfar Etzion.

It seems that Headquarters was unaware of the entire course of the battle. It did not know that in view of the strength of the enemy in the center of the Bloc it would be most difficult to establish contact between the various sectors, so as to recapture the strongpoints that had been occupied.

There was very little that the garrisons of the other settlements and Hirbet Zakaria could do to relieve the pressure on Kfar Etzion. The surrounding hills prevented them from observing the enemy's movements and what was happening around the village. Several Arab armored cars had taken up positions on Lone Tree Hill, commanding the internal road, and kept the forces in the northern sector pinned down. The three-inch mortar was dispatched to Ein Tsurim to operate against these vehicles, but it broke down after it had fired a number of shells.

Messages were sent to Jerusalem, stressing the urgency of the situation and appealing for evacuation.

From the accounts of members of Kfar Etzion (Continued)—May 12

Between two and five in the afternoon the shelling of Kfar Etzion died down, perhaps because the enemy was regrouping. Only sniper fire continued to harass the village.

The defenders made good use of the lull to restock the ammunition stores of the positions. Me'ir F. and David B.D. then volunteered to infiltrate into the fig orchard and to search for the anti-tank rifle that had been abandoned there by some of the men who had retreated from the Monastery. They could not find the rifle and were compelled to return when the enemy discovered their movements and opened up with heavy fire on them.

In the shattered dining hall Eliezer M. issued rations of water and food to the runners who had come in from the positions.

At 5:00 P.M. another spell of heavy shelling began. Several armored vehicles advanced upon the village from the direction of the air strip. Shimon S., of the Field Force, who was in the observation post near the gate, reported that tanks were approaching. The Piat in the defense position by the gate was got ready for action but the armored vehicles did not come within range. The enemy observed the men of the position as they were taking the Piat back, and blasted them with mortars and machine guns. David B.D. was hit and sent to the hospital.

The men heard a steady drone. At first they thought it was the sound of the motors of the armored cars, but it turned out that a plane was circling over the Bloc. The Arabs kept shooting at it.

From the account of a Squad Commander—May 12

Shortly before 5:00 P.M. an armored column was observed coming up from the air strip towards the Kfar Etzion road. The column consisted of three tanks, one Palmah armored car, and an Egged bus (the last two had been taken as booty at Nebi Daniel). The column advanced slowly, preceded by two Legionaries with mine detectors. Two platoons of the Legion's infantry took up the rear of the armor.

When the column was about two hundred and fifty yards from Rock Hill, the squad stationed there opened fire. The sudden rapid spurt of fire scattered the Arabs, who retreated to Lone Tree Hill. As they fell back they destroyed the bulldozer parked by the air strip, and a small plane.—YITZHAK W. (As recorded in the diary of Uriel O.)

On Rock Hill

From the account of the Commander of the Rock Hill position—May 12

At 6:00 A.M. I got orders from the Settlement Commander of Massuot Yitzhak to occupy Rock Hill, which commands the road entering Massuot and Kfar Etzion. There were thirteen men in the unit I commanded: five riflemen, two men armed with Stens, two members of the Breda machine gun crew, three of the two-inch mortar crew. I was armed with a Tommy gun.

When we arrived I saw that the enemy had captured the Mukhtar's Saddle and was getting ready to storm Kfar Etzion. Three armored vehicles carrying mounted guns tried to advance along the road leading to Kfar Etzion from the Saddle. They were followed by infantry, whom they shielded from Kfar Etzion's fire. The infantry, however, was exposed to us, and I ordered my men to creep up as close as possible to the edge of the strongpoint. Then I ordered the machine gun to open fire at eight hundred and fifty yards. The advance was held up, two of the vehicles slipping off the road and getting stuck, and blocking the way of the third.

Immediately afterwards we were reinforced by another detachment of settlers from Massuot.

Meanwhile I noticed two armored vehicles with mounted guns on Russian Hill and two others between Hirbet Sawir and Lone Tree Hill. Other armored vehicles were moving along the feeder road of the Bloc. The road leading to Massuot Yitzhak and Kfar Etzion seemed to be seriously threatened. We decided, therefore, to establish a position behind the rocks overlooking the fork in the road, thereby covering the flying strip with enfilading fire. We placed the Breda, the Spandau which Yitzhak W. had brought with him from Russian Hill, the two-inch mortar, and four riflemen among the rocks. The remaining men took up positions facing Kfar Etzion's fig orchard.

Armored vehicles, including an armored Egged bus, began to move along the air strip towards the fork in the road. When they were about four hundred yards away I ordered our men to open fire with everything we had. The Legionaries turned about and retreated. Several times they tried to come closer but our fire and the psychological effect of the mortar was too much for them. The machine gun fire which the enemy aimed at us was not very effective, for they did not know exactly where we were.—SHMUEL L.

From the account of a settler of Massuot Yitzhak stationed on Rock Hill—May 12

During the afternoon we succeeded in repulsing a number of attacks on Kfar Etzion by the armored vehicles, though our only "heavy" weapons were a two-inch mortar, the Spandau, and an Italian machine gun. Despite the fact that the sights were broken, the mortar kept up a rapid fire. Avraham B. and Moshe P. did fine work. I was the look-out.

"Range four hundred meters. Almost on the mark! The range is good, a little to the right!"

Then the enemy emplaced a heavy mortar behind the second armored car. "Range four hundred and fifty yards. Fire!" I called out.

The shell began its journey, with a shrill screech. I watched it with an aching heart. Then its trajectory was broken and it began to drop. It exploded and a cloud of smoke rose from behind the second armored car. The shell had done its work well. The mortar and the Legionaries who had served it were incapable of further action.

The riflemen did nice work too. Their rifle barrels were hot, their shoulders were sore, their hands sweated, but they kept up the good work. "Boys, aim at the wheels, at the loopholes! Let them come close to the edge of the field! Fire!" the voice of Shmuel L. thundered.

They had already begun their retreat. The Legion armored cars and their crews were running away from rifle fire!—ELAZAR I.

From the accounts of members of Kfar Etzion (Continued)—May 12

Just before evening the following message was sent from Kfar Etzion to Jerusalem Headquarters:

> Heavy shelling has been resumed. Send planes immediately. In the strongpoints captured by the enemy, everything has been destroyed. A large number of automatic weapons have been lost. Ammunition running low. You must bring up as much arms and ammunition as you can, especially anti-tank mines. Reinforcements absolutely essential. Propose that you risk several vehicles and send men tonight. Try and work quickly. Inform us of prospects.

During the day most of the buildings of the village had been badly damaged, including the dining hall, the kitchen, the pump house and the hospital. Nveh Ovadia, which stood out in the middle of the village, was very badly knocked about. There were huge shell holes in the walls and the roof had almost collapsed. The German Monastery building, where the Command Post, radio station, and shelter were located, had also suffered a number of direct hits. Fire broke out in the evening in the straw shed and the metal workshop.

The fighting of the day showed that, generally speaking, most of the positions had stood up to the attack, notwithstanding the large number of direct hits they had suffered. Despite the fact that the communication trenches were not deep enough and that there were stretches where there were no trenches at all—forcing the runners to expose themselves—the number of casualties was comparatively small.

In the Command Post

From "A Report on the Final Battle of Kfar Etzion"—May 12

The Command Post, radio station, and shelter had been located in the large chamber of the store of the German Monastery, from which a door led to the wood. The building had been badly battered. Several direct hits had been scored upon its thick walls but it still held. Shells and bullets penetrated through the window, and Ya'akov and his aides had to take cover from time to time.

Avraham F. was on the Saddle with the ambush party and Ya'akov alone conducted the defense of the village.

After a two-inch mortar had been put out of action, the crew—Aharon Y., Ya'akov Z., and Yosef Z.—were stationed in the Command Post and served as runners. In addition there were Yosef B., the sapper, Aryei H.Z., a number of men of the "Airborne Platoon" who had withdrawn from the Saddle, and drivers of the Nebi Daniel convoy. They served as a reserve force and undertook various missions during the day. . . .

The radio operators, Ben Zion G., Shlomo R., Hadassah N., and Aliza F., worked in the storeroom. They remained calm throughout and maintained contact with Staff and Regional Headquarters, sitting on the steps of the bunker. Later they went down to the cellar to operate their sets, because of the interruptions. Several times they climbed onto the roof, despite the fierce enemy fire, to repair the antenna. Whenever it grew quiet they went upstairs to carry on their work.

They kept busy throughout the day and relieved each other from time to time. It was an arduous job on the steps of the bunker, watched by dozens of anxious eyes. Each one of us tried to guess from their faces the content of the radio messages being transmitted and received. But they never lost their composure.

Towards evening Rahel W. and Rahel Z. were sent to the kitchen to prepare food for the defense posts and for the people in the cellar. In the Command Post, Ya'akov, who was already exhausted, sat on the bed briefing Shmuel B. of the Palmah on a proposed attack on the Arab armor stranded on the Saddle.

Then Yehoshua S., who was in command of Post Seven,

came in and asked for help to extinguish the fire in the straw shed and to bring water. He reported that the enemy vehicles on the Saddle were on the move again. The attack was called off. Avraham S. who came into the Command Post was ordered to bring the Striking Squad back to the village.

Shmuel A., Shalom G. and Tsvi T. entered the Post to talk to Ya'akov. Later they told me that they had asked Ya'akov to contact leaders of the Yishuv and to inform them of the seriousness of our position. Ya'akov had replied that in the morning he had asked Headquarters to get in touch with the Red Cross in order to evacuate the Bloc but that he had received no reply. He added that it is useless to talk about negotiations with the Arabs as he did not believe in surrendering to them. "We have no alternative but to fight to the last," he said.—SHA'UL R.

Ya'akov continued to give orders with his usual composure. From time to time, however, the lines on his forehead and around his eyes testified to his mood and the strain to which he was subjected. Listening to him give his orders you would have never realized that for months he had been convinced our situation was hopeless. He knew what we had to expect. His smile and the jokes that he allowed himself from time to time were deceptive. But a close look at his eyes, inflamed as they were by lack of sleep and deprived of all hope, revealed how much effort and courage were necessary in order to conceal his true despair. He knew all along that Kfar Etzion could not possibly hold out under such conditions. But having accepted the task, it was our duty to carry it through to the bitter end.—DAVID B.D.

In the Shelter

From the diary of a wounded member of Kfar Etzion—May 12

As soon as I heard the alarm bell in the early morning, I hurriedly put on some clothes and rushed to the cellar in the German Monastery to which the wounded had been posted. Within a short time the place was filled with those other wounded who were able to arrive unassisted, and with those girls who were not on duty. From time to time stretchers came in, bringing the wounded who had been transferred from the hospital. We crowded together to make more room for those who were badly hurt. Soon the cellar was packed.

The hours passed slowly and a deep depression settled like a pall over all of us. We were completely ignorant of what was happening outside, in the defense posts, and the strategic positions. Only the dull crack of rifle shots and the boom of artillery came to our ears.

Then the wounded began to come in from the Russian Monastery, gloomy and dispirited. From them we learned something of the progress of the battle. We heard of the death of a number of our comrades and of Mosh. Our depression deepened.

During the morning, Rafi N., who had commanded the Russian Hill post and who had succeeded in withdrawing, was brought in, wounded in the head. The nurses dressed his wound carefully and laid him on some blankets to rest, for he was weak from loss of blood. He protested staunchly that he had to go out again to one of the positions. It was only with difficulty that the girls persuaded him to lie down. After some time, one of the girls suddenly asked, "Where is Rafi"? They searched in the cellar of the German Monastery and in the rooms above, but he was gone. Unnoticed he had taken a rifle and slipped out. I never saw him again.

Hunger began to oppress us. We had eaten nothing since the previous evening. The hours dragged slowly by, filled with gloomy thoughts. A heavy bombardment was destroying the settlement, the construction of which had cost us so much effort. Would we ever be able to build it up again?

I recalled two fateful meetings, with far-reaching consequences, which had been held in the *kvutza.*

The first had taken place in the winter of 1943 in the dining hall of Kvutzat Avraham, at our preparatory labor camp near Kfar Pines. We were discussing the Jewish Agency proposal that we settle at Kfar Etzion. Members got up and warned us against accepting the proposal. Our settlement would be in the heart of the perilous Hebron district. Could we hope to overcome the dangers that would threaten us?

Then Shalom K. took the floor to refute these arguments. The settlement of Kfar Etzion was an historic mission, he declared. It would constitute a reply to the catastrophe that had engulfed our people in Europe. We must not hesitate to undertake the task, he urged, despite all the perils involved. The other *haverim* were infected with his enthusiasm and they voted to accept the proposal. We were to settle at Kfar Etzion.

Five years later. The United Nations had voted on the establishment of a Jewish State and the Arab disturbances had begun. The members of the *kvutza* had gathered in Nveh Ovadiah, our cultural center, to discuss the defense of our village. Once again the more cautious members of the group spoke soberly, sensibly. There was no longer any prospect of developing our settlement, they declared. Our decision to remain must be guided solely by military considerations. We must take advantage of the proposal advanced by the Zionist colonization authorities to rebuild our settlement elsewhere in the country. But other *haverim* protested vehemently. They would not discuss any suggestion that contemplated evacuation. The words of Shlomo R. echoed in my ears: "I was among the first to come here," he said. "I will not be among the first to leave." Now he was sitting at the transmitter, appealing to Jerusalem for help. Had not some cruel logic confuted that rock-like faith?

I recalled another occasion upon which we had met—on Rosh HaShana, 5708 (1947). Our *haverim* together with the guests of the rest resort, had assembled in the large hall of Nveh Ovadia, for the *Mussaf* Service. The worshippers were in a solemn mood. The Reader stood in front of the Ark repeating the *Shmone Esrei.* Then suddenly the congregation grew silent and we heard the voice of Shalom K. chanting part of the prayer—a Hassidic melody which he had brought to the *kvutza* and had introduced into our Rosh HaShana service.

> And Thou shalt behold the sacrifice of Isaac,
> When Abraham, our father,
> Sacrificed his son on the altar.

The congregation took up Shalom's sorrowful melody, so suffused with religious devotion, and was swept up in his ardor, giving voice to a prayer that surged up from the heart.

A tremor passed through my body and a prayer came from the depths of my heart: "Not that, O God! Only not that! Let not this battleground be our altar!"

I began to think of other things. I recalled our wives and children in the Ratisbonne Monastery in Jerusalem. My heart went out to them. What were they thinking of in the halls of that Monastery, far away in the city? Did they have any idea of what was happening in this former German Monastery, in their own village?

I thought of the girls who had remained with us. Most of them were new immigrants, arrived in this country from concentration camps barely a year ago, hoping to find a haven, after years of homelessness and tragedy. Among them were a number who had begun to build up their homes again in our midst; others had been prevented from doing so by the outbreak of war. What would become of this pent-up treasure of love, of hope, of maternal tenderness, which shone in their eyes? Should not their merits insure our deliverance?

The arrival of Yosef B. and Aryei H.Z. broke the thread of my thoughts. Were there any wounded who felt able to replace some of the weary *haverim* at their posts? A number of men responded.

It was already dark. The darkness of the cellar was only slightly relieved by a small kerosene lamp. The air was very stuffy. Bread and sardines were brought from the dining hall and sandwiches and water were distributed. The wounded lay down and tried to sleep. I fell asleep. Suddenly Tsvi T. came in from the defense post, and turning to my neighbor said: "I would like to tell you what to do with my son, Menahem." Then he stopped himself and continued, "What am I talking about! Who can tell who will survive?" I was shocked. Had we come to such a pass?—Dov K.

From the accounts of members of Kfar Etzion (Continued)—May 12

After nightfall the shelling died down. The relative quiet was broken by the fire of snipers. The positions were instructed to prepare food and water for the next day. . . .

At half-past-seven in the evening, Moshe Y., the Settlement Commander of Massuot Yitzhak, arrived to discuss the next day's plans. He asked for the dispatch of anti-tank weapons and ammunition to Rock Hill. He also suggested that we attempt to retake Yellow Hill.

Ya'akov was opposed to the men of Massuot Yitzhak undertaking the assault, as he wanted to intrust it to the other sector of the Bloc, namely Revadim, Ein Tsurim, and the Hirbeh. The men of Massuot must strengthen the force holding Rock Hill as much as possible. It was resolved to transfer the wounded to Massuot; a squad from that settlement that had come to attack the armored vehicles was ordered to accompany them. Ya'akov told us that Jerusalem Headquarters had assured him that everything possible was being done for us.

The men of the Striking Squad, who had lain in ambush all day in the orchard near the Saddle, came back. They were unhurt. Tired and hungry they immediately took up positions together with the other defenders. Avraham F. made the rounds of the defense posts and gave orders for the night. Akiva G. distributed straw and kerosene in the defense positions and reported that a promise had been received from Headquarters that planes would bomb the enemy at night. When the order was given, the men were to light bonfires in the corners of the farmyard to enable the pilot to distinguish between our area and that of the Arabs.

During the night Avraham Sh. and Yosef B., the sappers,

discussed the laying of mines with David B.D. who was in the hospital. They planned to mine the areas where the enemy was expected to concentrate, and also the approaches to Kfar Etzion and Massuot Yitzhak. A section of sappers came from Massuot Yitzhak to help, and went out to lay the few anti-tank mines that were still left. Three mines were laid on the road near Rock Hill leading to the Lone Tree, and two others on the road leading to Massuot Yitzhak.

At midnight a message was received at Massuot Yitzhak from Ein Tsurim to the effect that in Jerusalem and Tel Aviv the possibility of evacuation was being discussed. Azriel R. was sent to ask for Ya'akov's opinion.

Ya'akov's reply was: "Kfar Etzion prefers to remain where it is, if it is possible to send reinforcements. If that is not possible then we agree to evacuation."

During the night Ya'akov A. and Alexander N. succeeded in contacting the Bloc's representative in Jerusalem. They informed him that Kfar Etzion had been heavily bombed and that many of the buildings had been destroyed. The situation was very serious and if substantial aid did not come from Tel Aviv by plane or otherwise, the fall of the village was inevitable.

The reply they received was that the General Staff in Tel Aviv had promised air support. Heavy planes would take action against the enemy during the early hours of Thursday morning, before the attack on Kfar Etzion was renewed.

During the night the following messages were sent:

> Situation in regard to men, arms and ammunition, grave. Do everything you can, tonight.

What about the contact with the Red Cross? We can't attend to the dead and wounded.

At that time General Staff Headquarters radioed Jerusalem as follows:

You must contact the Red Cross immediately and make arrangements for the evacuation of the wounded from Kfar Etzion. Inform us of the results.

Jerusalem replied:

We have transmitted the appeal to the Red Cross. We have contacted all possible authorities.

In Jerusalem During the Battle

From the accounts of members of Kfar Etzion in Jerusalem —May 12

There were two days to go before the British left the country. The High Commissioner, the Chief Secretary, and the General Officer Commanding British troops in Palestine had all packed up and were ready to go. Access to their offices was fraught with danger, even virtually impossible. The Jewish institutions in Jerusalem too were being transferred to Tel Aviv, the seat of the incipient Government. Most of the leaders of the Yishuv were no longer in Jerusalem, and only a number of officials remained. Between the latter and Tel Aviv only a tenuous link remained.

The military spheres of competence were also divided between Jerusalem and Tel Aviv. The command of military operations was in Jerusalem, but the authority to conduct negotiations with the enemy must come from Tel Aviv. The calls for help were addressed to Jerusalem, but the only

source from which aid could come, by air, was in Tel Aviv.
—SHLOMO H.

We learned of the battle at midday on Wednesday, May 12, and sensed that the situation was critical. We received no further news until evening. We were then informed that the fighting had stopped. In the middle of the night, purely by chance, a radio message from one of the settlements of the Bloc fell into our hands. It was full of despair and contained an appeal to save the men. The Regional Commander was not in Jerusalem. We went to the officer in charge at Headquarters and asked for immediate action in order to arrange a cease-fire and, if there was no other alternative, to surrender. We were told that the matter came under the authority of the General Staff in Tel Aviv. We were assured that Tel Aviv had been contacted and that we would be informed of the steps that were being taken.

But we were not satisfied. We appealed to Chief Rabbi Herzog to contact the Red Cross. Rabbi Herzog got into touch with Regional Headquarters and asked for permission to do so. He was given an answer similar to the one we had received. He was told that the General Staff was being contacted and that as soon as surrender was considered necessary they would inform us. We called upon Dr. Leo Kohn, then Political Adviser of the Jewish Agency. He, too, declared that without the permission of the Regional Command he could do nothing. Before morning we were informed by the Regional Command that they had got in touch with Ben-Gurion and had been told that planes carrying heavy loads of bombs were being sent to the Bloc.
—HA'IM TS.

At Hirbet Zakaria

From the account of a Squad Commander—May 12

Darkness descended on the Hebron Hills. It was a clear night, lit by the stars, a night hostile to the enemy. To us it was an ally and protector. . . .

Suddenly bright lights shone in the wadi between Hirbet Zakaria and Lone Tree Hill. Vehicles, with their headlights full on, were traveling confidently along the stretch of road near the hill. Movements in the wadi increased; broken cries, a suspicious rustling. Perhaps they were getting ready for an assault.

But they did not come. They were afraid of the surprises of the night. We could see tanks moving behind the Lone Tree, withdrawing to the enemy's rear. The infantry, entrenched in our former strongpoints, sniped at us.

Suddenly there was a flood of light between the hills, from the northeast, from the ridges to the north of Ein Tsurim and Revadim, and from the wadi near Massuot Yitzhak. What was the matter? Were they trying to impress us? No. Quite simply they were shooting at an Auster, using tracer bullets. We contacted the pilot. He was confused but unafraid. He wished to drop his load over them. We must give him directions. We gathered twigs and branches and in a position concealed from the enemy we lit the beacon. Our wireless operator was directing him. His voice was quiet, but you could sense the emotion. "Drop your carnations six hundred yards south of the beacon. Knock them out!"

The pilot continued to circle at great peril to himself. The bombs began to drop. One fell in the wadi in front of us, lighting up every figure moving on Lone Tree Hill. Apparently the tanks had scattered. The bombing, however, brought no change in the situation. The Auster vanished. The enemy's sniping continued. Then slowly silence reigned again over the hills.—DAVID K.

The Transfer of the Wounded

From the accounts of settlers and of Dr. Kornblueth—May 12

Around midnight Dr. Windsberg examined the wounded on the veranda of the hospital and the order was given for their transfer. Thirty-five wounded men, many of them stretcher cases, set out in three groups for Massuot Yitzhak, supported by nurses and medical orderlies and escorted by a squad of settlers that had come previously from Massuot. The doctors left in the third group.

The procession proceeded by way of Rock Hill over a trail covered with rocks and thorns. When they turned off the internal road of Kfar Etzion, the men were overtaken by a group of sappers who were moving towards the settlement's gate to mine the feeder road. As the file of men and women wound its way over the hill their route took them within a distance of barely two hundred and fifty yards from the lit-up vehicles of the Legion, parked at the foot of Yellow Hill. However, the Arabs were unaware of their movements and the three groups arrived at Massuot without mishap.

Night in Kfar Etzion

From the description of a member of Kfar Etzion—May 12

The straw shed burned in the night, the flames twisting in the darkness. Only a few men had the strength to try and extinguish the flames. There was no more water; even the turbid water from the cattletroughs had been used up. The flames gave off a macabre glow conjuring up ancient memories of the burning of the Sanctuary.

Tracer bullets shooting through the air like rockets, were fired from the hilltops, flying through the night. Guttural cries could be heard. Apparently the Arabs were nearby. The night was dark and we were tired out.

"How many of you are there in the position?" someone asked suddenly in a worried tone.

"Five. We must be relieved."

"There is nobody to relieve you. Get food and water ready for tonight and tomorrow."

"Where shall we get water from? The pipes have all been blown up."

"Let someone go to the cistern and draw water."

The man hurriedly made his way to the next position and once again we were alone, facing the darkness and the enemy concealed among the rocks.

T. went out of the post. He swayed as he walked. He had been lying inside the post all day and his limbs were numb. The ground was pitted with shell holes. The roads had been destroyed; broken tiles and strips of galvanized iron covered the ground. It was pitch dark. Terror gripped him in the darkness, when he sensed the destruction of the village. Only yesterday everything had been so quiet and peaceful and then, in one day, all had been destroyed. There was an acrid smell of smoke in the air that boded no good. His legs led him to his own room. The building in which he lived still stood. Broken stones lay strewn on the floor and the pale light of the moon penetrated the gaping shell holes.

He looked around for his roommates. None of them was in the room. Were they still unhurt?

He prayed silently that the night might continue without end. At last, dull hope still flickered that somehow a miracle would happen and that in the morning the battle would end. In the darkness he came up to the white building near Post Seven. On the floor dark bundles lay heaped like the clothing of sleeping men. He stumbled over them, but no one moved. Were they asleep, too exhausted to move? Or were they dead? He retreated hurriedly in horror and awe. He began to weep like a child, and walked back to the building of the ruined village. Perhaps he would find someone to tell him what had happened in the course of the day, and who was alive and who dead.

He groped his way through the ruins and his brain shrieked, "The village is destroyed."

Two shadows were leaning over the cistern and drawing water. T. could hear the sound of water running into the buckets. The cistern had not been damaged. In the light of the moon the water looked pure and clean. He drew some water for the next day.

Suddenly he came upon Yehezkel lying with his Italian rifle among the stones.

"Yehezkel," he cried out "What is the matter?" He tried to rouse him but Yehezkel did not move. He was as stiff and unyielding as the stones among which he lay.

T. was astonished that no one had noticed Yehezkel's death. There were no bloodstains around him. He removed the rifle and the bandolier and with two rifles on his shoulder he wandered about the ruins thinking: "Now I have two rifles and only yesterday how enviously I looked at every ancient weapon still capable of firing a shot. Where were the men to remove the arms of the fallen and to take their places? A lone band was fighting to death unremembered on this rocky hill."

Something was moving in the farmyard. Preparations were being made for the next day, when the battle was to be resumed. A group of shadows were moving towards the defense posts. A number of men entered Post Seven together with him. The post was crowded, and he was ordered to go to the Command Post and ask what must be done with the men for whom there was no room in the position. In the Command Post tired and broken fighters were getting ready for the trial ahead. In a quiet voice Ya'akov told them to move to Post Five.

Defenders slipped by with their rifles and bandoliers to Post Five. The slope facing them was surrounded with Arabs. Two tanks had taken up position on the crest of Russian Hill. The dawn of a new day was heralded by a nervous burst of shooting.—YA'AKOV ED.

19 The Battle of Kfar Etzion —May 13

From the accounts of members of Kfar Etzion—May 13

The assault was renewed at half-past four in the morning. A number of armored cars advanced along the road leading to the village and covered the farmyard with a strong barrage of shells. Squads of uniformed soldiers could be seen advancing in battle order to the sound of bugle calls. At 5:10 A.M. the following message was transmitted to Headquarters:

> The Arabs have launched an all-out attack from the north, under cover of heavy artillery, mortar and machine gun fire. Our men are ready in their positions. Send help. In a few minutes the outcome may be decided.

At 5:30 A.M. there was an attempted assault from the direction of Russian Hill. Posts Three and Four permitted the Arabs to come right up to the settlement, and then opened fire. The two-inch mortar, and also from time to time, the Lewis gun opened fire.

At dawn a detail of settlers from Massuot Yitzhak relieved the men on Rock Hill who had been on guard throughout the night. The armored cars shelling Kfar Etzion could be seen on the ridges roundabout. Three armored vehicles and two tanks were stationed on Russian Hill. On Lone Tree Hill there were six vehicles and on the Mukhtar's Saddle eight vehicles and tanks. The infantry tried to close in under cover of heavy fire, but they were beaten back, suffering heavy casualties.

Six armored gun-carriers and two armored cars started to move up from Lone Tree Hill in the direction of Rock Hill, but were greeted with heavy fire and retreated. Again and again they tried to advance, but with the same result.

During the morning the following message was sent to Headquarters:

> Send bombers immediately. The village is under heavy artillery fire. The ammunition dropped by the planes fell into the hands of the Arabs. Let the planes try and drop ammunition, well-wrapped in straw, as soon as possible, for every minute is precious.

Planes came. Some dropped bombs; others, among them a two-engined aircraft, dropped weapons, including a three-inch mortar, shells, and batteries for the transmitter—but none of it reached the hands of the defenders.

In the defense posts the position was grave. After a day of battle and a night on guard the men were exhausted. Those men of the reserve force—the Palmah, the Field Force and the drivers—who had not yet been assigned to positions were distributed in the various posts. Only a few of the heavier weapons were still in working order: five light machine guns, one heavy machine gun, one two-inch mortar and one Piat. Ammunition was running short in the posts and runners were sent to the Command Post to get supplies.

At about seven in the morning, while the shelling and the assault were in progress, the last radio message was sent to the wives and children of the settlers in Jerusalem:

> Yesterday a heavy attack was launched upon us. We were attacked from the Saddle, the Valley of Brakha, and Russian Hill, by artillery, tanks, machine guns, and mortars. Many of the buildings were hit and Nveh Ovadia was badly damaged. We have repulsed all attacks. Yehezkel B. was killed and Aryei Kl., Yehuda G. and others were wounded. Our spirit is strong. It is quiet now.

This was followed by a message from Ya'akov A.

> About a quarter-of-an-hour ago tanks, artillery, and mortars resumed the attack. I know that you are in a difficult position. We hope you are able to hold out. Our spirits are strong. *Lehitra'ot.*

After this message had been transmitted, the commanders of defense posts were contacted to report on their men and arms. Just when they were about to report, however, communications were disrupted. The assault was renewed with very great intensity.

From the account of a Squad Commander stationed on Rock Hill—May 13

At 8:00 A.M. we noticed a large number of Arabs infiltrating from Russian Hill to just below the fig orchard, near the northern fence of Kfar Etzion, and preparing for an attack. They were men of the Arab Liberation Army. The squad on the forward sector of Rock Hill allowed them to mass without revealing its whereabouts and without the enemy apparently knowing that they were there.

At 8:45 A.M. the assault began. Shrieking *"Aleihum,"* and spurred on by bugle calls, they rushed forward in the direction of Kfar Etzion. The men in ambush—whose operative weapons had by now diminished to only four rifles and a number of Stens—opened up with withering flanking fire. The results were astonishing. The Arabs were so stunned by the unexpected attack that some of them ran headlong into it. In a few minutes the whole wadi was emptied, those who were unhurt rushing panic-stricken back to Russian Hill. Then an armored car came down into the wadi and cruised back and forth, picking up the survivors. The position of the ambushers had not yet been discovered and our men could rest awhile, keeping a close look-out over the battleground. Even when the armored vehicles began to shell the hill, the explosions only sent stones flying, and did not do much harm.

Two armored gun-carriers, of the column of six near Lone Tree Hill, managed at 9:00 A.M. to force their way into the feeder road leading to Kfar Etzion, reaching the fence of the fig orchard in front of the gate. We aimed our fire at the other four vehicles and succeeded in puncturing the tires of two of them. The other two withdrew. The two vehicles on the feeder road—when they saw what had happened to the others—followed suit. Another armored car was put out of action by a two-inch mortar shell, frustrating all further attempts at an advance. The fight with the armored vehicles lasted until about eleven o'clock.—YITZHAK W. (As recorded in the diary of Uriel O.)

From the accounts of members of Kfar Etzion (Continued)—May 13

Under cover of a hail of fire the enemy advanced, wave after wave, upon the village: in the northeast, from Wadi Shahid to the fig orchard; in the southeast, from Russian Hill and the Valley of Brakha; in the southwest by way of Wadi Piretrum, and apparently also from the west, from the Mukhtar's Saddle. The defenders allowed the enemy to approach until they were quite near and then opened heavy fire. The two-inch mortar was very effective and scored direct hits on the enemy concentrations.

Posts Two and Three, in the northeastern sector, were hit by a number of shells but no casualties were sustained. When the Arabs attempted to storm the positions they were beaten off by the defenders. The two-inch mortar and a Bren-gun were sent to reinforce this sector. A grenade launcher, fired from a nearby trench, gave effective support to the defenders.

When the attack from the direction of the Valley of Brakha grew in intensity, Yirmiyahu R. and Dov S. were transferred to Post Five with the Lewis gun. The gun had been operating all morning against Russian Hill and had prevented the Arabs from advancing on Kfar Etzion. Apparently other machine guns circulated between the various posts as the direction of the onslaught changed.

At mid-morning the following message was received at village Headquarters, signed by David Ben-Gurion, head of the Provisional Government:

> The Provisional Government and the entire Yishuv are following with awe and anxiety the unequal battle it is your lot to fight. Your stand in previous battles has not only been glorious, it has helped directly and indirectly to save Jerusalem. We are confident that you will continue your fearless defense.

Headquarters informed Kfar Etzion that a plane would come to clear the air strip and to drop arms and reinforcements. It also reported that it was in contact with the other settlements of the Bloc, which were not under heavy pressure. Avraham F. went round the posts to give the men the news, which was greeted with rejoicing. The ordnance men made the rounds of the defense posts, despite the heavy fire, replenishing supplies of ammunition and repairing the weapons.

A plane appeared in the sky. The movement of the vehicles was interrupted and every Arab weapon on the battleground was aimed at it, forcing the craft to fly high. Its bombs dropped wide of the mark. When it disappeared the attack was resumed.

Another plane then appeared and scored a direct hit on the enemy concentration on Lone Tree Hill. The hut on the hill was destroyed.

One of the airmen described one of these operations as follows:

> Three Austers stood ready on the Tel Aviv airfield to take off for the Etzion Bloc. We had a threefold objective: (1) to bomb the enemy; we knew that Austers could not decide the course of the battle, but this was the only support which could give the garrison even a short respite; (2) to drop batteries for the transmitters; (3) to contact the defenders at close range, to get information about the battle, to transmit instructions, and to render various services.
>
> At the flying field I received my final briefing regarding contact and bombing, and climbed into the machine of Chibbi, who was in command of the flight. Ten minutes after we had taken off, Chibbi called my attention to something. At first I could not understand what he wanted, but soon I saw two British Spitfires circling round us. The British intended leaving the country in a day or two. Our flight was still illegal and the barrels of the Spitfires' machine guns upset us a little. I contacted base and was ordered to continue to my objective but not to begin operations as long as the British planes were in the neighborhood. The Spitfires accompanied us for about ten minutes and suddenly disappeared from view.
>
> As we approached our objective, we succeeded in contacting the defenders to inform them of our arrival and to obtain details of their situation. They warned us against enemy fire. Indeed, as soon as we were flying over the area, we ran into heavy concentrated

fire. Within a matter of minutes three bullets had hit the plane, but fortunately neither of us was hurt. Chibbi kept changing his course to keep out of the way of the dozens of machine guns firing away at us. He was only partially successful, however, because the Auster is slow and not very maneuverable. I began to drop my load when suddenly I heard something and noticed that another bullet had entered the plane through the windscreen. I saw Chibbi slump down, the nape of his neck covered with blood. The bullet had passed between us and had scratched his neck. I dressed the wound with a personal bandage. He lost a lot of blood but continued to fly for another fifteen minutes through a hail of enemy bullets, until I had dropped all my bombs, and had communicated with the various strongpoints. Chibbi's face was pale with the effort but he succeeded in bringing the plane back safely to base. We counted fourteen bullet holes in the plane.—(Abridged from *Hail Avir*)

Later Kfar Etzion transmitted the following messages to the Regional Command:

The plane has dropped incendiary bombs in the wood near the Monastery, apparently inflicting casualties on the enemy. The bombing has encouraged the men. The plane returned after radioing that a bigger craft would come.

In the event of an enemy attack which might capture the village, we intend destroying the instrument. Confirm.

The tanks are alongside the Kfar Etzion fence. They are concentrating in the fig orchard. The parachutes have fallen in Arab territory.

From the accounts of members of Kfar Etzion (Continued) —May 13

At half-past ten the sound of bugle calls was heard from the direction of Russian Hill and platoons of the enemy again deployed in the wadi leading to the fig orchard. As the enemy reached the fence of the fig orchard, the four riflemen stationed on Rock Hill opened up with heavy enfilading fire. In the course of this phase of the battle, which lasted forty-five minutes, each of the four men fired about one hundred rounds. Dozens of casualties were inflicted and the enemy beat a hasty retreat back to Russian Hill.

But the whereabouts of the garrison on Rock Hill had already been discovered by the enemy. An armored column was advancing by way of the feeder road and swept Rock Hill with machine guns and artillery. The positions behind the high rocks, however, were strong and were not damaged. At 11:45 a heavy barrage of fire was directed at Kfar Etzion. Post One, in the northern section of Kfar Etzion, tried to contact the men on Rock Hill to ask them to call the Settlement Commander of Massuot Yitzhak for an urgent consultation, but their voices were drowned in the din. There was no hope whatever of a runner getting through the terrible barrage of shells. Once again enemy armor began to advance. When they were about one hundred and fifty yards from the gate, the men of Post One brought up the Piat but it wouldn't fire. All their efforts to get it to fire were in vain. The intensity of the enemy bombardment increased. From Rock Hill and from all other positions fire was opened up. The infantry fell back to Wadi Shahid, the armor to the Lone Tree, and there was a lull in the fighting. It seemed that the attack had been broken.

But the enemy was regrouping and preparing to press the attack. It was then that the Rock Hill position had to be abandoned.

Two of the members of the Rock Hill picket described the situation as follows:

"Strong reinforcements of armor reached the enemy at Lone Tree Hill. Their vehicles numbered twenty. We were weary and broken. Our ammunition was running out. Menahem G. and Yitzhak S. tried to get ammunition through to us, but in vain. We were cut off from the settlement; the telephone line to Massuot Yitzhak was our only means of communication. Soon the enemy would surround us completely. We had only two or three mortar shells left and a small supply of bullets. Our position was desperate.

"Just then we got orders from the Massuot Yitzhak Settlement Commander to withdraw immediately to defend the settlement from within. We took our arms and the telephone, crawled to our inner positions and began to run towards Massuot Yitzhak. A hail of bullets accompanied us, but none of us was hurt. As we came near the fence of the settlement one of our own planes bombed us; apparently the pilot had taken us for Arabs. Fortunately no one was injured."—ELIEZER S. and SHMUEL L.

The last messages transmitted from Kfar Etzion to the Regional Command were as follows:

> The Arabs have advanced from the north to within one hundred yards of the fence and attempted a charge but have been beaten back. They are now concentrating on the south and southwest. Our men are standing firm.
>
> The armored vehicles have held up their advance, after one struck a mine and the wheels of the two others were damaged. Shelling is continuing from Russian Hill.

20 *The Last Hours*

From the accounts of survivors of Kfar Etzion—May 13

As the men who had been posted on Rock Hill were withdrawing from their positions they observed a motorcyclist going from one concentration of the enemy to another. It appeared that he had orders for a renewed attack. Immediately afterwards heavy shelling of Kfar Etzion began and the armored vehicles advanced on the feeder road towards the village. There was no force now to hold up their advance upon the northern fence. Enemy pressure on the positions in the southern section of the village increased meantime, and men were dispatched from the center of the village to reinforce it. The men of Post One, facing the feeder road, were ordered not to retreat. The Piat was not working so they were told to use Molotov cocktails and hand grenades against the armored vehicles in the event of another attempt to force the gate.

From the account of the Officer Commanding the Legion's armored platoon which penetrated into Kfar Etzion—May 13

[This would be the last attempt, I told myself, after all our previous efforts had failed because of the unexpected fire aimed from the Jewish positions among the rocks (Rock Hill).

As we were advancing towards the end of the air strip, I noticed a group of Jews running westwards but we did not stop for them, and continued to move towards the gate of the village. We traveled as fast as we could over the broken ground on the left of the road to avoid mines. We reached a point where the fence of the fig orchard meets the road—about two hundred yards northwest of the village, and from there we opened up softening fire round the gate and the buildings commanding it. Then I ordered one vehicle to storm the gate and to enter the farmyard. The armored vehicle collided with the gate, pushed it aside, and entered the farmyard but it was greeted with Molotov cocktails and heavy fire and was forced to retreat. We continued to give covering fire and then another vehicle succeeded in forcing its way into the farmyard.]—LIEUTENANT NASRI EFFENDI (as reported in *Maoz Etzion,* published by Ma'arakhot)

From the accounts of survivors of Kfar Etzion (Continued)—May 13

As the armored cars approached, David D., who was stationed in the first building, tried to explode the electric anti-tank mine near the gate, but for some reason the mine did not blow up—perhaps the wire had been cut during the bombardment. One shell was fired at the gate and forced it open. The men of the post threw Molotov cocktails and grenades at the armor. Only some of the cocktails ignited. Two armored vehicles standing near the gate retreated, but soon resumed their advance under heavy covering fire, traveling at great speed into the settlement. The men of the position withdrew under fierce fire to their secondary post within the farm compound. Only one man, who was severely wounded, remained behind. The rest lay in the post near the Nveh Ovadia library and kept up steady fire at the gate, which the armored vehicles now succeeded in negotiating.

In their wake came the Arab gangs and a number of soldiers who occupied the first building. All around on the slope we could see a huge rabble cheering and descending in the direction of the settlement. A comparative lull reigned.—NAHUM Z.

When the report that the Arabs had forced their way into the settlement was received, a radiogram was sent to General Staff Headquarters in Tel Aviv. (This was the last message sent from Kfar Etzion.) Then we got an order to destroy the transmitter and burn all documents. Ya'akov A. ordered me to go up on the roof and to hoist a white flag. He went out to the positions. Avraham F., relying on the close contacts he had had with the notables of the district, went out to negotiate with the Arabs. When I went up on the roof I saw that the Arab armored cars were already in the middle of the farm compound.—ALIZA F.

The men in the secondary post observed the Settlement Commander, Avraham F., a bandage round his head, proceeding along the path leading from the rest resort dining hall to the building nearest the gate. An Arab emerged from the building and pointed his rifle at him. Avraham raised his hands above his head and called out, "*Halas*" (it is finished). He said something else in Arabic, but the Arab fired at him and Avraham fell backwards into the shrubs. The men in this position kept firing at the advancing Arabs, especially those who had broken into the first building and could be seen through the window, busy looting. On hearing the order "cease fire" the men of the post made their way to the center of the village.

It seems that the order to cease fire did not reach all the

posts. The structure of the hill on which the settlement was built prevented the men in the posts on the southern and eastern sections from observing the tanks forcing their way into the compound, together with hundreds of Arabs who soon occupied the buildings on the northern side. The men in the southern and eastern posts continued firing at the thousands of Arabs descending from the surrounding slopes.

Yitzhak B.S. describes the situation on the northeastern section as follows:

"Post Three kept up steady fire at the Arabs until the men were ordered to cease fire. The men did not know what to do, as the shooting had not stopped and large numbers of Arabs were still advancing upon the settlement. But when the commander of the position saw men in uniform on Russian Hill waving a white flag he realized that something had occurred. He went over to Post Two to inquire, and found Ya'akov A. there. He asked Ya'akov if orders had been given to cease fire, to which Ya'akov replied, 'Yes.'

" 'Why?'

" 'We have surrendered.'

" 'What does Jerusalem say?'

" 'The Arab tanks are in the village. We have no contact with Jerusalem.'

" 'What must we do now?'

" 'Destroy your weapons.' "

Yitzhak returned to the post. The men began to destroy their arms and ammunition and went to the German Monastery building in the center of the village.

Meanwhile Aliza called out to the posts on the southeastern section, "Stop firing, men. We are surrendering." The men from the various positions began to muster near the German Monastery building. Some of them had destroyed their weapons. Others still held them in their hands and refused to do so. On the porch leading to the cellar a number of weapons and some ammunition were piled. A white flag fluttered from the water tower near the Monastery, but the shooting continued.

The men who had come from Post One reported the killing of Avraham F. From the southwest came Ya'akov K., the Section Commander, David M., his runner, and Tsipora R., who had served as medical orderly of the section. The men stationed in Posts Six, Seven, and Eight were not seen among those gathered near the Monastery. Seven armored cars and half-tracks stood parked on the inner road of the farm, toward the west, their guns trained on the farm compound. A number of Arabs advanced from Nveh Ovadia towards the Monastery building. Meantime other Arabs were looting.

These moments are described by a settler, who was in Post Five:

"The shooting was dying down gradually. Shells were falling in the wood. A number of *haverim* walked up and down like living shadows, waving pieces of white cloth. Had we been defeated? We looked at our rifles, the good friends who had accompanied us throughout all these months. Had the time come to part? It was hard to believe that we were surrendering. Some inner voice insisted, 'No. It is impossible.'

"We came to the Monastery where we found other *haverim* returning from their positions. David D., who was covered with dust, sank to the ground wearily. 'The anti-tank weapons did not operate at the decisive moment,' he said. 'The Molotov cocktails missed their mark. The wire of the electric mine laid by the gate was cut by a shell. Avraham F. who went out to surrender was killed. The tanks are already in the middle of the farmyard.'

"Tsipora came up, weary, covered with dust, and weeping. 'Why have we surrendered?'

"Who had ever thought that this would come to pass?"—YA'AKOV ED.

From the account of the OC of the Legion's armored platoon—May 13

[When I observed another group of Jews coming out with a white flag I shouted to the mob to cease fire, although the Jews on the eastern side of the village were still shooting. I contacted my commanding officer for orders. I was told to accept the surrender and stop all shooting at once. A little while later, however, my wireless operator got a message that a direct order had been received from the British colonel that the *fellahin* must be allowed to finish the Jews off.] —LIEUTENANT NASRI EFFENDI (as reported in *Maoz Etzion,* published by Ma'arakhot)

From the accounts of survivors of Kfar Etzion (Continued) —May 13

It was fairly quiet. Many of the *haverim* who had left their positions believed that everything would turn out all right. They continued to destroy their weapons to prevent them from falling into the hands of the enemy. Meanwhile they gathered on the empty lot between the Monastery and the school building. A number of Arabs came up. First they ordered the Jews to sit down and then to stand up and raise their hands. One of the Arabs aimed his Tommy-gun at us and another wanted to throw a grenade, but others prevented them from harming us.

Then a photographer dressed in European clothes and wearing a white *kaffiyeh* came on the scene and photographed us. Suddenly an armored vehicle came up from the direction of the dining hall and stopped near the school. The barrels of the machine guns could be seen projecting from the side.

When the photographer had finished, fire was suddenly opened on us from every direction. Most of the assembled *haverim* were hit. Those who were not struck in the first volleys shoved the Arabs aside and ran. A number fled into the shelter in the cellar of the Monastery. Others grabbed their weapons. A huge mob of Arabs rushed upon the men standing in the middle of the village and fell upon them. Nahum Z. testifies that heavy fire came from the Vickers guns in the armored cars on the west of the farm compound.

Aliza F. a radio operator relates:

"After we had been photographed the Arabs started shooting and we scattered. I jumped into a ditch near the school. Suddenly an Arab approached and aimed his rifle at me. I cried out. When the Arabs heard my cry they stopped firing and pulled me out of the ditch. Two Legionaries grabbed me and took me through the farmyard to the wood. We trod on dozens of bodies. I recognized many of our men, but there were also many of theirs. I saw many pools of blood. The smell of the blood made me giddy. A mob was busy looting the school. The Arabs were shooting at each other.

"When we came to the wood the Legionaries tried to attack me. I resisted with all my strength. Suddenly I heard two volleys from a sub-machine gun. The Arabs fell to the ground, covered with blood. It was an officer of the Legion who had saved me. He promised me solemnly that he would do me no harm. He led me to the gate and put me into the armored car which took me to the Arab base on Lone Tree Hill.

"When the battle subsided, the officer took me back to the village and demanded that I show him where the arms caches were. When we passed by the doorway of the shelter under the German Monastery, he put a grenade into my hand, pulled out the pin and ordered me to throw it into the shelter. I held the grenade in my hand, for I was prepared to kill myself rather than to obey this order. The officer took it from me and threw it himself into the shelter.

"I saw many wounded—some of them in their last agony—both Jews and Arabs, in the farmyard. Anyone showing any sign of life, the officer shot and killed.

"Later he took me back to the armored car, in which I traveled to the Hebron Police Station."

The men who escaped the massacre by running to the east saw many others trying to flee, but they cannot remember who they were. Ya'akov Ed. and Yitzhak B.S. fled to the "Song of Songs" wood, and the latter recalls that near the poultry run he saw Amnon D. of the Palmah struggling with an Arab from whom he succeeded in wresting a rifle.

Ya'akov and Yitzhak remained in the wood for about a quarter-of-an-hour. They heard continual sounds of firing, explosions, and shouting from the direction of the village. Suddenly they noticed an old Arab approaching the rocks where they were hiding. He had a *tefillin* bag hanging from his neck, into which he was putting some bullets he had found. The Arab assured them they would not be hurt. They could see a large number of Arabs descending from the village with their loot. A number of Arabs approached with the intention of killing them, but the old Arab who had found them prevented this. He took them by way of the path to Russian Hill, where the armored vehicles were stationed.

On their way they met Arab notables wearing red *tarbushes* who helped Yitzhak, who was wounded in the foot, to walk. The notables assured them in Hebrew that the prisoners would not be harmed. Near the armored cars they found Captain Hikmat Bek and an Arab Legion Major, who had been directing the attack. "Why are you still shooting at our men, when they have surrendered?" Yitzhak asked through an interpreter. The answer was: "Your men are still fighting."

The two prisoners were placed on a truck, in which there were a Piat gun and a radio plundered from Kfar Etzion. Captain Hikmat Bek and the Major sat in the driver's cabin. There were four soldiers on the truck. Near the crossroads leading to Kfar Etzion they were photographed together with Arab notables, including the Mayor of Hebron. Then they were taken to Bethlehem escorted by an Arab Legion armored car. There was a lot of traffic on the road. From time to time the truck stopped to allow the crowds to cheer. The soldiers fired a number of shots to prevent the crowd from coming closer. From Bethlehem they were taken to Jericho, where Yitzhak's wound was dressed, and put into a cell in the Police Station. Here they were interrogated. On May 16 they were taken to Amman in Trans-Jordan, and on the following day to Zerka, where they were again interrogated, and then transferred to a prisoner-of-war camp in Um Jamal.

Nahum Z., who stood in the front rank of the *haverim* who had mustered in the center of the village, was wounded in the left hand in the first burst of fire. He rushed past the Arabs in the direction of Nveh Ovadia. He made his way westward past Post Eight and took shelter near the buildings. Turning south to the metal workshop, he came across two men of the Palmah, one of whom he described as tall and dark and the other as having a blond beard. They had a machine gun. Nahum called to them to follow him, but one of them was wounded and so they remained in the village. He passed under the southern gate and while doing so he was wounded again. He managed, however, to get to the vineyard on the southwestern slope, where he hid behind the trellised vines. As he lay bleeding in the vineyard, he heard the sound of an explosion in the village and saw flames rising from the supply store. The Arab mob was surging up all roads to the village, and trucks loaded with loot were driving away.

Quiet reigned at nightfall. In the darkness he made his way carefully through the orchards to the road leading to the Saddle and then to the young woodland skirting Abu Rish. He looked for a sub-machine gun that had been left behind the previous day but could not find it. Then he crawled to Massuot Yitzhak. During the night he heard the sound of voices and the rumble of motors coming from Kfar Etzion.

From the statement of a survivor

David B.D., who in November, 1949, crossed the Armistice lines with the Chief Chaplain of the Israel Army to collect the remains of the defenders, relates in his report:

> In the northern positions where the break-through occurred, I found single corpses. Apparently the men occupying these positions had retreated to the center of the compound. Near the German Monastery and in the places where the men had remained in their positions in the southern section, I found whole groups of corpses.
>
> Fahri, a young Arab, who accompanied me on my tour of the ruins of Kfar Etzion, told me:
>
> "When we tried to penetrate into the village from the south we encountered heavy fire from these positions and many were killed. When we had succeeded in silencing them we advanced into the farm compound. There we encountered total confusion: firing and deafening cries; Jews and Arab villagers and Legionaries were shooting at each other."

David B.D. continues:

> While we were clearing away the ruins that covered the cellar of the German Monastery I heard a Legionary telling a group of Arabs standing nearby that he had taken part in the battle of Kfar Etzion. He related that when the Arabs attempted to penetrate into the cellar they encountered fierce resistance and had to throw inside a number of hand grenades. Later the Legion's sappers dynamited the building. Not one of the defenders remained alive.

In Jerusalem

From the account of a member of Kfar Etzion—May 13

In Jerusalem we had no clear idea of the situation at the time when Kfar Etzion fell. The interruption of radio contact for several hours on end gave rise to the worst misgivings. In the late afternoon a report—which it seems, had been transmitted in the morning—was received, indicating the gravity of the position. Following a meeting with the officials of the Political Department of the Jewish Agency, it was resolved that the Chief Rabbi should endeavor to contact the British with a view to saving the defenders and opening negotiations for evacuation. Prior to this the representative of the Red Cross had been contacted, but in vain. It was impossible to get in touch with an authoritative officer of the Legion. The Arabs apparently refused to enter into negotiations.

We went to the Yeshurun Synagogue where a memorial meeting for the victims of the Hadassah convoy was being held and asked the Chief Rabbi to interrupt his sermon in order to try and save the defenders of the Bloc. Consultations, in which a number of officials of the Jewish Agency's Political Department took part, were held at the offices of the Chief Rabbi. The Chief Rabbi tried to get the High Commissioner, the Chief Secretary, and the Commander of the British troops in Palestine on the phone, but he was unsuccessful. The only replies he got were from subordinates who told the Chief Rabbi that their seniors were not in and were busy preparing for the evacuation of the country. Throughout that evening repeated but unsuccessful efforts were made to contact the British.

At nine in the evening we went to the Ratisbonne Monastery. Our *haverot* wanted to know how matters stood. We did our best to explain what was happening, trying at the same time to hold out some hope that the defenders could be saved. Someone switched on the radio and we heard: "Kol HaMagen HaIvri,"—the Hagana Radio Station—announce: "Today at 1:00 P.M. the enemy took Kfar Etzion by storm. The defenders fought a courageous hand-to-hand struggle until they were overwhelmed."

There was a stunned silence, followed by bitter weeping. —SHLOMO H.

The Fallen

One hundred and fifty-one defenders fell in the two-day battle. Twenty-four were killed on the first day and one hundred and twenty-seven were killed in the final phase of the battle of Kfar Etzion. Twenty-one of the fallen were women.

Only nine settlers of Kfar Etzion survived, of the eighty-eight who were in the village at the time of the battle: six wounded who had been evacuated to Massuot Yitzhak on the night of May 12, and the three who escaped the massacre.

Aliza F. was the only member of the enlisted personnel in Kfar Etzion to survive the final battle.

Ibrahim Hazboun, the tenant of the Russian Monastery, a man of saintly character who throughout had maintained good relations with his Jewish neighbors, and the members of his family, were among those who lost their lives in the last stand of the village. A Legionary told the captives that he saw their bodies among the ruins of the village.

Epilogue: The End of a Chapter

After the capture of Kfar Etzion, the southern road to Jerusalem was open to the Arabs. The Legion hastily withdrew its forces from the Bloc, to reorganize for the impending battle of the Holy City. Only a token force was left behind, and thus the main Arab forces facing the three remaining Jewish settlements and the Hirbet Zakaria strongpoint were the bands of the Arab Liberation Army and the unorganized villagers.

In Jerusalem, the unremitting attempts by the Jewish authorities to arrange for a formal surrender of the Bloc continued. The French Consul and the Red Cross representatives made especially vigorous efforts to influence the Arabs to agree to negotiations.

At Massuot Yitzhak

May 13

At 2:00 P.M. a long burst of firing was heard coming from the direction of Kfar Etzion. Suddenly the firing died down. A deathly silence reigned.

Sometime afterwards a message was sent to Jerusalem:

The Queen has fallen.

From the account of two Palmah soldiers—May 13

. . . In the meantime we had got ready to meet the enemy onslaught. A large barricade of farm carts, iron bars, and rocks had been constructed by the gate of the farm compound. Mines had been laid on the road leading to the settlement, while the squad stationed in the strongpoint facing Jabba had been ordered to withdraw to the settlement. A machine gun was trained on the gate. An ambush comprising three settlers armed with Molotov cocktails had taken up position, ready to attack any armored vehicles that approached the farmyard.

In the hospital the doctors and the nurses continued to take care of the wounded. Dr. Windsberg operated on all the seriously wounded.

One group began to plan a break-through to Jerusalem, through the hills. The Regional Command was informed of the plan and was asked to approve it. It refused however to do so on the ground that any such attempt was suicidal. At five in the afternoon the following message was received from Jerusalem:

> Hold on. Tomorrow the Red Cross will arrive. This is the only way. Soon airplanes will come. We have informed Tel Aviv of the situation.

Just before evening the planes did come and tried to parachute arms to us, but they fell in enemy territory. The bombs they dropped fell within the area of the settlement.—URIEL O. and NAOMI T.

At Revadim

From the account of a settler—May 13

At 2:00 P.M. we were stricken by the news that Kfar Etzion had fallen. Shortly afterwards we saw trucks, loaded with loot, hurrying down the strip of road visible from our settlement. Our men, weary and depressed, anxiously observed every car that passed, hoping to see prisoners taken at Kfar Etzion, but in vain. . . .

At dusk the movement of the Arabs on the hills and the spurs surrounding the Hirbet Zakaria—Ein Tsurim—Revadim triangle became more intense. The Arabs now took up positions among the rocks, keeping our settlements under constant fire. We could make out large groups of the enemy on Yellow Hill.

At eight in the evening, we contacted the secretary of Revadim who was in Jerusalem and urged him to make arrangements for the evacuation of the Bloc. His reply was that negotiations had entered the most critical stage.—DAN H. (As reported in *Shana BeSograyim,* published by Sifriat Poalim)

At Ein Tsurim

From the accounts of settlers—May 13

At two in the afternoon we heard the sound of firing and explosions from the direction of Kfar Etzion. The pilot who was circling above informed us of a large mob milling around the village. Then on the road near the Lone Tree we saw trucks loaded high with furniture and other loot from Kfar Etzion.

At 5:00 P.M. the following message was sent to Regional Headquarters:

> We are being heavily shelled by artillery and tanks. We cannot hope to hold our ground. Tonight represents the last chance for us to evacuate the village.

To which Jerusalem replied:

> Contact the local enemy commanders and arrange for a surrender.

Ein Tsurim answered:

> There is no chance whatever of entering into negotiations with the Arabs on the spot. Any attempt to do so means certain death. If we do not get a message soon about negotiations with the enemy our men will follow the route of the Thirty-Five.

An hour later Jerusalem reported that the negotiations with the Red Cross were in their final stages.

At midnight we received a message that a cease-fire had been agreed upon. We transmitted the message to the other settlements and to Hirbet Zakaria.—BEN ZION A., GERSHON SH., and ELIAHU B.H.

May 14

At 2:00 A.M., the following instructions were transmitted to the Bloc by the Jerusalem Regional Command:

> Contact has been established with the enemy through the offices of the Consular Commission and the terms of surrender have been agreed upon as follows:
>
> The men will be transferred under the supervision of the Red Cross to a prisoner-of-war camp. Those declared severely wounded by a doctor of the Red Cross, together with women and non-combatants, will be placed in the custody of the Red Cross and transferred to Jerusalem.
>
> Procedure: 1. The cease-fire will come into effect at 4:00 A.M.; 2. Representatives of the Red Cross will enter each settlement to transmit the conditions of surrender; 3. After due registration by the representative of the Red Cross all combatants will be taken prisoners; 4. Every person may take his personal effects with him.

At three in the morning, Jerusalem signaled to the Bloc as follows:

> The cease-fire will come into effect at 4:00 A.M. A convoy of the Red Crescent, representatives of the Consular Commission and

of the Red Cross, and a Jewish doctor will arrive between 7:30 A.M. and 8:00 A.M. Should there be any mines on the road, fire a volley as a signal to the car to halt. The conditions of the cease-fire remain unchanged.

From the account of a settler of Ein Tsurim—May 14

After the surrender terms were received there was a meeting of the Command of the northern sector together with the members of the settlement Secretariats. They discussed various matters to be done on the following day. It was decided: a) The village Mukhtars would represent the settlements in all negotiations; b) to surrender only to the Arab Legion and not to give up any arms until the men get into the trucks; c) all men of the Palmah and the Field Force would be included in the lists of the settlers; d) to destroy all the automatic weapons and a large part of the ammunition and to surrender to the enemy only part of the personal arms; e) a number of *haverim* would guard the women from molestation, until the latter were handed over to the representatives of the Red Cross.

The men all slept in their positions. All clothing and blankets in the store rooms were distributed to the settlers and to the men of the Palmah and Field Force.—GERSHON SH.

On the fifth of Iyar (May 14), the British Mandate came to an end—a day before its declared date of termination—and the State of Israel was proclaimed in Tel Aviv. While the Arab Legion completed the reorganization of its forces after the Etzion Bloc battle, the Jewish forces in Jerusalem, in a swift series of moves, exploited the inter-

regnum created by the British evacuation and captured most of the city.

In the Etzion Bloc, the anxious defenders of the three settlements and the garrison at Hirbet Zakaria, apprehensive of what the future held in store for them, prepared on the dawn of this fateful day to receive the Red Cross representatives.

At Revadim

From the account of a settler—May 14

The sun rose on an ordinary summer morning in the Hebron Hills. The enemy concentrations were already clearly visible. The Arabs encircled us in a strong, tight chain, and their raucous, hostile voices reached us clearly. We dared not provoke them. A cease-fire, a surrender, was in force. In the positions the boys lay exhausted, unnerved, ready to open fire if the rabble should come closer to the fence, or try to get into the settlement while we were still there.—TAMAR (As recorded in *Dvar HaPo'elet*)

At Massuot Yitzhak

From the diary of a Palmah soldier—May 14

As the first rays of the sun shone over the hills I climbed onto the roof of our rest resort, which served as the hospital, and hoisted two flags, one with the Red Cross and the other with a Red Shield of David.

Suddenly a dull explosion shook the air. Another Arab had struck a mine. I went outside and saw that Massuot was surrounded by thousands of Arabs prowling round the fence. Others were marching down in columns from Yellow Hill. The Arabs came closer but nevertheless kept at a respectful distance. All of them were armed, carrying rifles on their shoulders, but they observed the cease-fire conditions and did not shoot.—URIEL O.

At Ein Tsurim

From the account of a settler—May 14

At six in the morning, the Arabs who had concentrated on the ridges began to snipe at the settlement. We did not know what to do and contacted Headquarters in Jerusalem. We were advised not to reply, so as not to provoke any attack. The number of Arabs on the ridges grew steadily and indeed soon the slopes were black with spectators who had come to witness our surrender and to share in the loot.

The Arabs approached to within fifty yards of the settlement fence. We were nervous and worried. The non-Palestinian volunteers were concentrated on one side, the bands of the Mufti on the second, and Abdullah's men on the third. I decided to speak to the leaders of each group separately. I explained to each leader that we had refrained from answering his fire so as to abide by the cease-fire agreement, but if he and his men came closer to the fence we would open fire with machine guns and he, the leader, would be responsible for the consequences. At the same time I assured him that the moment we left he and his men would be the first to enter the settlement. The trick worked and each leader succeeded in keeping his men in check.—GERSHON SH.

At Hirbet Zakaria

From the account of a member of Revadim stationed at Hirbet Zakaria—May 14

In the half light of Friday morning we watched the Arabs

making their way towards the Hirbeh. I sent word round to all the posts not to open fire without orders. The sun rose and we saw that the surrounding hills were covered with thousands of Arabs advancing upon us. When those in the van approached to within two hundred yards of our positions, we shouted to them to halt and proposed that one of our representatives and one of theirs negotiate. They halted. One of them, Issa of Beth Umar, approached. Avraham R. went out to meet him. The Bren-gunner, who could not cover the spot where the two met, shifted his position to command the road. After some time Avraham came back and reported that it had been agreed to wait until the Red Cross arrived. We decided to call Barukh B., who spoke fluent Arabic, to help in the negotiations.—TSVI ST. (As recorded in the diary of Uriel O.)

From the account of a Field Force soldier—May 14

At 6:40 A.M. the car of the International Red Cross came into sight. It brought Dr. Zive, Dr. Halidi (an Arab), and two representatives of the Red Cross, Dr. Loehner and Dr. Fasel. They remained for about an hour in the section between Yellow Hill and Lone Tree Hill, apparently negotiating with the Arab commanders. Then they drove up to the Hirbeh. . . .

It is difficult to understand why the Legion withdrew from the Bloc, after the conclusion of the battle of Kfar Etzion, and before the surrender parleys began. Perhaps they had to regroup their forces. Or perhaps they wished to compensate the villagers and the members of the Arab bands for the heavy losses they had suffered and to leave the massacre of the surviving settlers and the plunder of the Bloc to them. Whatever their reasons, the fact that no representative of regular troops put in an appearance to accept the surrender, and that the cease-fire arrangements had to be concluded with the Arab bands and the rabble, gave rise to much anxiety.—H. A.

From the account of a member of Revadim (Continued)—May 14

The Red Cross car drove up. It was only with difficulty that I could make it out as it plowed its way through the Arab mob. Thousands of Arabs, armed with all sorts of weapons, completely surrounded us. Shlomo S. and David D., who spoke English, went out to meet the car in order to begin the negotiations. An armed Arab alighted, introduced himself as Haldi Bey Husseini, and informed us that we must give ourselves up to him. Our representatives replied that to the best of their knowledge they must surrender to regular troops only. The mob, which was growing impatient, surged about them, and they were soon in the middle of the Arabs, who were shouting their savage war cries. Our representatives declared that they held no positions of command and must return to the Hirbeh to report to their officers. They requested Haldi to give them an escort to accompany them through the mob, but he refused to do so, saying that he would lay down the conditions of surrender. The two were compelled to make their way back by themselves.

After they had reported on their talks with the Arabs, we resolved that we would not surrender to the mob and that if need be we would fight to the last bullet. After the Red Cross car had continued on its way to Ein Tsurim and the Arabs had resumed their advance, Barukh B. went out towards them and began to speak to one who seemed to be the leader. But the Arabs did not halt their advance. I was standing by the barricade behind the Bren-gun position, and told the Bren-gunner not to open fire without orders. I ordered the two-inch mortar position to get the shortest range possible and to wait for my instructions. The Arabs continued to surge forward. I put a bullet into the breach and shouted to them to halt. They refused to comply and called upon us to go out to them. I shouted to them again but in vain. They had come to within three yards of me and stopped for a moment. I did not order the Bren-gunner to open fire for fear of upsetting the cease-fire arrangements. I kept hoping that the regular troops would show up.

Suddenly a number of Arabs rushed at me. One of them lunged forward and grabbed my rifle. In that same split second I saw another Arab aiming his weapon at me and as I fell to the ground a bullet flew over my head, and I heard an answering volley from our Bren-gun. "This is the end," I said to myself. In the confusion I could make out the sounds of single rifle shots, volleys and explosions, and loud cries from the direction of the mosque of the Hirbeh. I raised my head slowly and saw that I was surrounded on three sides. The road behind me was clear but if I tried to retreat, I would attract attention. I called out to the Bren-gun post to give me covering fire when I fell back. As the Bren-gun opened up I jumped back into the pit in front of the position. Another leap and I was inside the position. In this post there were five men. We thought that these were our last moments.

Suddenly we saw Barukh running through the Arabs waving a scarf and shouting in Hebrew and Arabic: "Cease fire! Cease fire!" The shooting died down and we saw a police armored vehicle descending in our direction from the

Lone Tree. I came out from the post and advanced towards the armored car. Passing by the mortar position I saw Avraham R., lying on the ground with a terrible wound that ripped his whole stomach. Nearby was the safety-pin of a hand grenade. He had chosen to kill himself rather than fall into the hands of the rabble.

The armored car made its way towards us with its machine guns trained upon us all the time. I went towards it, picking my way past the bodies of Arab dead and wounded. Other Arabs who lay behind the rocks glared at me with wild eyes. I came up to the armored vehicle in which there were five Arab police constables and an officer wearing a *tarbush* who introduced himself: "Haj Yassin, Commander of the Arab Liberation Army." We shook hands and I made three requests: a) He should come into the Hirbeh; b) he should order the men in the armored vehicle to turn the turret around so that the machine guns would not point at our positions; c) he should order the mob to withdraw to at least one hundred yards from us.

The officer fired a number of shots in the air and the rabble made off. We entered the Hirbeh and the negotiations began. The officer apologized for the delay and promised that henceforth everything would proceed smoothly.—Tsvi St. (As recorded in the diary of Uriel O.)

The incident at the Hirbeh as seen in Revadim—May 14

In the distance we could distinguish the dark mass of thousands of human forms steadily approaching the Hirbeh. At the sight of the rabble just outside the Hirbeh, only a few yards from the defense posts, a number of *haverim* lost their nerve. Some fled to Revadim and Ein Tsurim, while one blew himself up with a grenade. The first of the fugitives from the Hirbeh began to arrive, bringing with them broken and fearful accounts of the morning's events. All of us rushed back to our positions and took up our weapons. We heard a sudden volley and saw the rabble scatter in all directions, leaving their dead and wounded behind them.

In one of the positions, Danny, a settler of Ein Tsurim, was posted at the Bren-gun, waiting for orders from Tsvi, of Revadim, who was parleying with the Arabs. He saw an Arab grab Tsvi's rifle and shoot at him. Tsvi dropped behind a low stone fence, separating him from the rabble. Danny, who thought that Tsvi had been killed, pressed the trigger and fired a long volley. The mob fled, leaving the bodies of fifteen Arabs on the ground. Three hundred Jews owed their lives to that single volley.

However, the mob halted again and a number of the figures once more advanced towards the Hirbeh. But before three minutes had gone by we saw vehicles coming down from the Lone Tree, approaching the Hirbeh, and then disappearing again behind a spur concealing it, and there was no more firing.—DAN H. (As reported in *Shana BeSograyim,* published by Sifriat Poalim.)

The Surrender of Ein Tsurim

From the account of a settler (Continued)—May 14

At about ten o'clock the representatives of the Red Cross came to the settlement. Two of our members met them. We informed them of our readiness to hand over our arms to the representatives of the Arab Legion, but that, if that was not possible, we would continue to fight. The representatives were astonished, asking how we could insist on such conditions when our very lives were in danger. But we refused to budge. The Red Cross delegates replied that they had no instructions for any such arrangement and that they would go and meet the Legion officers to discuss it. Dr. Zive remained in the settlement.

Meantime an Arab police officer from Bethlehem appeared and began talking with us. He said that he was prepared to escort us with our arms to Bethlehem on condition that we surrendered our weapons to him when we got there. He hinted that for a consideration he was prepared to see us safely to the Katamon quarter of Jerusalem. We rejected the offer, however, as we feared a trap.

At noon representatives of the Legion came up: two squads of soldiers without an officer. They wanted to disarm us. We refused to allow them to do so and declared that we would hand over our arms only when we got onto the trucks. We asked them to keep the rabble back, but they could not hold back the mob that broke into the farm compound. Firing broke out between the Legionaries and the mob. The villagers started squabbling among themselves over the loot and a number of Arabs were killed.

We waited for the arrival of officers of the Legion but they were busy with the settlers of Revadim. Our people gathered in the dining hall but when we saw what was happening in the yard we decided it would be better to leave. We took our bundles and marched in single file through the gate. We handed our arms over to the Legionary in command. At the gate Simha R. suddenly recalled that a *Sefer Torah* had been left behind in the dining hall, and, despite the fact that we could see Arabs on the rampage in the bungalow, Simha went in at considerable risk to himself and succeeded in removing it. We marched to Hirbet Zakaria,

the Legionaries escorting and guarding us. The men of the Hirbeh were waiting for us. They, too, had kept their arms until the last moment.—GERSHON SH.

The Surrender of Revadim

From the account of a settler—May 14

By the time the police officer came to Revadim, the settlement was completely surrounded by thousands of Arabs waiting for their chance to sweep down on it. All the villages from Jerusalem to Hebron, it seemed, had been emptied of their inhabitants, who had hurried to the Bloc with sacks over their shoulders.

The officer and the members of his escort entered the dining hall. Shortly afterwards the car of the Red Cross drove up. The representatives went into the clinic to conclude the terms of the surrender. The policemen scattered in the farmyard and tried to prevent the mob from breaking in. After all the arrangements with the Red Cross had been concluded, trucks of the Arab Legion arrived and their officers insisted that we hand over our arms. Our reply was that we would surrender them only after all our men were in the vehicles. We also demanded that the Commanding Officer send his men to relieve the settlers in the defense positions, with orders to prevent any attempt to storm the settlement. He complied immediately, sending Legionaries to the positions. Then our men began to get into the trucks.

Hundreds of Arabs were already crowding round the fences of the farmyard, waiting for the moment to break in. At any moment, it seemed, they would storm the village. As the *haverim* began to climb into the trucks with their little bundles in their hands, the rabble rushed into the farmyard. The villagers went frantic in their lust for loot. They ran from room to room, shrieking their war-cries, and even attacked one another.

At long last the convoy moved off. The trucks cumbrously climbed up the road to the Hirbeh. The slope was swarming with Arabs. "Will this handful of Arab Legionaries succeed in keeping off this mob of thousands?" I asked myself. My fears were groundless. The rabble was no longer out for blood but for loot. As the Arabs swept through the farmyard and the buildings, the settlers took a last look at their homes.

The convoy continued on its way. Near Hirbet Zakaria it halted to pick up the prisoners from Ein Tsurim and the Hirbeh garrison.—BARUKH B. (As recorded in the diary of Uriel O.)

In the Convoy

From the account of a settler of Revadim (Continued)—May 14

The prisoners-of-war convoy continued on its way towards the main road. In the van were the two trucks of Ein Tsurim, one carrying the men, the other the women. These were followed by the vehicles from Revadim: an ambulance with the wounded, one truck carrying the women and another the men. Six to eight Legionaries were seated in each of the vehicles. The convoy plowed its way through the thousands of Arabs that swarmed over the Bloc. The Legionaries remained vigilant, fearing an attempt to interfere with the progress of the convoy. From time to time, indeed, they shot into the mob to keep it off.

As we were passing near the Russian Monastery, a tremendous explosion rent the air. The truck carrying the men of Revadim had struck a mine, and half of them were thrown out into the road. Terrible confusion and panic resulted, because we were all ignorant of the cause of the accident. . . .

The Legionaries were sure that they had run into a Jewish ambush and were panic-stricken. One of them fired a long volley with his Tommy-gun into the men who had fallen from the truck and were rushing around in alarm. The outcome was tragic. Shmuel H. was killed by a bullet in the stomach. Sha'ul A. was also hit in the stomach. David H. was hit in the left elbow and later lost his hand. The Arab orderlies rendered first aid to the wounded.

Then the convoy started on its way again and when it reached the Jerusalem-Hebron highway it split up. The ambulance and the vehicle carrying the wounded turned left towards Bethlehem, while all other vehicles turned right, towards Hebron.—BARUKH B. (As recorded in the diary of Uriel O.)

At Massuot Yitzhak

From the accounts of settlers—May 14

Throughout the day a plane circled round the settlement, constantly on the watch.

In the morning Ein Tsurim signaled to us that the Red Cross delegation had arrived, and that we would be attended to last of all. . . .

In the early afternoon we were alone, the only settlement remaining in the Bloc. The settlers of Ein Tsurim and Revadim had been taken off in an unknown direction. From the cistern we watched what was happening to their settlements. The Arabs were in a scrimmage around the three bungalows of Ein Tsurim, destroying and looting. They seemed to be quarrelling fiercely over every article they found. Flames burst from the buildings. One after the other the bungalows collapsed, sending up huge showers of sparks. Only the small security building remained standing. From Revadim, too, a thick pall of smoke arose, covering the entire neighborhood.—MOSHE B. and ELIEZER S.

From the diary of a Palmah soldier—May 14

I was sitting in the operating room. The door opened and Moshe Y., the Settlement Commander, asked me to come outside. On the way Moshe explained: "I must leave the settlement to call on one of the Arab commanders and go with him to hurry up the arrival of the Red Cross delegates." We went up to the gate. It was still barricaded. Nearby was a defense position where the men were in a constant state of alert. Near the kitchen a number of other men had taken up their positions. About one hundred yards away the Arabs sat and waited for the moment when they could dash into the settlement and start looting.

Moshe called out to them in Arabic: *"Bas wahad"* (only one). Two Arabs came up. The younger of the two carried a rifle with two bandoliers round his body; the older, clean shaven, wore European clothes and shining topboots. We asked them why the Red Cross delegates were so long in coming. They replied, "The Red Cross and the Legion are transporting the men of Revadim and Ein Tsurim. When they come back they will take you too." "Where to?" we asked. "To Hebron," came the reply. And the older Arab added: "You need have no fear. No harm will befall you. You will be all right!"

We continued our tense watch.—URIEL O.

From a private diary—May 14

Hours passed and the Red Cross delegation had not come. . . . The sun was setting. Sabbath was approaching. I recalled that this was a great day in our struggle. The Mandate was coming to an end, and today the British would leave the country. Would the Jewish State be proclaimed as we had hoped? For days we had been completely cut off from the rest of the country. For a week no newspapers had reached us, and for three days the radio had been silent. But I was incapable of realizing the significance of the day. Too many thoughts and questions crowded my brain.

The defenders of Kfar Etzion had not lived to see the liberation of their people, the rise of the new Jewish State. Would our people appreciate the sacrifice of these unassuming and plain-living settlers and soldiers who now lay lifeless under the trees of the Russian Monastery garden, in the trenches on Russian Hill, on Hirbet Sawir, and among the ruins of Kfar Etzion? . . .

One of the *haverim* came up and said that Sabbath prayers would be held in the open. It was hard for me to attend a public service. In the morning too it had not been easy for me to pray. I had not reconciled myself to the catastrophe that had overwhelmed us. The verses of the prayers seemed at odds with my pain and sorrow. They did not express my sense of loss, they offered no answer to the questions that engulfed me. I could not submit to the decree of Providence. We had prayed for a miracle and for victory, but in vain.

How was I to pray when I was so troubled by doubt, together with all those people, many of whom had their own prayers to offer regarding their own future? But it was a religious duty, instilled in me since childhood and, putting aside my hesitation, I joined the congregation.

I could follow the Reader only with the greatest of difficulty. I recalled those moments of prayer during the Sabbath service in Nveh Ovadia. The tears ran down my face and I felt that I was beginning to accept what fate had been decreed. Together with the congregation I uttered:

> To declare that the Lord is righteous,
> My Rock in whom there is no evil.

Dov K.

In Jerusalem

From the account of a member of Kfar Etzion—May 14

Just before evening, Dr. Zive, who had accompanied the Red Cross delegation, returned from the Bloc, with the news that the delegation had succeeded in making arrangements for the surrender of Ein Tsurim, Revadim, and Hirbet Zakaria. All the settlers had been taken prisoner-of-war. The members of the delegation were not permitted to approach Kfar Etzion. The Legionaries had said that there was no need for haste; first the living must be saved. . . . The surrender of Massuot Yitzhak had not been arranged yet, but the talks would be concluded in the evening.

Dr. Zive could give us no information about Kfar Etzion. There was a rumor that two of the settlers had been taken prisoner by the Legion, but he did not know their names. What about the wounded? He had heard that the wounded had been transferred on the previous night to Massuot Yitzhak. He did not know their names. The burial of the dead would be dealt with later. . . .

It was Friday evening. The decisive battle for Jerusalem had begun. In Tel Aviv the Provisional Government had assembled to proclaim the State of Israel. In the offices of the Jewish Agency in Jerusalem, the few members of the Executive who remained in the city, the members of the Va'ad Leumi, and the leading members of other institutions, gathered to read the proclamation of the Jewish State. In the lobby and the corridors of the building reports of the fall of Kfar Etzion were discussed in whispers.—SHLOMO H.

The Surrender of Massuot Yitzhak

From the accounts of settlers—May 14

Downcast and lonely, we welcomed in the Sabbath with public prayer. We were still waiting for our captors. At half-past-seven that night, two Legion officers arrived with their men, accompanied by a settler of Revadim who spoke Arabic. The officers tried to set our fears at rest. They promised to remove us to a place of safety and to protect us from all harm.

We surrendered our arms to the Legionaries, who occupied our positions to prevent an attack by the mob.

We asked a Legion officer to permit us to take a Torah Scroll with us and he consented. We immediately extracted the *Sifrei Torah* and other religious articles from the pit where we had hidden them the night before.—MOSHE B. and ELIEZER S.

From the diary of a Palmah soldier—May 14

In the gathering darkness the first vehicles of the Arab Legion began to arrive: buses, trucks and the motor car of a Legion officer, and an Arab doctor. The officer informed us that the representative of the Red Cross would not come, as he had returned to Jerusalem after being given an undertaking by the Legion that the wounded and the women would be transferred to Jerusalem into Jewish hands. Contact by signals with Jerusalem remained uninterrupted. Regional Headquarters was asked, after the entry of the Legion, if we should trust them and the reply was, "Yes." The girls, the *Sifrei Torah,* and all personal belongings were concentrated near the dining hall. People began to climb up onto the trucks, dragging their belongings after them.

Dr. Shiyar, the Arab medical officer, went over to the hospital to inspect the wounded. Two buses drew up near the hospital and we helped the wounded to board them. It was hard work to cram forty to fifty wounded men into two tiny buses, but Dr. Windsberg utilized his experience in the Polish Army, and soon all the men were either lying down or, somehow or other, sitting down inside.

When the girls had taken their places in the trucks the last of the men left their positions and jumped up too. They handed their arms to the Legionaries.

At 8:00 P.M. the last signal was sent to the Regional Command in Jerusalem from Massuot Yitzhak:

THE MEN AND WOMEN ARE BEING TAKEN TO HEBRON, THE WOUNDED TO BETHLEHEM. REGARDS TO THE MASSUOT GROUP IN JERUSALEM. TONIGHT WE SHALL NO LONGER BE HERE. SO ENDS THE CHAPTER OF THE ETZION BLOC.

URIEL O.

Postscript

The captives of the Etzion Bloc were removed to a prisoner-of-war camp in Um Jamal, Trans-Jordan, where they were interned for nine months. In February, 1949, they were released and returned to Israel.

At the beginning of November, 1949, an Israel Army detail, acting on a decision of the Israel-Trans-Jordan Mixed Armistice Commission, and headed by the Chief Chaplain of the Israel Armed Forces, gathered the remains of the Etzion Bloc defenders and exhumed the bodies in the cemeteries of the Bloc.

They were laid to final rest in the Israel military cemetery on the slopes of Mount Herzl in Jerusalem on November 17, 1949, in a State funeral.

THE STAND OF THE ETZION BLOC IN THE ISRAEL WAR OF LIBERATION

By General Yigael Yadin *

The purpose of these lines is to provide a proper evaluation of the strategic significance of the Etzion Bloc campaign for the war in Palestine on the eve of the proclamation of the State of Israel.

As the date of the British evacuation of Palestine drew closer and the prospect of an invasion by the armies of the Arab States more certain, the General Staff was convinced of the absolute necessity of a number of operations of strategic importance, which must be concluded at all costs prior to May 15, to ensure that the interior of the country was safely in our hands and that we were able to face the invaders. Command of the lines of communications, the subduing of the forces and centers of resistance of Kaukji's army and the Mufti's bands, as well as the dozens of other guerilla centers of the Palestine Arabs, constituted a vital strategic necessity. All these aims had to be realized with the utmost dispatch, if we were to concentrate and move our small forces freely wherever they might be needed.

Plans to meet the Arab invasion called for the solution of a complex of problems; our major fear, however, was

* General Yadin was Chief of Operations of the General Staff in the Israel War of Liberation. This article has been abridged from the Introduction to *Maoz Etzion,* published by *Ma'arakhot,* Tel Aviv, 1949.

that, in resisting the invaders, our forces would be handicapped by the need to establish lines of supply to various parts of the country which had been cut off. Thus we would find ourselves fighting, without proper lines of communication, against regular troops in Western Galilee, in the Negev, in Jerusalem and in the Etzion Bloc. We foresaw that such a situation—guerilla warfare in the interior and regular warfare on the borders—would be catastrophic.

This ruthless appraisal forced us to solve our problems swiftly but separately. It was a task involving a supreme effort. In the concentration of our forces and the planning of the various phases of the operations, a system of priorities had to be established on the basis of military considerations alone. Our calculations were made on the basis of the state of supply in the settlements, their morale, their ability to hold out and to resist local attacks, and so on.

We knew that, if we were successful in solving our various problems before May 15, cleared our internal lines of communication, defeated the semi-regular and irregular enemy troops, and succeeded in getting through a quantity of supplies to the various settlements, thereby enabling them to hold out for some time after May 15—we should be able, once the British had left, to solve our supply problems, and at the same time defeat the invading armies.

The means at our disposal were meager, the tasks facing us immense, and the time in which to tackle them minimal.

For weeks Western Galilee had been cut off from other centers of Jewish population; none of our attempts to force through convoys had succeeded, despite the heavy toll of lives taken. The Eastern Galilean salient was almost completely surrounded and threatened with isolation; Safed was cut off, and there was a danger that it might be converted by the Arabs into a powerful base for operations against Galilee and the Valley of Jezreel; the noose round Jerusalem was steadily being tightened; every effort to supply the Negev and the southern settlements involved constant engagements with the Arab villages and bands dominating all main highways. By now it was virtually impossible to supply the Etzion Bloc, Hartuv, Nveh Ya'akov, and Atarot by normal means. If these problems were not solved before May 15, any clash with the Arab regular armies might spell disaster. The need for a speedy solution was crystal-clear. It now became more imperative than ever to establish a list of priorities.

The Etzion Bloc, that mountainous district, the most completely isolated Jewish area in the country and at the same time of the utmost importance for the defense of Jerusalem, which so far had withstood the enemy attacks with outstanding courage, called for immediate relief. It was vital to get through food, arms, and materials for fortifications, at least in quantities to enable it to hold out until the end of May. A giant convoy was organized. Every single armored vehicle available on the Jerusalem front was thrown into this operation. It called for a high degree of courage on the part of the General Staff to make this decision, but we knew beforehand that if the convoy failed to get through, the Bloc was doomed.

The convoy did get through, bringing sufficient supplies to last to the end of May. But on its way back, at Nebi Daniel, it was overwhelmed, though some of the vehicles succeeded in withdrawing to the Etzion Bloc, reinforcing it with men, armored cars, and arms. The Bloc breathed freely for a while, but we had sustained a savage blow. We had lost all the vehicles that had been engaged in the transport of supplies to Jerusalem. Now the problem of keeping Jerusalem supplied became one of paramount importance. We were compelled to concentrate upon the problem of providing food for Jerusalem's one hundred thousand Jews, so that they could hold out at least until the middle of June. We concentrated all the forces we could muster, and perhaps even more than normally we should have allowed ourselves. "Operation Nahshon" was launched, whose purpose was to force the way through to Jerusalem and to bring up the supply convoys.

After the defeat sustained by the convoy on its return journey from the Etzion Bloc to Jerusalem, the Air Force worked day and night, supplying the Bloc with arms and building materials for the fortifications, at the same time carrying out its operations in Western and Eastern Galilee and in the Negev. Jerusalem and the Etzion Bloc, however, were still given top priority.

Western Galilee, too, was appealing desperately for aid. But we could not respond, as other calls were regarded as more urgent. Eastern Galilee, too, was in distress. It too, was required to hold on until such time as we could divert forces to its aid. The Officer Commanding the Negev Area called upon us again and again at Operations HQ to plead for action against the Arab villages blocking the road to the Negev. Here again we insisted on patience.

Towards the end of April the situation in Galilee took a turn for the worse. It was clear that Safed must be taken before May 15, whatever the cost. We assembled a number of Palmah units, and, reinforcing them with some Field Force troops, organized an independent brigade, which was entrusted with the execution of what we called "Operation

Yiftah,"—to liberate Eastern Galilee and, above all, Safed and its environs. This brigade and the task it was to undertake imposed on us a new and heavy responsibility. We scraped together whatever we could from our Air Force and attached it to this brigade. We established for it special supply bases in Eastern Galilee. As a result our reserves were dangerously depleted. Our other problems were still demanding our attention, but Eastern Galilee urgently demanded a solution to its problems, for it was necessary to get ready to meet the imminent invasion.

Reports from Jerusalem Intelligence indicated the prospect of an earlier evacuation of the City by the British than originally had been scheduled. The necessity of solving several of Jerusalem's problems—the maintenance of communications with isolated South Jerusalem, the Sheikh Jarrah Quarter, the center of the city, and the like—became more acute.

We transferred to Jerusalem most of the forces that had been concentrated for "Operation Nahshon." We established the Harel Brigade, and, in "Operation Jebus," in which all the forces in the City, together with the reinforcements that had been dispatched, were engaged, we began our drive on Katamon, Sheikh Jarrah, the center of the city, and its environs. The intervention of the Arab Legion and of the Arab villagers south of Jerusalem might have decided the fate of the City. Consequently, new tasks were imposed upon the Etzion Bloc which, when carried out, proved of considerable assistance to the troops concentrated in the district and to those engaged in Operation Jebus. But they weakened the forces defending the Etzion Bloc. We knew, however,—as did the defenders of the Bloc—that their very existence depended upon Jerusalem, and that every effort had to be made to save the City.

The attacks launched by the Arab Legion and the irregulars on the Etzion Bloc at the end of April and the beginning of May made the dispatch of new reinforcements necessary. A substantial proportion of the small amount of arms which had reached us from abroad during Operation Nahshon was allocated to the Bloc. The most capable officers of the General Staff worked upon the problem of keeping it supplied and reinforced by air.

But our needs multiplied in other theaters also. In Western Galilee the situation was deteriorating. Delegations from the settlements who had managed to get through to us gave us dismal accounts of their position. It became clearer and clearer that action could no longer be delayed, and that the issue had to be decided before the invasion by regular troops began. Haifa Region and the Carmel Brigade were ordered to liberate Western Galilee in "Operation Ben Ami." The task was put off from day to day owing to our inability to supply the Command of this operation with the necessary forces.

The Haifa Regional Command mobilized all available forces. They were reinforced by Palmah units, a number of armored vehicles, and a quantity of "heavy arms" (which, according to the concepts current at that time, meant machine guns and mortars). Together they were to carry out the liberation of Western Galilee in the week between May 8-15. The Air Force, which was already busy enough flying its tiny planes ("birds" as we called them at the time) to the Etzion Bloc, Jerusalem, Eastern Galilee, and the Negev, was called upon to support the attempt to force a passage through to Western Galilee. The objections of certain of our commanders were rejected. We hoped that the Etzion Bloc, with the aid of the supplies and the inadequate arms at its disposal—though by the standards of that time the quantity of these was not inconsiderable—would succeed in holding its ground until May 15.

The High Commissioner, the OC British Troops in the country, His Majesty's Government, had all solemnly undertaken that not a single soldier of the Arab Legion would be in Palestine before May 15. After that date, we thought, we should be able to force our way through to the Etzion Bloc by a large concentrated effort after the pattern of "Operation Nahshon" in the Jerusalem area, "Yiftah" in Eastern Galilee, and "Ben Ami" in Western Galilee.

We assumed further that after May 15 the Bloc would be in a better position to defend itself as the only approaches open to regular troops were via Jerusalem in the north and the Negev in the south—both of which we hoped to control.

But the Arab Legion and the British also realized that if the Etzion Bloc was not captured by May 15, it would constitute a major obstacle on their road to Jerusalem. They mustered against the Bloc a large concentration of troops, and particularly of armor and artillery, the like of which had never before been mustered against any of our settlements. The Bloc's defenders fought heroically, but they were vastly outnumbered, and inadequately equipped with anti-tank weapons to repulse enemy armor (though we had succeeded in getting through to them two Piats—weapons that were rather rare at the time). The Bloc was defenseless against the enemy guns, and was overrun.

The fall of the Etzion Bloc was one of our most serious defeats. Its capture on the day before May 15, when the

Arab armies were simultaneously to invade the country, intensified the apprehensions entertained by many of us regarding our ability to repel regular troops equipped with heavy weapons. The fall of the Bloc forced us to close ranks. It was necessary to strengthen fortifications, accelerate the dispatch of heavy arms and, above all, sternly refuse to order the evacuation of a number of other frontier outposts, regarding our ability to hold which there were some apprehensions. Nevertheless, we decided to withdraw from Atarot, Nveh Ya'akov, and Hartuv. All these steps were influenced to a considerable extent by the capture of the Etzion Bloc.

On the other hand, the heroic stand of the defenders, the spirit of self-sacrifice that had inspired them, and particularly the high price exacted from the enemy for the victory, strengthened our confidence in ultimate victory.

The fall of the Etzion Bloc was tragically heroic. It had executed almost all of the tasks imposed upon it with courage and fortitude, diverting enemy forces threatening Jerusalem from the south, enabling the defenders of the City to consolidate their positions and to prepare for the attack of the Legion, which was now compelled to recuperate from its losses and to reorganize its forces before the attack on the City.

The Hagana High Command had been widely advised at the end of April to evacuate the Bloc, and also to withdraw from the Negev and Galilee. But if we had adopted such a policy where would it have ended? The heroic stand of the Etzion Bloc, of Manara, Kfar Szold, Yehiam, Yad Mordekhai, Kfar Darom, Negba, Gat, and Gallon, contributed to our victory no less than the larger-scale military operations. The stand of these settlements, and especially that of the Etzion Bloc, will occupy a prominent place in the history of our people and of the Israel War of Liberation.

THE ZIONIST SETTLEMENT MOVEMENT AS A MILITARY FACTOR IN THE ISRAEL WAR OF LIBERATION

By General Yig'al Allon *

> They that built on the wall and they that bore burdens laded themselves, every one with one of his hands wrought in the work and with the other held a weapon.
>
> (Nehemia 4:11)

In the course of the seventy years which elapsed between the beginning of the Zionist settlement in Palestine and the proclamation of the State of Israel, the establishment of Jewish right of tenure over any area in the country was identical virtually with settlement in that area. The extension of the borders of Zionist colonization deeper into the interior of the country, besides reinforcing the Jewish community's economic and social foundations and increasing its capacity for self-defense, ensured that an ever-increasing area was brought under the ultimate authority of the Jewish people. The occupation of the land not only created the instruments for the development of the national economy, for the social consolidation of the Yishuv and the advancement of the political struggle. It also strengthened the basis upon which Jewish national aspirations rested, and brought the Jewish State closer to ultimate realization.

---

* General Allon is the former National Commander of the Palmah. This article has been abridged from the Introduction to *Gush Etzion BeMilhamto.*

The uncertain state of public security in Palestine and the recurrent outbreaks of large-scale organized violence led to a situation whereby land acquisition and settlement policy were governed as much by strategic considerations as by the quality of the soil and the prospect of development. In the initial stages of establishing a new settlement, the strategic position of the site weighed most with the settlers. Even the initial attempts at settling Jews on the land in Palestine, sponsored by Baron Edmond de Rothschild at the end of the nineteenth and beginning of the twentieth century, had as their motive not only to penetrate into vital areas but to establish a chain of villages on one continuous area of Jewish land. This policy received even more emphasis when the Zionist Organization undertook colonization. Responsibility for military planning and the defense of the new settlements was placed in the hands of the Hagana, a national defense organization under the command of a properly constituted General Staff. A special branch of the General Staff determined the location of each village in conformity with local conditions and the broader strategy of district and national defense. The Hagana High Command gave final approval to settlement plans, supplied the necessary arms for self-defense, provided for the training of the settlers and trained the local commanders. Under its direction the villages were so fortified that they were simultaneously civilian settlements and military strongpoints.

When the Israel War of Liberation broke out, the Jewish settlements which, in the British Mandatory period, had been primarily territorial defense units, were transformed into military bases in the full sense of the term.

The Arabs fully appreciated the importance of the agricultural settlements as the backbone of the Yishuv. For that reason, indeed, their offensive concentrated upon the villages in order to capture them and to remove what prevented them from attacking the main centers of Jewish strength in the cities. The persistent attempts made to cut the main arteries of Jewish communications in the initial phase of the War were intended primarily to isolate the settlements—and also some of the towns—from the main centers of Jewish population, preparatory to capturing them. But each settlement had already been converted into a strongpoint, each bloc of villages a major stronghold integrated into the national defense pattern.

The villages, however, did not confine themselves to defensive operations. The strategic considerations which had underlain the plan of Zionist settlement decided in large measure the fate of many regions of the country, including areas largely or entirely settled by Arabs, such as Tiberias, Tsemah, Beit She'an, Acre, Haifa, and Jaffa, all of which were surrounded by Jewish villages. In Jerusalem events would certainly have taken a totally different course had the city been supported by an agricultural hinterland and linked to the coast by a series of Jewish villages. On the other hand, lacking the few outposts which were established on its outskirts, there is little doubt that its fate would have been sealed.

Those areas of Jewish settlement further inland, in the heart of Arab-controlled territory, constituted forward bases, whose function was to hold out at all costs until the advance of the main body of troops could extricate them.

There are two reasons for the maintenance of isolated outposts in enemy territory: a) the absolute necessity to divert an enemy advance upon large civilian centers; b) when the forces under attack intend to mount an offensive soon, in order to unite with the settlements that had been cut off. Both of these conditions obtained during the War of Liberation. It was absolutely necessary to hold up the Arab advance towards the sea. At the same time it was vital to relieve enemy pressure in a number of sectors—primarily on the Jerusalem front—and to gain time for the deployment of the main body of Jewish troops for the decisive battle.

The fact that the settlers themselves manned these outposts reduced the number of regular troops needed for tasks of static defense, and thereby increased their mobility and striking power. This strategy of territorial defense proved highly advantageous despite the losses it entailed. Evacuation of the outlying villages would have permitted the Arab troops to advance more rapidly, would have increased Jewish losses, and, it is reasonable to suppose, would have considerably diminished Israel's ultimate gains.

The settlements to whom this task fell suffered severely, far more indeed than other sectors of the front. The majority of them were successful in holding out, despite enemy pressure, until they were relieved. Some, however, fell after fighting a desperate battle, literally to the last bullet and hand grenade, against an enemy overwhelmingly superior in men and equipment.

Much has been written—and remains to be written—about the heroic defense of the Etzion Bloc settlements and of the Hagana units dispatched to reinforce them. Strategically and otherwise the four settlements of the Etzion Bloc, occupying a tract of land among the Hebron Hills commanding the only road leading southwards from Jerusalem, were in a peculiar situation. Together they constituted a Jewish enclave in the heart of hostile Arab territory, whose function was to serve as a basis for further Jewish colonization. Their fate was sealed when war broke out before they could consolidate their position in their unfriendly neighborhood.

From the military point of view the situation of the Etzion Bloc possessed both advantages and drawbacks. The principal drawback, of course, was the fact that it was far from any other center of Jewish population and could easily be cut off from its sources of supply. On the other hand, the four settlements occupied a series of hilltops favorably sited for defense, even against regular troops. In retrospect it is reasonable to assume that with more adequate fortifications, anti-vehicle obstacles, anti-tank guns—even of the lighter variety—and larger reserves of food and ammunition, the Bloc would have been able to hold out for a longer period until it could have been relieved.

A striking feature of life in the besieged Bloc was the total integration of social and economic activity into the life of a garrison on a war-footing. All of the settlers, without exception, took an active part in the defense of their villages. A study of the settlement Journals and the personal diaries of individual settlers proves how harmoniously they combined their functions as settlers and soldiers. They remained farmers, though they did their stint of guard duty and participated in other military operations. As long as circumstances permitted they tilled the soil and maintained essential services. The settlers and the settlements, it must be remembered, constituted the hard core of the Bloc's defensive system. The Hagana troops came and went—and the defense of the Bloc would have been inconceivable without them—but the farmers remained, wedded to the soil.

The part played by the womenfolk is worthy of special mention. In the kitchen and in the clinic, in the fields and barns, in the forward defense posts, and in the convoys they did their duty, a constant source of encouragement and inspiration for all the defenders.

The Etzion Bloc was one of the most important fronts of the War of Liberation. Its stand was hopeless and bloody, but essential. Its orders, like those given to Jewish soldiers and settlers in other sectors of the front, were to hold out at all costs. The men and women of the Bloc fell not only in defense of their settlements and homes; they died to save Jerusalem. In the Hebron Hills they fought the battle of Jerusalem and played a far more decisive role than if they had fought within the city itself.

War and immense sacrifice in men are only too often the price of liberty and national independence. The War, which the Jews did not will, was a struggle for existence and for that reason alone there was no alternative but to take up the challenge.

The Sources for This Book

The material upon which this book is based has been derived from various sources. Hundreds of people took part in the defense of the Etzion Bloc, and many of them recorded in various forms the events they experienced.

At the beginning of hostilities many of the settlers committed to writing their impressions of the fighting and the problems of the siege. These documents were collected in the Archives of Kfar Etzion together with reports and other material dealing with events in the area. Part of this material was copied and sent to the womenfolk of the settlements, who had been evacuated to Jerusalem.

The Secretariat of Kfar Etzion wrote every two or three days to the representatives of the Bloc in Jerusalem and Tel Aviv and to the women quartered in the Ratisbonne Monastery in Jerusalem. These reports, too, described life in the Bloc, the moods of the settlers, the public discussions and various events. Practically all of this material has been preserved. The minutes of important meetings were also transmitted to Jerusalem; some of these are reproduced in this volume.

The Journal of Kfar Etzion dealing with the period of the siege, extracts from which are included in this volume, is based upon these letters and diaries.

During the siege the settlements continued to publish their internal news-sheets containing accounts of and comments on developments in the Bloc. Apart from this, there were members who recorded the events in the Bloc, as they occurred, in their private diaries, and at frequent intervals sent these accounts to their wives in Jerusalem. A great deal of this material has also been preserved.

The representatives of the Bloc attached to the various colonization and defense institutions in Jerusalem and Tel Aviv kept a record in their journals of the matters they dealt with and of the reports they submitted to the settlers. It has been possible to include many of these accounts in this book.

Important contributions were also made by members of settlements and by enlisted men who served in the Bloc. Interviews were held with many of the men who took part in the various battles, and their accounts are also recorded here.

The description of the final battle consists of reports from several sources. These include the survivors of Kfar Etzion, who were taken prisoner, and who were able afterwards to record details of the final battle in which they had taken part. They made every effort to corroborate the facts they reported in the light of the evidence of members of the other settlements and men serving in the Palmah and the Field Force. These accounts were published in a stenciled booklet, "A Report on the Final Battle of Kfar Etzion."

A very significant source is the diary of Uriel Ofek, of the Palmah, who collected the testimony of many of the settlers and soldiers who had fought on various sectors during the final battle.

We have also utilized the wealth of historical material on the fighting in the Etzion Bloc area preserved in the Archives of the Israel Defense Forces and of the Memorial

Department of the Ministry of Defense, and documents in the possession of the Central Zionist Archives, of HaKibbutz HaDati and HaPoel HaMizrahi.

Accounts and articles have also been taken from the following publications: *Ma'arakhot,* the Israel Defense Forces monthly; *Hail Avir,* the organ of the Israel Air Force; *Dvar HaPo'elet;* and the dailies *HaAretz* and *HaTsofe.*

The photographs were contributed by the Keren HaKayemet and Keren HaYesod, as well as by the individual photographers to whom credit is given.

Almost every document included here is signed. In the *kibbutzim* it is customary for a signature to comprise the first name and the initial letter of the surname of the signatory. This was also the normal practice in the Bloc.

DOV KNOHL

Contributors

SIEGE IN THE HILLS OF HEBRON was compiled from the writings and eyewitness accounts of the following:

Ahiman, Hanokh
Aiges, Ya'akov
Aloni, Ben Zion
Altman, Ya'akov*
Ariel, Aryei
Arzi, Shmuel*
Auerbach, Yehezkel*
Azaria
Baraginsky, Moshe
Bar Hama, Eliyahu
Ben David, David
Ben Sira, Nahum
Ben Sira, Yitzhak
Ber, Moshe
Bombagi, Barukh
Braun, Elimelekh
Braver, Moshe
 (HaTsofe)
Damast, Yosef*
Deiksler, Mordekhai
Druzdik, Naomi
Edelstein, Ya'akov
Ehud
Eliyahu K.
Elston, D.R.
Feuchtwanger, Aliza
Fishgrund, Avraham*
Friedenfeld, Me'ir*
Galandauer, Akiva*
Granek, Shalom*
Grinspan, Naftali
Grodzenski, Ben Zion*
Hail Avir
Haimowitz, Shlomo
Holender, Shimon*
Horowitz, Dan
 (Shana BeSograyim)
Isaakowitz, Elazar
Kadari, Menahem Tsvi
Karniel, Shalom*
Katz, Yitzhak*
Kenoller, Yehoyakhin
Kfir, Aharon
Klapholtz, Ya'akov*
Knohl, Dov
Knohl, Shoshana
Kokhav, David
Kushnir, Rina
Leviatan, Aharon
Levinowitz, Yehoshua*
Livni, Shmuel
Me'ir, Aharon
"Military Correspondent,"
 HaAretz
Mittleman, Mordekhai
Muskal, Mordekhai
Narkis, Uzi *(Ma'arakhot)*
Ofek, Uriel

* Killed in action

Pinkerfeld-Amir, Anda
(Lamed Hei)
Porat, Yosef
Raz, Sha'ul
Rosen, Shlomo*
Sadiel, Yehoshua*
Saltzman, Tsvi
Schwartz, Shlomo
Segal, Shmuel
Shifman, Ya'akov
Shnur, Avraham*
Shnur, Natan
Shtaub, Gershon
Silberschmidt, Moshe ("Mosh")*
Staklov, Tsvi
Sternberg, Eliezer
Tamar
Teitelbaum, David*
Treinin, Avraham *(Ma'oz Etzion)*
Tsigler, Ha'im
Tulman, Naomi
Weiss, Yitzhak
Windsberg, Dr.
Yavnieli, Aharon*

---

* Killed in action

Glossary

Bachad	—The religious pioneering Zionist youth movement that originated in Germany in the 1920's.
Bedikat hametz	—Ceremonial search for leaven before Passover.
Bnei Akiva	—The religious pioneering Zionist youth movement that originated in Central Europe and Palestine in the 1930's.
Fellahin (Arabic)	—Arab peasants.
Field Force	—The mobile Hagana reserve force which was activated in periods of emergency.
Golah	—The Diaspora.
Hagana	—The clandestine defense force of the Jewish community in Palestine in the days of the British Mandate.
Haggada	—The liturgical text of the Passover Seder.
Hakshara	—Training farm for Zionist pioneers.
HaKibbutz HaDati	—The federation of Zionist religious collective settlements.
Halakha	—Jewish Religious Law.
Halutz (pl. Halutzim)	—Zionist pioneer.
Hametz	—Literally "leaven"; food forbidden in Jewish homes on the Passover festival.
Hanukka	—The festival of lights, celebrated eight days, to commemorate the victory of Judah Maccabee against the Hellenistic Syrians in the Second Century B.C.E.
HaPoel HaMizrahi	—The religious Zionist labor organization.
HaShomer HaTsair	—The left wing pioneering organization of the Zionist labor movement.
HaTikva	—The Zionist national anthem.

Haver (f. Havera pl. Haverim or Haverot) —Literally "member" or "comrade"; used to designate a member of a collective group.

Hevra Kadisha —Burial society.

Hol HaMo'ed —The intermediate days of the Passover holiday.

Kaddish —The mourner's prayer.

Kashrut —The ritual purity of food.

Keffiyeh (Arabic) —A kerchief used by the Arabs as a headdress.

Kehilla —An organized Jewish community.

Kibbutz (pl. Kibbutzim)—Zionist collective settlement; used almost interchangeably with *Kvutza.*

Kiddush —Literally "sanctification"; the act of sanctifying the Sabbath or festivals with wine.

Kvutza (pl. Kvutzot) —a) Zionist collective settlement; used almost interchangeably with *Kibbutz.*
b) A collective group.

Lehayim —Literally "to life"; salutation before a toast.

Lehitraot —*au revoir.*

Ma'ariv —The evening prayer service.

Mapai —The largest Zionist labor party in Palestine.

Minha —The afternoon prayer service.

Mitzva (pl. Mitzvot) —Religious precept.

Moshav (pl. Moshavim)—A smallholder co-operative settlement.

Mukhtar (Turkish) —Headman of a village during the British administration in Palestine.

Mussaf —The second part of the morning prayer service recited on Sabbaths and festivals.

National Institutions —The governing bodies of the Jewish community in Palestine, the most notable being the Jewish Agency.

Omer, Counting of —The ritual counting of the forty-nine days between Passover and Pentecost.

Oneg Shabbat —A celebration held on the Sabbath in honor of the Holy Day.

Palmah —The striking force of the Hagana, many of whose units were permanently mobilized.

Pessah —The Passover festival.

Purim —The festival which commemorates the deliverance of the Jewish people from Haman, as related in the Book of Esther.

Rosh HaShana —The Jewish New Year.

Seder —The order of service on Passover Eve, recited around the dinner table.

Sefer Torah (pl. Sifrei Torah) —Scrolls of the Holy Law.

Settlement Police —The supernumerary police force established by the Mandatory Government in Palestine.

Seuda Shlishit —A festive late-afternoon meal on the Sabbath.

Shabbat —The Sabbath.

Shabbat Shalom —Literally "a peaceful Sabbath"; salutation used on the Sabbath.

Sharav —Hot dry wind.

Shavuot —The Pentecost festival.

Shehehiyanu —A benediction recited on festive or joyous occasions.

Shema Yisra'el —"Hear O Israel"; the key declaration of loyalty to Judaism which is recited, *inter alia,* before death.

Striking Force —A squad of settlers which served as the active component of the Jewish village's defense system in the days of the Hagana.

Tefillin —Phylacteries.

Tsholent (Yiddish) —A Sabbath stew prepared of potatoes, beans, barley, and meat.

Va'ad Leumi —The representative body of the Jewish community in Palestine.

White Paper —The 1939 statement of policy of the British Government on Palestine which severely curtailed immigration and prohibited the sale of land to Jews in most areas of the country.

Yeshiva —Talmudic academy.

Yishuv —The Jewish community of Palestine.

Youth Aliya —The Zionist organization for the training in Palestine of homeless Jewish children.

Zemirot —Hymns sung during the Sabbath meals.

Siege in the Hills of Hebron *is set in linotype* CASLON. *The beginnings of this style of letter can be traced back to old Italian manuscripts calligraphed before printing was invented. The first printer to use the type, to which Caslon later gave his name, was Jenson in the 1470's. For more than two centuries the type face was perpetuated by various printers.*

In 1720 the Society for Promoting Christian Knowledge engaged William Caslon to cut a font of Arabic type for Oriental use. Under the Arabic type Caslon signed his name with letters cut in pica roman of his own design based on the letters written in the old Italian manuscripts, Jenson's type, and type used in the 1680's by Dutch type founders. Caslon's face, however, was more graceful and clearer. His signature was much admired, especially since English type founders of that period were not respected. William Caslon, who had served his apprenticeship as an engraver of ornaments on gun barrels, then cut several other fonts of Caslon type and in due time became world renowned. In the late 1700's the popularity of Caslon type faded, with the rise to fashion of the faces designed by Giambattista Bodoni. Only in the last fifty years had Caslon type returned to use.

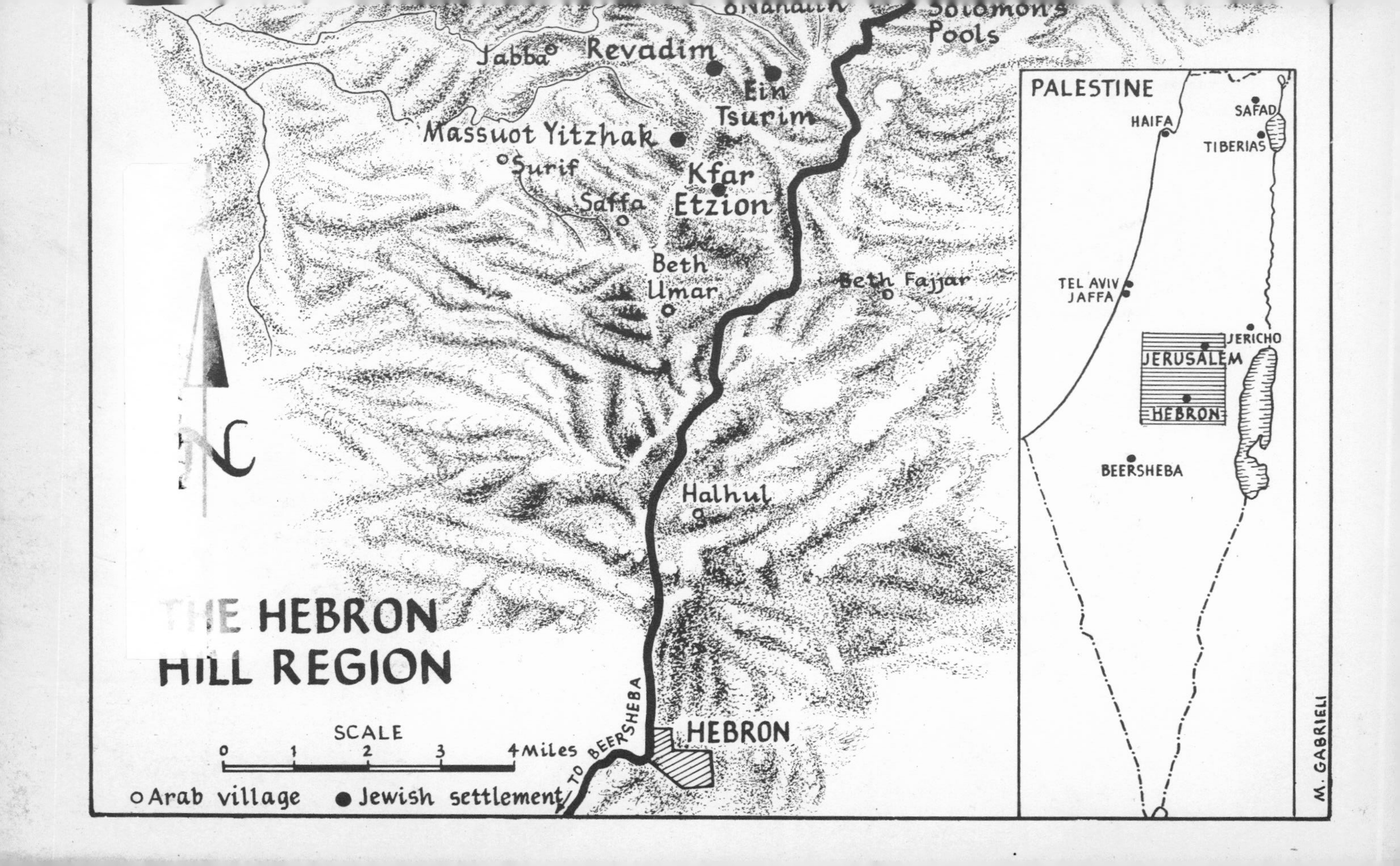
THE HEBRON
HILL REGION
N
SCALE
0 1 2 3 4 Miles
o Arab village ● Jewish settlement
Jabba
Revadim
Pools
Ein
Tsurim
Massuot Yitzhak
Surif
Kfar
Etzion
Saffa
Beth
Umar
Beth Fajjar
Halhul
TO BEERSHEBA
HEBRON
PALESTINE
HAIFA
SAFAD
TIBERIAS
TEL AVIV
JAFFA
JERICHO
JERUSALEM
HEBRON
BEERSHEBA
M. GABRIELI